PUBLICATIONS ON ASIA OF THE
INSTITUTE FOR COMPARATIVE AND FOREIGN AREA STUDIES
Number 29

The Jurchen
in Twelfth-Century China

A STUDY OF SINICIZATION

Jing-shen Tao

UNIVERSITY OF WASHINGTON PRESS

SEATTLE AND LONDON

Copyright © 1976 by the University of Washington Press
Printed in the United States of America

All rights reserved. No part of this publication may be reproduced or transmitted in any form or by any means, electronic or mechanical, including photocopy, recording, or any information storage or retrieval system, without permission in writing from the publisher.

Library of Congress Cataloging in Publication Data

Tao, Jing-shen.
  The Jurchen in twelfth-century China.

  (Publications on Asia of the Institute for Comparative and Foreign Area Studies; no. 29)
    Bibliography: p.
    Includes index.
    1. Ju-chen (Tribe)--History. 2. China--History--Sung dynasty, 960-1279. I. Title. II. Series: Washington (State). University. Institute for Comparative and Foreign Area Studies. Publications on Asia; no. 29.
DS751.T33   951'.02   76-7800
ISBN 0-295-95514-7

To my parents

Contents

Introduction ix

1. *The Origin of the People and Their Culture before 1115*   3

2. *The Rise of the Chin Dynasty*   14

3. *The Period of Dualism: 1115-1150*   25

4. *Sinicization: 1123-1161*   38

5. *Jurchen Bureaucracy and Political Recruitment*   52

6. *The Jurchen Movement for Revival*   68

7. *From Prosperity to Decline*   84

8. *Several Aspects of Sinicization in the Early Thirteenth Century*   95

9. *Conclusion*   111

Appendix	118
Abbreviations	119
Notes	121
Glossary	167
Bibliography	177
Index	207

Illustrations

Between pages 94 and 95

Chin Buddhist art: head of a lohan

Chin Buddhist art: lohan with a sack

Chin coins

Calligraphy of Emperor Chang-tsung

Scroll of the Tripitaka

On title page

Seal of Emperor Chang-tsung

Introduction

This monograph is a study of twelfth-century relations between the Chinese and the seminomadic Jurchen. It attempts to trace the political, economic, and sociocultural change among the Jurchen conquerors who tried to perpetuate their rule of the conquered majority in North China. It seeks to explain the fusion of Chinese and Jurchen cultures, and the consequent assimilation of the Jurchen by the Chinese.

Invasions of China by nomadic and seminomadic peoples from inner and northeastern Asia, and the effects of such invasions, constitute one of the important elements in Chinese history. As early as the first millennium B.C. nomads on the western and northern frontiers of China began a long conflict with their Chinese neighbors. Several times these peoples crossed the Great Wall and set up kingdoms. During the prolonged period of disunity (222-589 A.D.) North China was devastated and for most of the time controlled by them. After the tenth century, when the barbarian incursions were renewed, the menace from the north and the northeast became increasingly serious, resulting in the establishment of the Ch'i-tan and Jurchen states and the Mongol and Manchu empires.

The traditional Chinese view of Sino-barbarian relations suggests a monocultural system that could be achieved by melting down barbarian elements through peaceful persuasion and military enforcement. This traditional theory of assimilation has been restated in modern times, with emphasis on the amalgamation of various peoples in Chinese history. The peoples roundabout China, such as the Manchus, the Mongols, the Moslems, and the Tibetans, whose domains are now incorporated in China, have been considered as the peoples of the frontiers (*pien-chiang min-tsu*), not as foreigners, who have been at least partially assimilated by the Chinese. The ancestors of these peoples, together with those who were active in the past, such as the peoples of the Northern Dynasties, the Ch'i-tan, and the Jurchen, have been described as branches of the Chinese people (*Chung-hua min-tsu*). The history of the frontiers, whether in the past or in the present, is part of Chinese history in the broad sense. Needless to say, there has been a long process of sinicization, in which the peoples of the frontiers have been continuously assimilated by the people of the Han.[1]

In the West, a few different views have been propounded. Owen Lattimore depicts the nomadic society on the borders of China as "marginal society" and the nomadic state as a "reservoir," ready to invade and rule China. But the fusion of the society of China and the steppe society was never achieved; neither could absorb or even permanently subdue the other. Wolfram Eberhard's theory of "superstratification" probes into the feudalistic tendencies under nomadic rule. He distinguishes three types of nomadic rule: the Tibetan, the Turkish, and the Mongolian types. Even the T'o-ba, the most sinicized group among these nomads, were able to preserve many old customs.[2] In Karl A. Wittfogel and Feng Chia-sheng's monumental history of the Liao society, the authors utilized the theory of acculturation in anthropology and the sociological model of categorizing and comparing cultures and societies. Discussing the cultural borrowing between the Chinese and the Ch'i-tan, Wittfogel stresses the aspects of Ch'i-tan culture that were intact, and those of a mixed nature, which gave rise to a "third culture." Although Wittfogel's attack on the traditional "absorption" theory is effective, his assertion that "comparative analysis shows that none of the four major conquest dynasties of China confirms the myth of absorption, not even the last" seems sweeping and farfetched.[3] In the case of the Manchus, for example, Wittfogel's evidences in regard to the Manchu maintenance of cultural and ethnic iden-

Introduction

tity have been ably questioned by Mary C. Wright. Moreover, actually most scholars do not believe in the complete or absolute absorption theory, and the concept of a "dual" structure of the Liao society described by Wittfogel and Feng may not be entirely new. While Tsuda Sokichi's article on the dualistic structure in Liao institutions is "a classic for Japanese students of Liao society," Fu Lo-huan's study of the same subject has also become a classic for Chinese students.[4]

A few Japanese scholars have proposed to view the dynasties established by the northern peoples as dynasties of the north and suggested that the history of these peoples should be considered as the history of northern Asia instead of a part of Chinese history. Wittfogel's concept of "conquest dynasties" has been widely accepted by other Japanese scholars. The application of the term, however, should be limited to the Chin, the Yüan, and the Ch'ing, and the period from 907 to 1368 should not be considered, as Otagi Matsuo does, the era of conquest dynasties, ignoring the existence of the Sung.[5]

Based upon the above studies and other research, mainly on the Ch'ing dynasty, it is possible to draw generalizations on the rise and fall of conquest dynasties in China, and on the nature of the "Chinese world order."[6] These generalizations and theories will be tested and refined by more case studies.

This study is an attempt to deal with the case of the Jurchen Chin. The Chin dynasty is known for its occupation of North China as a rival state of the Southern Sung, and its eventual assimilation by the Chinese civilization. The obscurity of the Chin in other respects owes much to its less prominent position in Chinese history, in terms of wealth and power, than those of the mighty Yüan and the durable and stable Ch'ing. The Jurchen conquest of North China, however, is significant in that it marks the rise of conquest dynasties and that it sets up a pattern of alien rule in China, with its institutions being imitated and modified by subsequent conquest dynasties. The Jurchen conquest can be considered as part of a process of the barbarian encroachment of the Sung Empire, starting with the Ch'i-tan incursions, and served as the prelude to Mongol invasion. Indeed by the thirteenth century Eurasia has witnessed the upsurge of the military power of the nomads in Inner Asia. The technology and military strategy centering upon the use of the horse were perfected and effectively employed by these nomads to attack the agricultural societies. Military organization, together with political skills acquired from the sedentary societies, enabled them to rule the conquered areas and populace. The Jurchen mastered such techniques and skills, took advantage of the weakness of the Liao and Sung dynasties to destroy them, and became the first group of people from Manchuria ever to establish a kingdom in China.

There are two alien dynastic patterns: the nomadic Ch'i-tan and Mongols, and the hunting-fishing-farming Jurchen-Manchus.[7] Historians have tended to treat the Jurchen as a people similar to the Ch'i-tan and Mongols, simply because there have been more studies on the latter. But Jurchen and Manchus differed from the Ch'i-tan and Mongols in subsistence economy--farming was important to the former but not to the latter; and in that the former gradually transformed themselves into Chinese, but the latter never took over all Chinese institutions and customs. Further, dynasties set up by the Tungusic Jurchen and Manchus were more successful than any other alien dynasties in China. While the Ch'i-tan never intended or were able to control North China, the Jurchen stayed in that area for over a hundred years (1126-1234). Compared with the Jurchen, the Mongols maintained a longer rule in China--134 years in North China (1234-1368) and 89 in South China (1279-1368). They, however, could not match the achievement of the Manchus, who dominated China for over two and a half centuries.

The literature in Western languages on the Jurchen Chin is scarce. The only account of Chin history is C. de Harlez's French translation of a Ch'ing work. Recently there has been a growing interest in Chin historiography, art, and literature, and the literature on Chin society that should emerge will fill an important gap in our knowledge of the period between the Liao and the Yüan.[8] In China and Japan, substantial scholarship has been devoted to the Chin period. This study has been benefited by scholarly works of Shih Kuo-ch'i, Yao Ts'ung-wu, Liu Ming-shu, Mao Wen, Mikami Tsugio, and Toyama Gunji.[9] There are only two articles, however, on the sinicization of the Jurchen, in which the

Introduction

assimilation of the Jurchen by the Chinese is emphasized, neglecting Jurchen efforts in maintaining their cultural heritage and their influence on the Chinese civilization.[10]

The problem of sinicization in this study will be considered in the context of social and cultural change. Although there is a distinction between social and cultural change, they are closely interrelated, and according to Francis R. Allen, "change in human affairs is best approached through a combination of social and cultural change."[11] The sociocultural change in twelfth-century North China was complicated by the invasion and rule of the Jurchen. In analyzing this change, the conceptual tools of acculturation and assimilation are helpful. There are, however, some semantic confusions about these terms. Whereas anthropologists tend to view assimilation as a phase or a result of acculturation, sociologists consider acculturation as included in assimilation.[12] The term assimilation is used in this study in the sense of F. C. Anthony Wallace's statement that "in assimilation, the subordinate group attempts to abandon its existing inadequate culture by entering into the society of the dominant group and accepting its culture, almost *in toto* (retaining only token vestiges of their distinctive culture traits)."[13] The term so defined includes both acculturation and integration.[14] The concept of sinicization is employed in this study in the same sense as assimilation. Anthropologists generally agree on acceptance, syncretism, and reaction as possible results of acculturation. In addition to studies on these results, the research on diffusion and innovation provides valuable reference in analyzing historical data[15]

I am deeply indebted to Professor Ssu-yü Teng, my adviser at Indiana University, who from the beginning gave me suggestions, pointed out shortcomings, and advised a number of changes in the progress of this study. Professor Robert H. Ferrell carefully undertook the time-consuming task of improving the English, and made valuable suggestions both in organization and presentation of the material. I want to express my gratitude to the late Professor Ts'ung-wu Yao, my advisor at National Taiwan University, and Professor George Beech, my former colleague at Western Michigan University, who kindly read the manuscript. I also owe a great deal to

Professors Frederick W. Mote and Hok-lam Chan for their penetrating criticism and valuable suggestions. Mrs. Margery Lang offered me helpful editorial assistance in the final stage of preparation. I owe a debt of gratitude to the staff of the Indiana University Library, and those of the East Asian Library at Columbia University, the Harvard-Yenching Library, Libraries of National Taiwan University, the National Central Library, and the Fu Ssu-nien Library, Academia Sinica, for kindness and helpfulness. Finally, I am particularly thankful to Chia-lin Pao Tao, my wife, who has helped in preparing the manuscript and made a number of criticisms. The errors that remain are my own.

THE JURCHEN IN TWELFTH-CENTURY CHINA

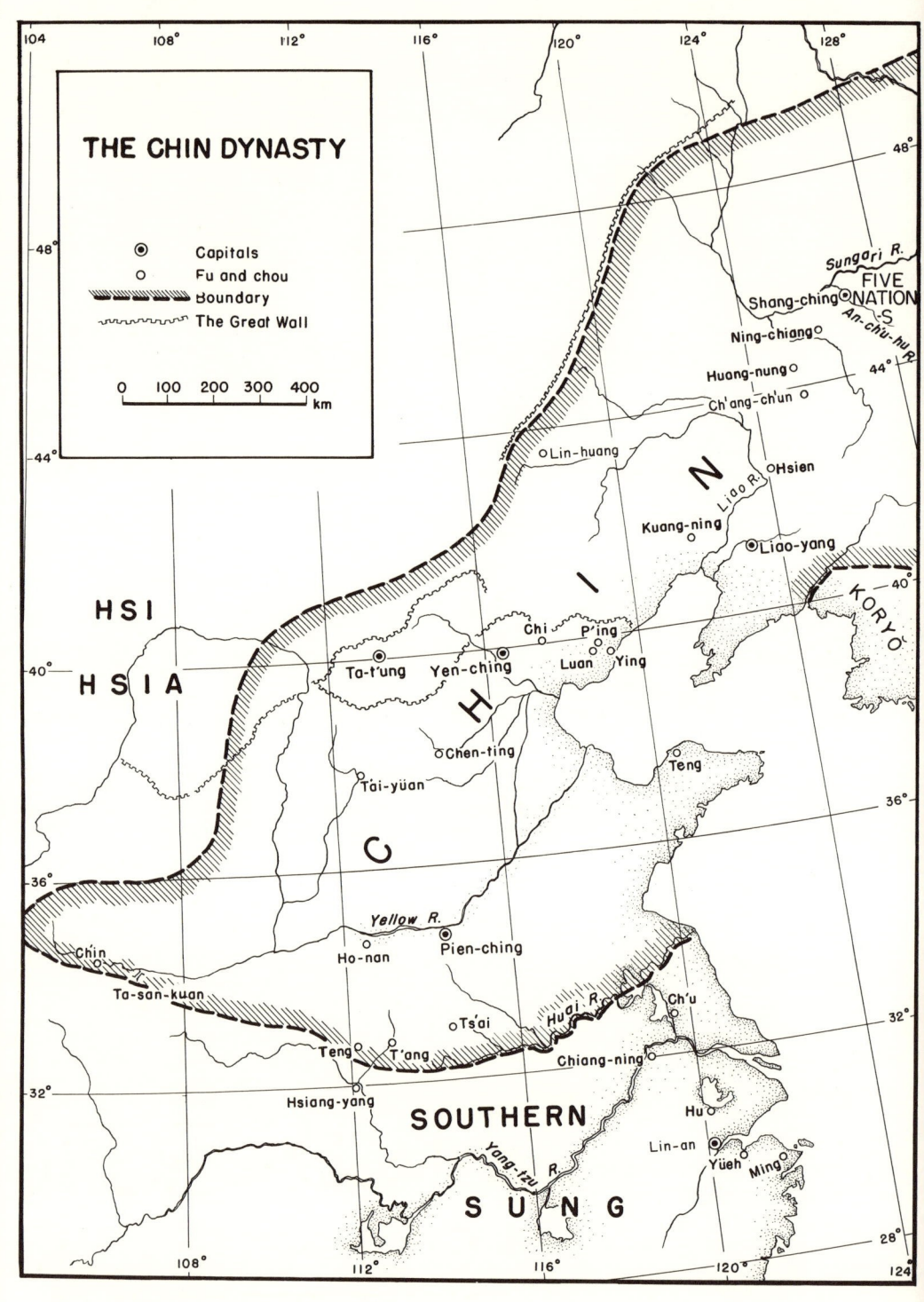

1

The Origin of the People and Their Culture before 1115

Origins

The name Jurchen first appeared in Chinese history in 903. There are several variations, such as Nü-chen, Nü-chih, Chu-li-chen, Chu-erh-ch'e, Chu-shen, Jurched, Jürced, and so on. In the Jurchen language, it renders as 賨谷, pronounced Jusen. In this study the designation "Jurchen" is used.[1]

As soon as the name Jurchen appeared in Chinese chronicles, traditional historians began to identify these people with others in Manchuria, the earliest being the Su-shen tribes in the sixth century B.C., who sent China tribute consisting of bows and stone-pointed arrows.[2] It seems that the writers of Chinese dynastic histories used the name Su-shen to designate almost all peoples in eastern Manchuria, regardless of possibly different ethnic origins. In writing a new chapter on the barbarians, the compilers of several dynastic histories simply took a group of people in the previous dynasty for a present group, though the two groups had different names. None explained why there were different names for the same people; none gave evidence for identification of a later group with an earlier one. In this manner they identified the I-lou from the third to fifth centuries A.D. with the Su-shen; the Mo-ho from the sixth to the eleventh centuries with the Su-shen and I-lou; the Po-hai in the ninth and tenth centuries with all the above.³ Thus most historians believed that the Su-shen were the remote ancestors of the Jurchen.⁴

One of the weaknesses in the notion that the Jurchen were descendants of the Su-shen is to assume that since ancient times there has been only one ethnic group in Manchuria. Modern archaeological and anthropological studies reveal that for millennia Manchuria has been an area where cultures and peoples met. The ocean cultural tradition was dominant during the sub-Neolithic stage; later the Yellow River and Gobi cultures made inroads, their influences becoming the most important in this region.⁵ Nor did ethnic elements in Manchuria originate from one source. The designation of any group's origin is difficult, for traditional Chinese records about aboriginal peoples are by no means the works of ethnographers; there is a lack of anthropological data.

One of the major cultural traditions in Manchuria, the ocean tradition, is characterized by a subsistence pattern of hunting, fishing, and some farming, and the practice of subterranean dwelling. Distribution of these inhabitants of Manchuria and eastern Siberia has been widespread since prehistoric times.⁶ Another major people, the Shamanist Tungus, whose economy was hunting, fishing, some farming, but principally stockbreeding, appeared later in Manchuria. Their early distribution may have been from the Lake Baikal region to the upper Amur River,⁷ and their ethnic makeup may have contained elements from the area south of Lake Baikal, the Gobi region. From the first millennium A.D. the Tungus who settled down in Manchuria have mingled with or even assimilated other peoples and have also adopted their customs.⁸

Modern historians and anthropologists no longer believe in the mono-ethnogenetic origin of peoples in Manchuria, and new interpretations of traditional Chinese accounts have appeared in the past several decades. Ling Ch'un-sheng thinks it is doubtful to regard the Su-shen as a Tungusic people, and P. Schmidt acknowledges that the I-lou and Po-hai belonged to the "Paleo-Asiatics." Ts'ao T'ing-chieh, Liu Chieh, and Ling consider that the names Wo-tsu, I-lou, Fu-yü, Wu-chi, Mo-ho, and Wu-che are all different transliterations of the same term, Wo-chi, which means "dense forests in the mountains." People bearing these names may all have been forest hunters and fishermen, the oldest population in Manchuria.[9] Recent studies of Chinese chronicles appear to confirm this assumption by considering that the Su-shen, Wu-chi, Fu-yü, and I-lou were related to the Hui and Mo people, who belonged to the ocean cultural tradition.[10] Archaeological finds in Hsi-t'uan-shan, Kirin, however, seem to suggest that the Hsi-t'uan-shan culture, which differs from other remains in Kirin, represents the culture of the Su-shen and the I-lou. According to archaeologists, the bones of Hsi-t'uan-shan belong to the Tungusic people, and among the remains, the bones of pigs are abundant, indicating an important element in the Tungusic way of life.[11] Historical records tell that both the Su-shen and I-lou raised pigs, and that the language of the I-lou was different from the Koguryŏ and Fu-yü languages, which perhaps were of the ocean cultural tradition.[12] In short, it seems that the Su-shen, and more probably the I-lou, were of Tungusic origin, whereas other peoples such as the Wu-chi and Fu-yü, were people with the ocean cultural tradition.

It is certain that there was an intimate relationship between the Mo-ho and the Jurchen. In the first place, traditional Chinese chroniclers unanimously thought the two were of the same origin. The brief statement in the *Sung-mo chi-wen* by Hung Hao reads, "The Jurchen are in the country of Su-shen in ancient times. They were called I-lou in the Yüan Wei period [A.D. 386-550] and Mo-ho in the Sui and T'ang dynasties."[13] A similar description in the *San-ch'ao pei-meng hui-pien* by Hsü Meng-hsin is probably based upon Hung's work. Another source, the *Ta-Chin-kuo chih*, attributed to Yü-wen Mao-chao (thirteenth century), adds that the Jurchen were the descendants of the Hei-shui Mo-ho.[14] Finally, description of the Jurchen in the *Chin-shih* (Dynastic History of the Chin) gives similar information: "The origin of the Chin was from the Mo-ho. Mo-ho were originally called Wu-chi, and Wu-chi were in the place occupied by Su-shen in ancient times."[15] If these evidences are not yet sufficient to support the thesis that the Jurchen had a long existence in Manchuria (for historians customarily copied from those who had gone before them), Korean sources point to the same conclusion--that Jurchen and Mo-ho were of the same origin. They show that Mo-ho, Hei-shui Mo-ho, and Jurchen were the same people. For example, there were thirty "Jurchen clans" at one time, and Korean chroniclers said that these clans belonged to the Hei-shui Mo-ho. Moreover, a chieftain of the Hei-shui was sometimes referred to as chief of the Eastern Jurchen, and in other times as that of the Hei-shui Mo-ho. Eastern Jurchen and Hei-shui are also synonyms.[16]

The interchangeability of these names may mean that Mo-ho and Jurchen had the same ancestors, but another difficulty arises, for in Chinese chronicles there is a distinction between the two. It appears that the Jurchen invaded the Ch'i-tan in 924, and the Hei-shui kingdom sent presents to China in 925. Mo-ho envoys went to Ch'i-tan court in the next year, and a Jurchen mission visited the Ch'i-tan in 927. A possible interpretation is that the Mo-ho may have mingled with the more ancient population long before the Jurchen, another group of Tungus, became powerful. The Jurchen may have been subject to the Mo-ho for a long time, and hence were also called Mo-ho or Hei-shui Mo-ho. This is common practice among peoples surrounding China.[17] When the Jurchen became the most influential tribe in Manchuria in 1100, the Mo-ho suddenly disappeared in history, probably because the Jurchen had subjugated all the Mo-ho tribes, and all the Mo-ho called themselves Jurchen. Thereafter historians referred to the two simply as Jurchen.

Culture

During the Liao dynasty of the Ch'i-tan the Jurchen spread over eastern Manchuria. According to the influence received from the Ch'i-tan, traditional historians roughly divided the people into three groups. The "civilized Jurchen" were those who moved and settled down at or south of Liao-yang. Those who lived in the area of the prefecture of Hsien (now Kai-yüan in Liaoning) to the middle Sungari River were under the military control of the Ch'i-tan. In the middle and lower Sungari the people were the "savage [*sheng*] Jurchen," who received the least Ch'i-tan influence. These last people were to become rulers of Manchuria and North China for 120 years.[18]

The original savage Jurchen culture was a mixture of hunting, fishing, agriculture, and stockbreeding. Much evidence shows that in many areas of Jurchen territory farming was predominant: oxen were requested as early as 1042 from the Koryŏ government by some chieftains;[19] archaeological findings related to the Liao-Chin periods in the middle Sungari region show remnants of iron plows; the people planted rice, millet, and wheat as their staples; and when they took up arms against the Ch'i-tan they sent soldiers to till the newly acquired land. In Jurchen ceremonies there was also an element of agriculture; when Wan-yen A-ku-ta (1068-1123) became emperor in 1115, he displayed nine farming tools in the coronation ceremony, indicating the intended conquest of good farmland, and before 1115 Jurchen chieftains had observed the ceremony of goading a clay ox in early spring to insure a good harvest.[20]

The construction of houses and walled towns is further evidence of the extent of their agricultural development. Several dozen wooden buildings or log cabins formed a village or walled town (*chai* or *ch'eng*). A Sung envoy took down many names of such villages as P'u-li po-chin chai, T'o-sa po-chin chai, and so forth. Walled towns certainly indicate a permanent, settled life style, and in the *Dynastic History of the Chin* there are quite a few such names as Liu-k'o ch'eng, A-su ch'eng, Tun-en ch'eng, Wu-t'a ch'eng, and Mi-li-mi-shih-han ch'eng.[21] The distance between villages or walled towns was from three or five *li* to a hundred *li* (one *li* is approximately one-third mile), permitting people enough land for farming but perhaps not enough for large-scale stockbreeding.[22]

Archaeological evidence confirms the existence of walled towns in the Liao-Chin periods. In the past few years, sites of small walled towns, spaced from ten to twenty kilometers apart, have been discovered in the middle Sungari region. In those identified as belonging to these periods, walls measure from 680 to 5,181 meters. Coins found in these sites are, in the main, of the Northern Sung dynasty, indicating that at least some of the towns may have belonged to the pre-Chin period, for during the Chin dynasty the people had their own coins and also used Southern Sung money.[23] The lack of Jurchen Chin and Southern Sung coins in the sites probably means that such towns had already been abandoned in the early years of the Chin, when a great number of the Jurchen migrated to North China.[24]

Further evidence of sedentary life is the use of

the *k'ang* in the Jurchen house. The *k'ang* was a bed built of bricks or clay, so that it could be heated with a fire underneath; in winter people sat and worked on it for warmth. Visiting the people in 1120, Ma K'uo, a Sung envoy, saw a *k'ang* in Wan-yen A-ku-ta's house.[25] A house with a *k'ang* would suggest a permanent abode.

Still another indication of agriculture in Jurchen life is pig raising.[26] Pigs could not follow the pastoralists, nor could they live in the Gobi, but for sedentary people they were good garbage disposers. The term *Tungus* probably derives from the custom of pig raising.[27]

The Jurchen clans lived in clearly defined regions and confined their activities there in the early twelfth century. When the Chin government compiled old records of the Jurchen, clans were distinguished from others by names, villages, and by the nearby rivers. Remote ancestors of the Wan-yen clan settled down near the P'u-kan River and lived there for a long time, later moving to the Hai-ku River region.[28] These two rivers are close to the present A-shih and Lalin Rivers, both of which flow into the Sungari.[29] The capital of early Chin, Shang-ching (the present A-ch'eng in Kirin), was on the bank of the A-shih River, and the name of the Chin kingdom also derived from the original name of the river, An-ch'u-hu or An-ch'un, which means "gold" in the Jurchen language.[30]

All of these aspects of at least a semiagricultural society, the walled towns, farmland, and domesticated animals resembled those in North China, to the extent that the Jurchen were not antagonistic to the agricultural society found there. It was much easier for them than for nomads to become full-time farmers.

There were, however, other aspects of Jurchen life --hunting, fishing and stockbreeding--activities that enabled people to endure hardship and to improve their fighting skills. These pursuits also offered a chance for recreation, as A-ku-ta once told Ma K'uo: "The happiest thing in our country is hunting." Ma followed A-ku-ta to hunt as far as 500 *li*. Large-scale hunting was called *ta-wei*, or hunting by encirclement, and Ma commented that Jurchen military maneuvers were just like hunting. Another source states that when the Jurchen had Shang-ching as their capital, they hunted throughout the year. Even after they moved the capital to

Origin and Culture

Yen-ching (present-day Peking), they still hunted in winter for more than a month. They were expert archers, exceeding even the Ch'i-tan.[31] The smallest trace of an animal enabled a hunter to find its hiding place, or to pursue and kill it. They used horns made of the bark of the birch tree for imitating calls to lure deer for the kill, and their skill was often employed by Ch'i-tan during the Liao period to entice deer.[32] The Jurchen on their part imitated the Ch'i-tan custom of camping or *na-po* in four seasons. They kept this practice, no matter how superficial, until they moved the capital to Pien-ching (Kaifeng), where there was no hunting ground.[33]

Skilled horsemen, the Jurchen used cavalry as their main force in warring, and had a great many horses when they rose to power.[34] Because every male adult member of the tribe participated in hunting and fishing, he was automatically a soldier in war. Before 1115 this was their only obligation to the tribe, for they did not pay tax, and in case of war the chieftains or a common chieftain of several clans would draft soldiers from the several *po-chin* over whom he had control. The *po-chin* was a chieftain or headman of a clan, and in war he became a *meng-an*, head of a thousand men, or *mou-k'e*, head of a hundred men.[35] In 1116 A-ku-ta organized 300 households into a *mou-k'e* and ten *mou-k'e* into a *meng-an*. Soldiers would bring their own supplies and weapons, and for each soldier there was an assistant called *a-li-hsi* to accompany him to the battleground. When the Jurchen rose against the Ch'i-tan, all warriors were mounted. Jurchen cavalry derived formidable strength and great mobility from its practice of providing each soldier with an assistant and several horses.[36] In short, hunting and stockbreeding, especially horse breeding, provided much mobility, one of the major reasons for the Jurchen conquest of Liao and Northern Sung, and also led many historians to consider the Jurchen a nomadic people.[37]

To have a more complete picture of the Jurchen way of life, it is necessary to mention other features of their culture, some of which bear Ch'i-tan, Koryŏ, and Chinese influences.[38] The ritual of "shooting willow wands" (*she-liu*) was probably an imitation of Ch'i-tan practice. The celebration of this ritual on the fifth day of the fifth month of the Chinese calendar, the

date of the Chinese Dragon Boat Festival, indicates
Chinese influence. Spread of Buddhism to the Jurchen is
an example of cultural borrowing from Koryŏ.[39]

As hunters and fishermen the people ate meat as
well as birds and fish. According to Hung Hao, they had
a special set of confections, including dried fruits,
honey, and glutinous rice; they also had cheese. Together with alcoholic liquor, the confections were
called *ch'a-shih* (tea and confections). People liked
liquor so much they became intoxicated whenever there
was a banquet.[40]

The Jurchen knew how to weave, plant hemp, and cultivate silkworms.[41] They dressed in linen in summer,
preferably in white, and wore furs in winter. Both men
and women liked to wear gold and silver earrings. Women
coiled queues around their heads, while men left their
queues hanging down their backs.[42]

The people seem not to have used much pottery;
utensils were mostly made of wood.[43] Introduction of
iron casting was reportedly late, when it was used for
making weapons. As for transportation, the Jurchen
rode horses, used oxen for carrying loads, and made
dugout boats.[44]

The Jurchen clans were patrilineal; each clan consisted of a few lineages, such as twelve lineages for
the Wan-yen clan, fourteen each for the T'u-tan and Wu-ku-lun clans, seven for the P'u-ch'a clan, and so on.
The Wan-yen clan had marital relations exclusively with
its neighboring clans, such as the T'ang-kua, P'u-ch'a,
Na-lan, P'u-san, Ho-shih-lieh, Wu-lin-ta, and Wu-ku-lun.
Some clans, such as Wen-tu and Hu-li-kai, never intermarried with the Wan-yen.[45] Most Wan-yen lineages
lived near the present A-ch'eng county. A few lineages,
such as those of Yeh-lan District, and of Ho-pao village near the Ma-chi (or Wu-chi) Mountain, were not in
this area, but they may have moved from the center of
the Wan-yen clan. Those clans that intermarried with
the Wan-yen clan were mostly close to this area.[46]

Lineages were the basic organizational units of the
Jurchen. Every lineage occupied a village or walled
town, the chieftain or head of which was a *po-chin*.
Certain villages and walled towns therefore bore the
names of their chieftains, such as T'o-sa po-chin chai,
Tun-en ch'eng, and so forth.[47] Before the rise of the
Wan-yen clan, all the *po-chin* were independent although

Origin and Culture

their sole authority over the clansmen was in the capacity of military leaders in the event of war. Such organization lasted for a long time; even long after the people settled down in North China they still had their villages and walled towns scattered among the Chinese population, with *chai-shih* (fort chiefs) as heads. It was also the original form of the *meng-an* and *mou-k'e* system. When the Wan-yen clan was able to control all the Jurchen clans, the *po-chin* became *meng-an* and *mou-k'e* in case of war, thus becoming the military officers of the Chin kingdom.[48]

Differentiation in social classes was not obvious in pre-Chin times. Wan-yen Wu-ch'i-mai (r. 1123-35) used to bathe in a river with his clansmen before he became the second ruler of the Chin, and his house, means of transportation, clothing, and food were the same as those of other people.[49] But slavery existed very early, an important source of which were the predatory wars against Liao and Koryŏ.[50] Social stratification became more evident after the people received more Chinese and Ch'i-tan influences. The Jurchen, in unifying all the clans and conquering other peoples, used prisoners of war as the slave class. For example, after one battle the Wan-yen men robbed the conquered clan; those who refused to submit were taken as slaves. In another battle the Wan-yen men destroyed *Liu-k'o ch'eng*, "took the property and slaves and came back."[51]

Slavery existed in another form. The early Jurchen law stipulated that in a case of capital punishment the family members of a criminal became slaves. If relatives of the criminal wanted to redeem their status, they had to pay a ransom of horses, cattle, and other property to the court. To compensate the plaintiff, the defendant had to give away members of his family as slaves.[52]

Corporal punishment was an important element in Jurchen law. Those whose crimes were not serious were subject to beating with willow wands, or to providing recompense with property. Criminals might lose ears or noses as marks of punishment.[53]

Before A-ku-ta enthroned himself, there was a rudimentary government as a result of efforts made by several generations of Wan-yen chieftains. The chieftain was usually a *chieh-tu shih* or commanding prefect of Liao, with a *kuo-hsiang* or state minister just second to him.⁵⁴ Later there were *po-chi-lieh* as the most important officials, and the *kuo-hsiang* became one of them. Every *po-chi-lieh* had an additional title, such as *tu po-chi-lieh, an-pan po-chi-lieh, kuo-lun po-chi-lieh, a-she po-chi-lieh, wu po-chi-lieh,* and *tieh po-chi-lieh*.⁵⁵ They did administrative work, but sometimes the chieftain, now with the title *tu po-chi-lieh*, would appoint a few *po-chi-lieh* as military commanders. Usually Wan-yen clansmen held all the prominent positions in the government, and members of the imperial lineage monopolized state affairs. Nevertheless, the government in 1115 was not despotic; there were tribal meetings in which all the people could participate and make decisions on important matters. The kowtow ceremony was not performed at A-ku-ta's court in early Chin.⁵⁶

The Jurchen had no written language as late as 1115. Up to that time, government gave orders in the form of lines inscribed on wood tablets, called "inscribed words" (*k'e-tzu*), matters of emergency being marked by three lines. But the Jurchen rapidly adopted the Ch'i-tan and Chinese languages. A-ku-ta in 1119 assigned the task of creating the Jurchen script to Wan-yen Hsi-yin, who imitated the Ch'i-tan system in using Ch'i-tan and Chinese characters.⁵⁷

The Jurchen practiced polygamy and levirate. When a man died, his brother could take his wife, or his son or his brother's son could take his concubine. Parents arranged most marriages. In marriage protocol the bridegroom went to the home of the bride with gifts, usually horses and cattle. After the wedding there was the custom of suitor service--the groom had to serve in his bride's home generally for three years.⁵⁸ An indigenous custom was levirate marriage, a kind of collateral inheritance, or inheritance by brother from brothers in preference to the children.⁵⁹ Later they adopted primogeniture with great difficulty, as manifested in disputes for several generations rising from contested succession to the throne.

The original religious belief of the people was shamanism. An important figure for the founding of the Chin kingdom and the inventor of the Jurchen language, Wan-yen Hsi-yin, was a shaman. The Jurchen believed that a shaman had the power to kill by magic, and could predict the sex of an unborn child. By his magic power

Origin and Culture

a shaman could also cure disease.[60] A custom related to shamanism was acquisition of mythical strength by cutting one's forehead with a knife and letting blood and tears roll down together. When used as a mourning ritual it was called "sending blood and tears" (*sung hsüeh-lei*).[61] When A-ku-ta swore to avenge the Ch'i-tan, he cut his forehead and made a demogogic speech to his followers. When a famous general, Wan-yen Wu-chu, was to fight his way back across the Yangtze in 1130, he sacrificed a woman, a white horse, and cut his forehead in a ritual for acquiring magic power. Such ritual was in part conducted as an act of worship of heaven. Like the Ch'i-tan, the Jurchen worshipped the sun, and this custom, later with Chinese modification, persisted until the end of the dynasty. Buddhism came from Koryŏ, and a brother of the founding ancestor of the Wan-yen clan was a Buddhist.[62]

As for funeral practices, they buried their dead without a coffin. When a noble died his favorite slaves and saddled horses were burned alive and buried with him. They burned the sacrificial food and alcoholic liquor, a practice called "burning the cooked rice" (*shao-fan*). A contemporary writer reported that the people had a peculiar way of preserving a corpse with salt and alum.[63]

From the above account one sees that by the twelfth century the Jurchen had received much influence from outside. Immersed in a long process of acculturation, the Jurchen culture was by no means primitive. Their success in conquests over the Ch'i-tan and Chinese was largely due to their military superiority, but other factors contributed to the founding of the Chin dynasty as well.

2

The Rise of the Chin Dynasty

Political Developments Prior to 1115

The rise of the Jurchen was partly owing to the breeding and use of the horse. Trade, the horse trade especially, with both the Liao and the Northern Sung, accelerated the growth of Jurchen economic and military power.

The Jurchen had close relations with the Liao Empire. As early as 903, when the Ch'i-tan had not yet established the Liao dynasty, they subdued the Jurchen with a military expedition. The latter sent tribute to the Liao in 927, becoming, some time afterward, Ch'i-tan vassals. By 968, Jurchen chieftains received official titles from the Ch'i-tan,[1] and when the Ch'i-tan were to invade Koryŏ in 1010, the Jurchen helped them with 10,000 horses. Occasionally the Jurchen were restless; they raided the Ch'i-tan in 924, 973, and 975. A punitive expedition against the Jurchen in 985-86 is said to have captured more than two hundred thousand horses, which seems an incredible number. In the early trade between the two peoples the major articles exported from the Jurchen to the Ch'i-tan were gold, cloth, honey, wax, and raw materials for drugs. The most important trading post was the prefecture of Ning-chiang (now Shih-t'ou-ch'eng-tzu).[2] It is noteworthy that the earliest account about the Jurchen did not mention horses as their livestock, but oxen, deer, and dogs.[3] Horses became increasingly important in trade, and sending tributary horses to the Liao became more frequent after 1080. In the mid-eleventh century the Jurchen even paid an annual tribute of 10,000 horses to the Ch'i-tan. Partly as a result, the Ch'i-tan herds flourished and increased to more than one million--so the records say-- in 1086.[4] Economic effects of the trade on the Jurchen are not clear, because of lack of data. One thing is certain: the tributary system in Chinese history was beneficial economically to tributary states or tribes; the Ch'i-tan tributary system, which was an imitation of the Chinese model, may not have been an exception.[5] There is evidence that Jurchen wealth increased at the time of Wu-ku-nai (1021-74) when the Jurchen could buy iron weapons from neighboring countries to enhance their military strength.[6]

Jurchen-Koryŏ relations were similar to those of Jurchen-Ch'i-tan. A Jurchen chieftain sent 700 horses, together with other native products, to Koryŏ in 948, marking the beginning of relations between the two peoples. The Jurchen furnished Koryŏ with information about the Ch'i-tan, revealing, in 993, a Ch'i-tan plan of invading Koryŏ.[7] Although the Jurchen paid tribute to Koryŏ and received official titles, they raided and looted Koryŏ borders, and even guided the Ch'i-tan to attack Koryŏ in 1013.[8]

Chinese-Jurchen relations began in 924 when the Jurchen paid tribute to the Later T'ang; they again sent presents with horses to the Northern Sung in 961.[9] Until the second decade of the twelfth century Sung-Jurchen relations had centered around the trade and tribute of horses. To encourage the horse trade the Sung court in 963 exempted the inhabitants of the Sha-men Island in the prefecture of Teng of Shantung from taxation, and ordered them instead to prepare boats for transporting horses from the Liaotung peninsula to Shantung.[10] A profitable trade did not materialize, for the Ch'i-tan cut off the horse route in 991.[11] Ninety years later the Sung court asked the king of Koryŏ to allow the Jurchen to trade horses with China through his territory, but the Jurchen did not come. In the 1110s, when the Sung Chinese tried to secure a Jurchen alliance against the Ch'i-tan, they still wanted to buy horses from the Jurchen.[12]

The Chinese and Ch'i-tan acquired Jurchen horses to maintain and improve their military power, a trade especially important to the Ch'i-tan, for they reckoned both their wealth and military strength in horses.[13] Thus Chinese and Ch'i-tan demand for horses may well have encouraged horse breeding among the Jurchen, who also bred horses for defending themselves against the Ch'i-tan. Prolonged exploitation and slavery was a challenge to the Jurchen to improve their military forces, especially cavalry.

One may say that on the eve of conquering the Liao and Sung the Jurchen were primarily agriculturists who had mastered the adroit use of the horse for military purposes. Chinese records reveal that in the later part of the first millennium B.C. horses already existed in Manchuria. It was only when the Jurchen employed them for large-scale warfare that they became the first people from Manchuria to set up a dynasty in China. Certainly the reasons for the success of the Jurchen are manifold, but the combined effect of a sedentary existence and horse breeding was an important contributing factor in the conquest first of Manchuria and later of North China.[14]

The rise of the people in the early twelfth century was also the result of a gradual growth of political power. Struggle for supremacy of the Wan-yen clan, later the imperial clan of the Chin, among the Jurchen and other tribes is an interesting story. The Wan-yen clan first appeared in Korean history when a Jurchen mission that included leaders of thirty clans paid tribute to Koryŏ in 1012. Korean historians recorded the surname of one of the clans as *Man-yin-i*, which is phonetically similar to Wan-yen.[15] The names of A-ku-ta's ancestors according to the *Dynastic History of the Chin* are given in table 1.[16]

The *Dynastic History* shows that Han-p'u came from Korea, which was Koryŏ (918-1392), not Koguryŏ (37-668), for there were only four "generations" between Han-p'u and Wu-ku-nai, who was born in 1021.[17] One must conclude that there was the practice of inheritance among brothers, as Ho-li-po, P'o-la-shu, and Ying-ko were brothers and belonged to the same generation.[18] It is safe to assume that Han-p'u moved from Koryŏ to Manchuria in the early or middle tenth century and settled in the Mutan River region. After four "generations" Sui-k'o moved to the banks of the Hai-ku River, near the present A-shih River. His successor Shih-lu began to

TABLE 1
Wan-yen Forbears of A-ku-ta

Name	Posthumous Title	Date of Birth and Death
Han-p'u	Shih-tsu	?
Wu-lu	Te-ti	?
Pa-hai	An-ti	?
Sui-k'o	Hsien-tsu	?
Shih-lu	Chao-tsu	?
Wu-ku-nai	Ching-tsu	1021-74
Ho-li-po	Shih-tsu	1040-92
P'o-la-shu	Su-tsung	1042-93
Ying-ko	Mu-tsung	1053-1103
Wu-ya-shu	K'ang-tsung	1061-1113

introduce law and order in the clan, which became powerful, and the Liao government appointed Shih-lu as a Liao official. Wu-ku-nai defeated two tribal chieftains of the neighboring Five Nations (*Wu-kuo pu*) for the Ch'i-tan, and received the title of "Commanding Prefect of the Jurchen Tribe" (*Nü-chen pu-tsu chieh-tu shih*).[19] The people then made weapons with iron, and all the neighboring clans and Wan-yen lineages obeyed Wu-ku-nai. After him Ho-li-po, P'o-la-shu, Ying-ko, and Wu-ya-shu also suppressed rebellious tribes for the Ch'i-tan, making the Jurchen the most powerful tribe in the middle Sungari region and the Wan-yen men firmly established in its central leadership. Among the four leaders, Ying-ko was the most ambitious and capable; he "endeavored in agriculture, collected grains, trained soldiers, and bred horses."[20] He stopped the sending of horses as tribute to the Ch'i-tan, and after 1100 he refused tribute to Liao and Koryŏ. He was interested in expanding his territory to the Koryŏ borderlands.

Ying-ko's ambition in Koryŏ engendered a clash with that country. Under the leadership of Wu-ya-shu the Jurchen defeated Koryŏ several times, forcing peace in

1113. Having eliminated the danger of fighting on two fronts, the Jurchen turned their attention to Ch'i-tan borders. At a banquet in 1112 A-ku-ta dared to refuse to dance for the last Ch'i-tan emperor. He repeatedly asked the Ch'i-tan to hand over a rebellious Jurchen leader who fled to Liao; but Liao replied with troops to reinforce the control of borderlands. A-ku-ta attacked the Ch'i-tan in late 1114, and in the following year enthroned himself as the first emperor of the Chin state.

It is clear that the Jurchen chieftains, acting as Ch'i-tan officials, not only maintained peace for Liao among tribes in eastern Manchuria, but built their own authority by punishing disobedient tribes. The police function worked to the advantage of these Jurchen chieftains.

From their earliest appearance in history to the establishment of the Chin state, the Jurchen experienced more than two hundred years of political, economic, and military development and by the year 1115 were no longer disorganized primitives. Culturally they had received Ch'i-tan, Chinese, and Koryŏ influences, which combined with an energy that both Liao and Sung lacked. Growth of military power, enlargement of territory, and aggrandizement of authority among other tribes in eastern Manchuria were conducive to the establishment of a tribal and marginal state on the borders of the Middle Kingdom.[21] When the time was ready, these ambitious Tungus would contest with the Ch'i-tan and Chinese for leadership in East Asia.

Conquest of Liao and Northern Sung

Attacks of the Jurchen on the Liao empire began in 1114. Within twelve years (1114-26) they not only destroyed the Liao, but also conquered North China and overthrew the Northern Sung. Their success was partly due to the internal weaknesses of the two declining dynasties.

With decay and increasing corruption of the Liao court in the last few decades of its existence, exploitation and slavery of peoples of non-Ch'i-tan origin intensified. One of the causes for which the Ch'i-tan drove the Jurchen to open rebellion was the Ch'i-tan demand for a kind of falcon called *hai-tung-ch'ing*,

Rise of the Chin Dynasty

which came from the northeastern seacoast of Jurchen territories and was trained by the Ch'i-tan for hunting. Missions sent by Liao to buy these birds went through these regions, and their wicked deeds incurred a deep hatred among the Jurchen.[22] Further, in business transactions Ch'i-tan officials and merchants often cheated the Jurchen, resulting in many Jurchen grievances. The immediate cause for rebellion, or A-ku-ta's pretext to provoke a war against their rulers, was Ch'i-tan protection of A-su, a Jurchen rebel. When Ying-ko expanded his domain to that of A-su, the latter fled to seek Ch'i-tan assistance. The Ch'i-tan refused to hand him over to the Jurchen, and instead, concentrated their army in Ning-chiang Prefecture. That move inspired A-ku-ta to resort to force.[23]

After the outbreak of war in the autumn of 1114, A-ku-ta defeated a Ch'i-tan army with only 2,500 men and took Ning-chiang Prefecture. He proceeded to disrupt another Ch'i-tan army at Ch'u-ho-tien (now on the south bank of Sungari, near Jen-chia-tien). By this time his troops had increased to 10,000 men. He marched to the prefecture of Huang-lung (now Nung-an, Kirin) and Ch'ang-ch'un (now Ch'ang-ch'un) in late 1115, destroying a huge enemy force reportedly containing 700,000 men under the personal command of T'ien-tsu ti, the last Liao emperor.[24]

Meanwhile the Ch'i-tan suffered from internal dissension. Yeh-lü Chang-nu and Kao Yung-ch'ang's rebellions in 1115-16 accelerated the disintegration of the empire.[25] Taking advantage of the situation, A-ku-ta overran the area north of the Liao River.[26] At this juncture the Northern Sung Chinese decided to ally with the rising Jurchen against the Ch'i-tan, to "use barbarians to fight barbarians." The Sung government sent envoys to negotiate with the Jurchen in 1118, and a treaty was concluded in 1120, in which the two parties agreed to attack the Ch'i-tan from two fronts. The Sung was to give annual presents to the Chin instead of Liao, providing the latter's destruction. Accordingly, A-ku-ta took the Central Capital (now Ning-ch'eng, Jehol) of Liao in 1120-21 (the Supreme Capital already had fallen into his hands in 1119), but the Chinese failed to take the Southern Capital (now Peking), and fell to the Jurchen in 1121.[27] With Emperor T'ien-tsu escaping westward, Sung and Chin further agreed upon return of Yen-ching and the so-called Sixteen Prefectures of Yen and Yün to the Sung, while Chin got the rest of Liao territories, roughly the area north of the Great Wall.[28]

The death of A-ku-ta in 1123 did not halt the expansion of Jurchen influence. After Wu-ch'i-mai's enthronement, the Hsi Hsia kingdom submitted to the Chin as a tributary state in 1124, while Koryŏ followed suit in 1126.[29] The Jurchen captured the Liao emperor in 1125, thus ending the Liao dynasty.[30] The remnant Ch'i-tan forces fled to the west under the leadership of Yeh-lü Ta-shih, the founder of the Qārā-Khitay kingdom (Hsi Liao).[31]

The declining Sung now had to face the rising Chin. Sung policy makers, including the poet-emperor Hui-tsung, failed to realize that their weak military forces and the few thousand soldiers called the Ever Victorious Army (*ch'ang-sheng chün*) led by Kuo Yao-shih, who had defected from the disintegrating Liao, were unreliable.[32] The Sung court attempted to recover from the Jurchen all the territories lost to the Liao during the Five Dynasties (907-60), even demanding the return of the prefectures of P'ing, Luan, and Ying, places not included in those ceded to Liao.[33] The Jurchen refused, on the ground that according to the treaty of 1120 the territories supposed to be taken by the Chinese did not include these places. They delayed and even refused to return northern Shansi, which A-ku-ta had promised to hand over to the Sung.[34] Although many people in the Yen and Yün regions preferred Sung to alien rule, the Sung government was too weak to protect them, even allowing the Jurchen to take properties and move wealthy families from Yen-ching to Manchuria. When Chang Chüeh, a Chinese official under the Chin, rose against the Jurchen and asked for Sung protection, the Sung authorities, unable to provide it, killed him and sent his head to the Jurchen.[35] This affair caused much disappointment and disillusion among the Yen Chinese, some of whom were so bitter that they urged the Jurchen to invade Sung, and provided them with important information and guidance.[36]

Wan-yen Nien-han, Wan-yen Wo-li-pu, and other Jurchen generals favored a preemptive war to prevent the Sung Chinese from stabilizing their new position in the Yen-yün region. Their pretext was that Sung had sent

Rise of the Chin Dynasty

spies to disturb Jurchen territories and protected rebels who escaped from Chin-controlled areas, in addition to Sung's unwillingness to give annual presents to the Chin.[37] The Jurchen dispatched two armies into North China in late 1125; one, led by Wo-li-pu, the right vice-marshal (*yu fu-yüan-shuai*), was called the Eastern Army, which marched southward after taking Yen-ching. The other was led by Nien-han, the left vice-marshal, who invaded Shansi. While Nien-han's Western Army was surrounding T'ai-yüan in Shansi, the Eastern Army met little resistance after surrender of Kuo Yao-shih, and laid seige to Pien-ching in the spring of 1126. Wo-li-pu brought Emperor Ch'in-tsung (Hui-tsung had abdicated in early 1126) to terms: Sung was to cede to Chin three garrison posts in Hopei and Ho-tung (Shansi), in addition to paying a large indemnity.[38] After Ch'in-tsung acceded to the demands, Wo-li-pu withdrew his army.

As soon as the Jurchen released pressure on the Sung capital, the war faction dominating the Sung court refused to give up the three garrison posts. War broke out again when the Jurchen accused the Chinese of enticing Yeh-lü Yü-tu, Nien-han's ranking general who had defected from the Ch'i-tan, to rebel against his new masters. Wo-li-pu returned with Nien-han, who had broken the defense at T'ai-yüan; the two generals besieged Pien-ching for a month (from December 10, 1126, to January 9, 1127), took it, captured the two Sung emperors, and escorted them to Manchuria. The whole imperial clan, a large number of courtiers, as well as priceless treasures, were also taken there. After setting up a puppet regime in Pien-ching, called the Ch'u, with Chang Pang-ch'ang as the emperor, who supposedly would rule the ex-Sung territory south of the Yellow River, Nien-han and Wo-li-pu divided the land north of the Yellow River and ruled with full authority.[39]

Jurchen Military Power

The Jurchen military achievement in the early twelfth century was as surprising as it was brilliant. The compilers of the *Dynastic History of the Chin* commented:

When the Jurchen rose, they employed their army as if with divine power. They won victories and took territories without a match in the world. Within less than ten years they had achieved the establishment of their dynasty. The causes for such swift success were that their customs were fierce, giving them great strength, and that the people were tenacious and vigorous. All the brothers, sons and nephews were talented generals. All the tribes and basic units were good soldiers. In addition, their land was small and poor, and products few. In peacetime they worked hard in the fields to earn a living; in case of war they devoted themselves to fighting in order to capture booty. They constantly practiced physical exercise so that they could endure cold as well as warm weather. The way they drafted and sent soldiers to the battleground was like a family affair. Therefore the commanders were brave and had one spirit; the soldiers were skilled and all possessed great strength. Once they rose and transformed themselves from a weak tribe to a formidable one, they were able to conquer a vast population with a few people.[40]

Chinese writers of this period for the most part attributed Jurchen victories to the cavalry. It has already been pointed out that Ma K'ou's observation of Jurchen hunting led him to conclude that Jurchen military maneuvers were based upon hunting skills. Comments from other Chinese writers are: "When the Jurchen at first rebelled (against the Ch'i-tan), all soldiers were mounted"; and "The Jurchen were experts in riding, and they often won battles with cavalry."[41] The soldiers were well equipped with heavy armor, and in some cases several horses were attached together with chains to form a horse team (the famous *kuai-tzu ma*).[42]

The *San-ch'ao pei-meng hui-pien* provides a striking description of an engagement between 17 Jurchen horsemen and 2,000 Chinese foot soldiers in 1126:

When the peace negotiations were concluded the Jurchen sent seventeen horsemen to report to their government, en route to Tz'u prefecture. Considering that he had responsibilities as a military officer and that the government order to repel the Jurchen was still in effect, Li K'an commanded 2,000 troops and militia to attack the Jurchen forces. When the troops encountered the seventeen horsemen, the latter said, "It is unnecessary to fight, for peace has already been concluded at Pien-ching. We are sent by our prince to report it to our government." K'an did not believe them and wanted to fight. The seventeen horsemen then divided themselves into three groups: seven of them came to the front and five each were disposed on the left and right wings. As they approached the [Sung] government forces, the seven horsemen charged and the government soldiers retreated a little. The two wings took advantage of the retreat and rode into the government forces, shooting arrows. The government forces were dispersed and almost half of the troops were lost.[43]

The military organization seems to have been another important factor in their success. The *meng-an mou-k'e* system as a sociopolitical organization stimulated the morale of the people, for they could occupy new land for their clans and families. The booty acquired by organized raids attracted non-Jurchen, too. Adopting the far-sighted policy that took the shortage of Jurchen manpower into consideration, the Jurchen rulers recruited a number of collaborators to fight for them. One famous example is the Ever Victorious Army led by Kuo Yao-shih, which turned against the Northern Sung and guided the Jurchen to take Hopei.

As brilliant warriors the Jurchen were quick to master Chinese strategies and to borrow Chinese weapons. They developed effective war machines to attack walled towns in a seige, including various kinds of ladders and bridges, catapults, and heavily covered carts carrying sand bags for filling up the moat around the town.[44] The most remarkable weapons they borrowed were firearms. With modifications and improvements, the firearms included bamboo guns, cannons, grenades, and even rockets, all of which were employed on a large scale during the seige of Kaifeng in 1233 to defend the city against the invading Mongols.[45] This famous battle was the first in human history in which gunpowder was used effectively.[46]

These horsemen, however, were not accustomed to fighting on the water and were at a loss when the demands of battle took them from the field, as when the fleet of the Southern Sung prevented them from crossing the Yangtze River in 1129-30. The fourth Chin emperor, Liang, was defeated in 1161, again on the Yangtze, in another attempt to conquer the south. Although the Jurchen did build a navy by employing Chinese artisans and shipbuilders, even naval captains who defected from the southern state, their aspirations suffered a great setback in 1161 when the new navy was shattered and burned by the Southern Sung navy.[47] The Jurchen could not conquer the Southern Sung without a good navy and as a result, the two states coexisted in the twelfth and early thirteenth centuries.

3

The Period of Dualism: 1115–1150

Early Social and Political Changes

The very suddenness and swiftness of the Jurchen conquests surprised the Jurchen themselves. Certainly they were not prepared to move into North China and rule the vast Chinese population. It was quite natural for the new rulers to adopt the Ch'i-tan method of employing Chinese institutions to administer the Chinese populace, while preserving their own tribal structure for the Jurchen.

One of the major effects of expansion of Jurchen territory, and the increase of population under their rule, was that Jurchen tribal organization was no longer adequate to administer the new state. New political and military institutions gradually came into being. The conquerors encountered two urgent problems: how to control and govern the heterogeneous populace, especially the preponderant Chinese; and how to establish among the Jurchen people the dominant position of the Wan-yen clan, especially that of the imperial lineage. The solutions to these problems, which were closely related, seemed at this stage to require the selective adoption of certain Chinese institutions and the establishment of centralized control.

As discussed earlier, the Jurchen political and military institutions in the early twelfth century were the *po-chin* or *po-chi-lieh* and the *meng-an mou-k'e*, which in fact were one system at first. With expansion of the Wan-yen clan its chieftain became the common chieftain of a Jurchen confederation. The Jurchen rulers used a Chinese character *tu* (supervising) to designate the common chieftain as *tu po-chi-lieh*. Having become emperor from the position of *tu po-chi-lieh*, A-ku-ta set up the *po-chi-lieh* institution composed of a number of *po-chi-lieh* as high-ranking government officials, with different titles to denote their functions. For example, the *po-chi-lieh* next to the emperor was the *an-pan po-chi-lieh*, meaning the great *po-chi-lieh*, who was the heir apparent of the emperor.[1]

The *po-chi-lieh* institution, however, was by no means well organized. Frequently A-ku-ta created new titles of *po-chi-lieh*, and abolished others whenever he thought it necessary to give positions to important Jurchen leaders.[2] A-ku-ta seems to have known that to establish a central authority in his state he had to diminish the influence of certain powerful leaders. He managed to achieve this, tactfully and peacefully, by taking over their political and military power. His first object was to deprive his cousin Sa-kai of power. Sa-kai was the eldest son of Ho-che, who was the eldest son of Wu-ku-nai, A-ku-ta's grandfather. A-ku-ta and Sa-kai's relationship is shown in the genealogical chart (table 2).

TABLE 2
Genealogy of A-ku-ta

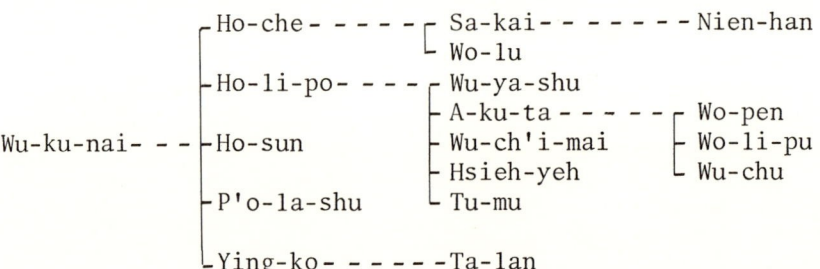

Perhaps because he lacked ability as a leader, Ho-che did not succeed Wu-ku-nai as general chieftain of the Jurchen. Nor did his sons, Sa-kai and Wo-lu, succeed Ying-ko after the latter's death. But Sa-kai, Wo-lu, and Sa-kai's son Nien-han did exert an extremely important influence on the founding of the Chin and early developments of the state. At the time of Ying-ko, Sa-kai was *kuo-hsiang* or state minister, and before 1115 he ruled about half the Jurchen territories. His opinion was decisive when A-ku-ta hesitated over waging war against the Ch'i-tan.[3]

Having founded the state in 1115, A-ku-ta made his brother Wu-ch'i-mai *an-pan po-chi-lieh*, and Sa-kai *kuo-lun hu-lu* (or *tu*) *po-chi-lieh*. Remaining powerful in the central government, Sa-kai nevertheless lost authority in the Lalin River region. In 1116 A-ku-ta appointed Sa-kai's brother Wo-lu as *tieh po-chi-lieh*, another central government post. Wo-lu had been chief commander in southern Manchuria. Having become *tieh po-chi-lieh*, he also lost his local authority.[4] Such measures were A-ku-ta's first steps toward centralization of power in his government.

The highest local authority was assumed by the chief commander and *chün-shuai* or military commander as heads of prefectures.[5] Basic officials were *meng-an* and *mou-k'e*. The *meng-an mou-k'e* system, like the Eight Banners system of the Ch'ing dynasty, was not only a military but a sociocultural institution. The army units in both the Chin and the Ch'ing were also the basic units of their tribal society. The settling of these units at strategic places with the additional task of cultivating land was a practice of both the Jurchen and the Manchus. Politically the *meng-an* and *mou-k'e* were local officials, as in the early Chin the Military Commanders were often *meng-an*.[6] Militarily the *meng-an* and *mou-k'e* functioned as police, garrisoning strategic posts and watching over conquered peoples in their domain.[7] Socially the system maintained the tribal organization of the Jurchen, keeping the conquerors in a dominant and privileged position among the conquered.[8]

The absorption of foreign elements into Jurchen administrative and military organs accompanied their growth of power. With expansion of his territory, A-ku-ta sent *meng-an* and *mou-k'e* to the new land and exercised military rule. He appointed tribal chieftains and Ch'i-tan officials who had surrendered to or collaborated with the Jurchen as *meng-an* and *mou-k'e*. In general, although *meng-an* and *mou-k'e* garrisoned key posts in the conquered area, the old Ch'i-tan local government structure of prefect (*chou*) and counties (*hsien*) remained almost intact. The Jurchen employed former Ch'i-tan bureaucrats and influential landlords as local officials, under supervision of Jurchen personnel. During and after Jurchen attacks on the Liao, many Chinese officials went over to their side.[9] The Jurchen gave titles of *men-an* and *mou-k'e* to those who contributed militarily.

Nineteen Chinese, two Ch'i-tan, six Po-hai, and two Hsi received these titles, according to the *Dynastic History of the Chin*.[10] A method of controlling these foreign associates was to keep their relatives as hostages.[11]

In general, Jurchen policy toward conquered peoples was to treat them leniently. It was a conciliatory policy, if not appeasement. A-ku-ta declared that he only wanted to attack the Ch'i-tan, not the Po-hai, who together with the Jurchen were "originally of the same family." Further, he proclaimed in 1116 that all peoples who surrendered to the Jurchen, including the Ch'i-tan, were to be treated kindly and their chieftains appointed Chin officials. He forbade soldiers to disturb the people, especially their agriculture. Meanwhile A-ku-ta and Wu-ch'i-mai quelled uprisings, most of which were staged by the Chinese. Wu-ch'i-mai not only invited people to join him but also distributed land and helped the impoverished.[12] Most of this compassion and leniency occurred in Manchuria, for the Jurchen army killed a large number of Chinese civilians in North China.[13]

In addition to some relief measures, the Jurchen reduced taxes imposed on the people by the Ch'i-tan, and leveled the unequal taxation between Ch'i-tan and the common people. An important measure was emancipation of Ch'i-tan slaves, which A-ku-ta did in 1116; later, surrendered Ch'i-tan slaves became commoners. Wu-ch'i-mai repeatedly ordered release of the Jurchen originally under Ch'i-tan rule and members of the Wan-yen clan who had become slaves were redeemed with money paid by the government.[14]

To increase tax revenues and the productive power of the new state, Jurchen rulers took many northern Chinese captives to Manchuria. A-ku-ta, for example, transplanted captives to the Shang-ching area during the early years of the war against the Liao. After

Period of Dualism: 1115-1150

taking Yen-ching he moved wealthy families and artisans there to the "interior" of Chin, that is, Shang-ching.[15] Wu-ch'i-mai in 1123 transferred people living near present Shan-hai-kuan to the prefecture of Shen (now Shenyang), and sent some other tribes to Manchuria. People living in Shensi, Honan, and Hupei were forced to move to Hopei. All in all, a contemporary writer reported that after the Jurchen conquered the Northern Sung, more than one hundred thousand Chinese migrated northeastward.[16] The conquerors sustained their troops by making themselves part-time farmers, but most of their revenues were taxes collected from Chinese peasants. To move the Chinese to Manchuria was to facilitate tax collection, an imitation of Ch'i-tan policy.[17] Enforced transfer of Chinese peasants to Manchuria also proved that during the reigns of A-ku-ta and Wu-ch'i-mai the Jurchen had no intention of becoming masters in the Middle Kingdom.

Chinese Influences at Shang-ching

During the time of the first two Chin rulers, Shang-ching became the center of Jurchen culture. There the new Jurchen script created in 1119 was taught.[18] What is more, Chinese influences prevailed there--a result partly of Wu-ch'i-mai and his followers' interest in Chinese civilization, and partly from concentration of Chinese scholars, books, and all sorts of influences from China to Manchuria. While A-ku-ta, Nien-han, and Wo-li-pu led the armies to conquer the Liao and Northern Sung, Wu-ch'i-mai as *an-pan po-chi-lieh* stayed in Shang-ching and ruled Manchuria. He and his most important assistants, Wo-pen, Hsieh-yeh, and Mou-liang-hu, quelled uprisings, pacified refugees and unruly local thugs, reduced taxation, emancipated slaves, and brought Chinese peasants to Manchuria. They encouraged agriculture, tolerated Chinese and Po-hai scholar-gentry, and set up new government institutions.

The Chinese and the sinicized Po-hai, whose achievements during the early Chin periods were as important as those of the Chinese, exerted influence on the Jurchen in Shang-ching. A-ku-ta's chief political adviser was Yang P'u, who, as a sinicized Po-hai, held a Ch'i-tan *chin-shih* degree. Yang was probably the first man at A-ku-ta's court to advocate Chinese administrative practices, such as rules concerning audience with the emperor, and formation of a hierarchy of officials. A-ku-ta knew the value of employing literati; as early as 1117 he chose Chinese scholars to write imperial proclamations and orders and selected capable men to be government officials.[19]

Wu-ch'i-mai seems to have been an enthusiastic protagonist of sinicization. His righthand man, Wo-pen, together with Hsieh-yeh and Mou-liang-hu, proposed to set up a Chinese bureaucracy, and Wu-ch'i-mai implemented the plan in 1126. This government organization was revised and modified in 1134.[20]

The adoption of the Chinese bureaucratic system in 1126 was the result of the initial Chinese influence, which, however, did not change the Jurchen power structure. The *po-chi-lieh* institution retained its main functions, while the Chinese organizations only operated for administration of the non-Jurchen population.[21] Wu-ch'i-mai's attempt at centralization of authority in 1132 suggested reform of the *po-chi-lieh* system. The ever-changing system under him was stabilized and simplified by the creation of a left *po-chi-lieh* and a right *po-chi-lieh* under the *kuo-lun po-chi-lieh*, an organization resembling the Sung Presidential Council, in which under the *shang-shu ling* there was a left and a right minister.[22]

It was said that half of Wu-ch'i-mai's servants were Chinese.[23] Chinese scholar-gentry, especially those of Yen and Manchurian origin, contributed a great deal to the adoption of Chinese institutions. These scholar-gentry included some sinicized Po-hai, such as Yang P'u and the Chang and Li families of Liao-yang.[24] Famous Chinese officials from the Yen region and southern Manchuria were Han Chi-hsien, Tso Chi-kung, Liu Yen-tsung, Shih Li-ai, Meng Hao, Chang T'ung-ku, and Han Fang. Han Fang was once a teacher of Tan (1123-49), the third Chin emperor, and Chang Yung-chih, a Chinese, was the tutor of the fourth emperor Liang (1149-61), and Liang's sons.[25]

Among the Chinese officials Han Chi-hsien was by far the most influential. In the opinion of Wu-lu (1161-89), the fifth emperor, Han was the wisest Chinese prime minister, responsible for establishing many government institutions. He also helped make decisions on important policies in the inner court. As Wu-lu com-

Period of Dualism: 1115-50   31

mented, although Han's contributions to the state could hardly be acknowledged by people outside the court, "of all Chinese prime ministers who served the Chin dynasty, no one could match the achievements of Han."[26]

Besides these Yen and southern Manchurian Chinese, there were some important figures from the Northern Sung. Most important was Yü-wen Hsü-chung, captured by the Jurchen while an envoy to the Chin. He became General Hsi-yin's adviser, and teacher of his sons.[27] He introduced many T'ang and Sung administrative institutions. In Hung Hao's opinion Yü-wen was the chief progenitor of Chin government organization, rank and salary scale, rules of bestowal of honorific titles as well as awarding of hereditary privileges, and regulations for observing the taboo characters and for assigning imperial posthumous names.[28]

Not only Chinese and Po-hai intellectuals gathered in Shang-ching, but people of various professions as well. A-ku-ta, Wu-ch'i-mai, and some generals moved wealthy families and artisans from Yen-ching, Pien-ching, and other places in North China to Shang-ching, together with many Chinese products and treasures.

Among the people brought were: about 470 imperial clansmen; erudites and students of the imperial academy; eunuchs; medical doctors; artisans; prostitutes; imperial gardeners; artisans of Imperial Constructions; actors and actresses; astronomers; musicians. These totaled several thousand men.

Goods imported were: spice and incense, rhinoceros horns, and ivories in the Imperial Treasury; court costumes; sacrificial instruments; medicine; nine bronze tripods and eight imperial seals; books and maps; original copies of proclamations of amnesty; letters accompanying tributary missions from Hsi Hsia; imperial carriages and sedan chairs; weapons of the imperial guards; games and gambling equipment; and numerous treasures.[29]

There was also Ch'i-tan influence, of which probably the most important was Buddhism, the Ch'i-tan state religion. Buddhist temples, such as those at Ch'ing-yüan and Hsing-yüan existed as early as 1123. A famous priest went to Hsing-yüan temple in 1124 and began to study and preach there.[30] Lu I, a Sung envoy, saw Ch'i-tan documents, actors, and musicians at the Jurchen court and observed the practice of Ch'i-tan

etiquette there. In Wu-ch'i-mai's coronation ceremony
the Jurchen used Chinese procedure and music, and sacrificed to heaven and earth according to Chinese custom. The Jurchen custom of revering the sun was converted to the Chinese style in 1126. As early as 1117
A-ku-ta prohibited marriage between two persons having
the same surname, another Chinese practice.[31]

The city plan of Shang-ching was an imitation of
Chinese cities, particularly Pien-ching, although it
was much smaller. According to the archaeologist Torii
Ryuzō, there were two cities side by side in the Chin
period; the northern city was the new one, built by
Tan, the third emperor. Palaces at the time of A-ku-ta
were not much more than tents.[32] Wu-ch'i-mai ordered a
Chinese, Lu Yen-lun, to build a new city in 1124, and
he constructed official buildings as well as private
residences, systematically, with new architectural
methods. Wu-ch'i-mai's Ch'ien-yüan palace was completed
in 1125. The Jurchen in 1123 built the earliest imperial
ancestral temples and tombs, which the two captured Sung
emperors visited in 1128. Thereafter ancestral temples
appeared in all the five capitals of the kingdom.[33]

Dualism and Feudal Forces

The period from 1123 to 1150 was the era of dualism, which was an imitation of the Ch'i-tan dual state,
composed of pastoral tribal elements of the north and
sedentary Chinese of the south.[34] There was, however,
no clear regional division of the Jurchen state. Manchuria and the territories north of the Great Wall
constituted the Jurchen "proper," where the central government ruled both the Jurchen and other peoples, with
the dual administrative system established in 1126.
Furthermore, Jurchen rulers considered the Yen region
and North China a peripheral part of the state. A-ku-ta
organized a sinicized Bureau of Military Affairs (*shu-
mi yüan*) to govern the Chinese sector. The Bureau of
Military Affairs was at first stationed at Kuang-ning
(now Pei-cheng) in 1123,[35] largely manned by Yen Chinese such as Tso Chi-kung, Liu Yen-tsung, and Han Chi-
hsien.[36] Theoretically this organization was under
supervision of the Office of the Grand Marshal (*tu yüan-
shuai fu*) created in 1125 when Wu-ch'i-mai decided to
invade the Northern Sung. The grand marshal was sub-

ordinate in turn to the *an-pan po-chi-lieh* or heir apparent to the emperor.[37] Practically, in the early Chin the two vice-marshals, Nien-han and Wo-li-pu, possessed almost absolute authority in civil administration and military affairs over North China.[38] Besides drafting soldiers, the duty of the Bureau of Military Affairs included employing and promoting local officials, and collecting taxes. It sponsored examinations to select local officials in 1127. Having captured Chen-ting (now Cheng-ting, Hopei) in 1128, Wo-li-pu also held civil service examinations to recruit government officials.[39]

Wu-ch'i-mai's institutional reforms in 1126 seem to have exerted little influence on the political structure in North China. The limit of power of the central government is indicative in the case of Han Chi-hsien, who was in charge of the Bureau of Military Affairs in 1128, and stayed in Shansi. He was appointed left prime minister of the superficial Presidential Council as early as 1129. Since Chinese officials only administered Chinese affairs, he did not go to Shang-ching and have an audience with Wu-ch'i-mai until 1134, when he was appointed chief of the Presidential Council of the newly reformed governmnent.[40]

The Bureau of Military Affairs moved from Kuang-ning to Yen-ching in 1124 and to Ta-t'ung in 1128. There, where it could rule North China flexibly, it remained until 1135.[41] When the Jurchen intended to occupy North China, the power of the bureau extended to the area north of the Huai River, as it did in 1127-30. When they were unable to control the whole of North China, the bureau only ruled the region north of the Yellow River, as in 1130-37.

Another aspect of political dualism in the early Chin was the establishment and support of puppet regimes in China. It aimed at employing Chinese to rule Chinese for two reasons. First, the Jurchen at the time of A-ku-ta and Wu-ch'i-mai were unable to control the whole of North China, not to mention destroying the Southern Sung. A pro-Jurchen satellite was a good solution to the problem. It could act as a buffer state between the Chin and Southern Sung, avoiding direct clashes between them when political and military conditions were unfavorable to the Jurchen. Meanwhile the Jurchen could deal with internal problems and consolidate their position in the area north of the Yellow River.[42] Second, in a more positive sense the Jurchen could use the Chinese against their own people, weakening the Southern Sung and even keeping the Chinese puppet regime from growing too strong.[43] The Jurchen could then spare time and energy to prepare for becoming masters of North China.

The first attempt at establishing a puppet regime in China failed almost immediately after the Jurchen evacuated from Pien-ching. The ninth son of Hui-tsung, Chao Kou, became the first emperor of the Southern Sung in 1127 (his posthumous title was Kao-tsung; r. 1127-62), and destroyed the Chang Pang-ch'ang (the Jurchen puppet emperor) regime. He ordered the capable general Tsung Tse (1059-1128) to defend Pien-ching, and planned to recover the lost territories. Kao-tsung, however, never dared to return to Pien-ching. Meanwhile the Jurchen sent Wu-chu to eliminate the new Sung government. After Tsung Tse died in deep frustration, Kao-tsung could not resist Wu-chu's attacks and escaped southward, crossing the Yangtze River in 1129. Wu-chu pursued him to Chiang-ning (now Nanking), Hu-chou (now Wu-hsing), Hangchow, and Yüeh-chou (now Shao-hsing). The Jurchen general captured Ming-chou (now Ningpo) in 1130 and Kao-tsung was forced to seek refuge on the sea, only to return after Wu-chu failed to capture him in a long pursuit and had left for the north.

While Wu-chu was pursuing Emperor Kao-tsung in South China, other Jurchen generals took all the land north of the Yangtze River. The most powerful of these generals were Nien-han and Ta-lan, who carried out a short-lived Jurchenizing movement. They forbade the Chinese to wear native dress, and ordered them to have their hair cut in Jurchen style. The Office of the Grand Marshal proclaimed in 1126 the *t'i-fa ling* or the Head Shaving Act:

> Now all places have submitted to our dynasty. It behooves to have a unified custom. Therefore the people are expected to shave their hair and wear short dress with the lapel opening on the left. Those who dare to disobey this order will be considered loyalists of their former dynasty and be severely punished according to the law.[44]

This move, by causing the execution of many disobedient Chinese, terrorized the masses.[45]

Generally, the Jurchen still maintained a policy toward the Chinese of sponsoring a puppet regime. Ta-lan, whose influence was in Hopei and Shantung, found a good collaborator in Liu Yü, the former prefect of Tsinan. With Kao Ch'ing-i's assistance, Liu Yü secured Nien-han's consent, and finally Wu-ch'i-mai's permission to set up another puppet regime in 1130, called the Ch'i. The capital was at first at Ta-t'ung, and later moved to Pien-ching (1132). The domain of the Ch'i covered present-day Hopei, Shantung, Honan, and Shensi, land between the Yellow River and the Huai River.[46] Actually the Chin emperor treated Liu as a "son," while the generals made all important decisions for him, and sent troops to garrison some key posts to keep an eye on him.[47]

In order to establish itself as a legitimate Chinese dynasty, several times the Ch'i attempted to overthrow the Southern Sung during the eight years of its existence, but to no avail. The Jurchen in the same period concentrated on solving internal problems and weakening the power of the great generals. Nien-han died in 1136 and Kao Ch'ing-i was executed for alleged treason shortly afterwards. Meanwhile Liu Yü lost Ta-lan's favor and confidence. Since nobody supported the puppet regime, the government abolished it in 1137. Ta-lan proposed to return Ch'i territories to the Southern Sung and make peace. The government, after a heated debate among generals and administrators, adopted Ta-lan's policy of giving up the land south of the Yellow River. But Ta-lan's peaceful coexistence policy finally failed, and Tan deprived him of military power, reoccupying the area below the Yellow River down to the Huai River.[48]

When the Ch'i ceased to exist in 1137 the Jurchen set up two Mobile Presidential Councils (*hsing-t'ai shang-shu-sheng*) at Pien-ching and Yen-ching respectively, the latter being originally the Bureau of Military Affairs at Yen-ching. Returning the land south of the Yellow River to the Southern Sung in 1139, the Jurchen moved the Mobile Presidential Council from Pien-ching to Ch'i Prefecture (now An-kuo, Hopei). After execution of the rebellious Ta-lan, O-lu-kuan, and P'u-lu-hu in 1140, Wu-chu was in charge of the Mobile Presidential Council (now merged into one), and moved it back to Pien-ching. It continued to function until

1150, but its power became much more curtailed than before, for the central government put the Yen region under its own control in 1141, and the grand marshal controlled Shansi as well as the tribal people further north. The function of the Mobile Presidential Council was the same as that of the Bureau of Military Affairs, but as its name indicates, it was a branch of the Presidential Council, not an instrument of the grand marshal. Nevertheless, in the early years the Jurchen always considered civil affairs secondary to military, and both the Bureau of Military Affairs and the Mobile Presidential Council were under the control of the grand marshal and some powerful generals. This type of rule persisted until 1150 when the central government abolished the Mobile Presidential Council, mainly because the central government was not strong enough during 1123-50, and not ready to rule North China directly.[49] The major obstacles hindering centralization were the generals in China. Seen from this viewpoint, the period of the dual rule was one in which North China was semi-independent of the central government, and the Bureau of Military Affairs and the Mobile Presidential Council a sort of buffer or compromise between the central power and local forces of warlords in North China.

Under these Jurchen warlords there seems to have emerged an incipient feudalism in North China. After A-ku-ta's death, Wu-ch'i-mai could not control the generals in China, who had absolute authority. Wu-ch'i-mai in 1123 permitted them to act as circumstances might require and entrusted them with North China. He issued them silver tablets and proclamations without titles with which the generals could appoint and promote officials, and when they did this it was unnecessary to consult the emperor. An edict issued in 1124 to officials in Yen-ching further stipulated that they must report everything to the generals rather than to the central government.[50] Each of these generals had his clique of advisers: Wo-li-pu had Liu Yen-tsung, Nien-han had Kao Ch'ing-i, Shih Li-ai, and Han Chi-hsien, and Hsi-yin had Yü-wen Hsü-chung as principal advisers.

The generals also made foreign policy in early Chin. According to the *Dynastic History of the Chin*, Wo-li-pu sent an envoy to the Hsi Hsia asking for the last Ch'i-tan emperor, while Nien-han accepted Hsia's tribute and in exchange ceded some land to the western kingdom in 1124. Wo-li-pu persuaded Wu-ch'i-mai to invade the Northern Sung, and Nieh-han insisted that Shansi not return to Sung. Wo-li-pu and Nien-han invaded the Sung, captured the two Sung emperors, and sponsored two puppet regimes. Their power was so great that the people of North China called their respective offices the Eastern Court and the Western Court.[51]

Following the deaths of Wo-li-pu and Liu Yen-tsung, Nien-han became the most powerful general. Later Wu-chu and Ta-lan emerged as influential warlords, but Wu-chu was always loyal to the imperial court. Nien-han and Ta-lan supported the Liu Yü regime, and of course, had decisive authority over it. With assistance from Hsi-yin, Nien-han even convinced Wu-ch'i-mai to make Tan the heir apparent, instead of Wu-ch'i-mai's own son P'u-lu-hu (Tsung-p'an). Favored and supported by Nien-han, Hsi-yin, and Wo-pen, Tan, the first son of A-ku-ta's first-born and a boy of only fourteen, became *an-pan po-chi-lieh* in 1132. His uncles did not particularly like him, but considered him easy to handle.

Feudal forces came into being because the expansion of Jurchen territories was too rapid for the central government to absorb, and because the remnant tribal influences were still strong. In North China a few generals and royal kinsmen such as Nien-han, who was from the powerful family of Ho-che and Sa-kai, ruled like feudal lords. It is a case of superstratification imposed upon the conquered by the conquerors.[52] Wu-ch'i-mai and his successors disliked such feudal forces and hoped to establish a state with a strong central government. To attain this goal these rulers had to employ Chinese ideas and institutions; they could not do otherwise, for their own experience did not offer solutions to the unprecedented problems.

4

Sinicization: 1123–1161

Administrators versus Generals

From the time of A-ku-ta there had been a trend toward adoption of Chinese institutions and ideas in order to consolidate the new state and to build a new social-political order. Old tribal political practices bearing some "democratic" tendencies gradually disappeared, whereas some of the methods in tribal politics tinged with barbarism were introduced into the Chinese political system.

The fading of the equitable and democratic practices is indicated in the emergence of an unequal relationship between the tribal ruler and his subjects. As described earlier, Wu-ch'i-mai had taken his bath in the river with his Jurchen tribesmen, and A-ku-ta did not require the officials to perform the kowtow ceremony at his court in the early years of his reign. In addition, there was a tribal council in which important policies were discussed and determined collectively. It seems that a few important decisions were still made in this manner during the reigns of Wu-ch'i-mai and Tan. One example is the debate at Tan's court over the policy toward territory south of the Yellow River when the inept puppet regime was abolished in 1137. It is interesting to note that such debate did not ease any tension among the leaders and only provoked political struggle at the court.[1] The adoption of Chinese values and symbols centering upon the exaltation of the emperor created a gap between the ruler and his officials, not only that between the ruler and his subjects.

In general, the reigns of Tan and Liang witnessed two developments. First, there was the brutal elimination of tribal influence on politics as represented by the warlords and by the incipient feudalism in North China. Second, together with and especially after the destruction of the warlords and feudal forces, Chinese institutions, values, and customs were borrowed on a large scale. During the struggle between the central government and the regional forces, men in the government continuously drew experiences and methods from the Chinese to deal, along with coercion and suppression, with the recalcitrant generals and imperial clansmen. Consequently when Chinese institutions were introduced, most tribal practices had to go, with the exception of the military organization on which the new state was founded. But a centralized control was also carefully devised in this respect.[2]

It seems that in the new state the rulers were divided into two groups. One group of bureaucrats led by Wan-yen Wo-pen (Tsung-kan) remained loyal to the emperor and advocated institutional reforms. The other group of generals and aristocrats, such as Nien-han and Ta-lan, wanted to have a weak government so that their own authority in their respective domains could be enhanced. The bureaucrats favored sinicization whereas the generals were against it. Since it was extremely difficult for the two groups to iron out their differences, a final showdown became almost inevitable. Thus bloodshed and terror plagued the reigns of Tan and Liang. In addition, Tan seems to have become a madman in his last years. Moreover, Liang, who murdered Tan, was a usurper. Both were extremely suspicious of their own tribesmen and both were compelled by the rapidly changing circumstances to resort to naked force to achieve their goals.

As noted previously, Wu-ch'i-mai the administrator was a different ruler from A-ku-ta the conqueror. Interestingly, the internal strife that succeeded them seemed to be between the administrators and the warlords. The administrators and bureaucrats were innovators who reconstituted the government and established a centralized bureaucracy patterned after that of China. They also wanted to adopt the principle of primogeniture to regulate the problem of imperial succession, and a centralized control of all territories of the state. One of the most important leaders of this group during the reign of Tan was Wan-yen Wo-pen (Tsung-kan). Not a military man, Wo-pen was distinctly different from the other leaders in the early Chin period, who were almost always formidable warriors and brilliant strategists. Wo-pen seldom left the capital in Manchuria, and his family was under strong Chinese and Po-hai influence. He hired Chinese teachers for his son and also for Tan, who was raised in his home. Wo-pen had taken in Tan's mother after the death of Tan's father. As a result of this education, Tan reportedly could write Chinese poems, loved Chinese classics, and "lost all the Jurchen manners and attitude." Resembling a young Chinese scholar, he even regarded the old founders of the dynasty as "ignorant barbarians."[3]

Another protagonist of Chinese culture was Wan-yen Hsi-yin, originally a shaman. Hsi-yin was so fascinated by Chinese classics that he collected a great number of books when the Jurchen captured Pien-ching. He treated Chinese scholars kindly and always tried to learn from them. Like Wo-pen, Hsi-yin also employed several Chinese scholars to teach his sons and grandsons, whose classical education was sufficient to enable them to compose Chinese poetry. The poems must have been of good quality, for they exchanged them with Hung Hao when he was detained in Manchuria.[4] And the sinization was advanced to the point that one of Hsi-yin's sons was among the first Jurchen to have a Chinese wife. Yü-wen Hsü-chung, a prominent scholar and teacher hired by Hsi-yin, induced Hsi-yin to introduce many Chinese institutions in the early Chin.[5]

Some Jurchen administrators were dynamic in adopting Chinese institutions. Men like Wan-yen Hsi-yin and Wan-yen Tsung-hsien favored Chinese political organization and proposed a selective borrowing of old as well new elements. Tsung-hsien thought it unnecessary to imitate Ch'i-tan dualistic institutions and probably this was the consensus among the administrators, for the Jurchen did go beyond the Ch'i-tan and assumed direct control of North China.[6] This flexible attitude perhaps contributed to the establishment of a bureaucracy comprising not only Sung but also T'ang elements.

The warlords favored a strong regionalism in order

to maintain authority in their respective domains. The
most important warlord was Wan-yen Nien-han, who had
taken part in putting Tan on the throne. Another was
Ta-lan, who together with Nien-han sponsored the puppet
Liu Yü regime in North China, and later convinced the
administrators in the aforementioned debate to return
ex-Ch'i territory to the Southern Sung. Nien-han and
Ta-lan seem to have resisted sinicization, and were
responsible for the launching of the Jurchenizing movement in the early Chin, in which the Chinese were forced
to adopt Jurchen hair style, clothing, and customs. The
descendants of Wu-ch'i-mai, in particular P'u-lu-hu,
were also against centralized control. All these warlords eventually lost their powerful positions, even
their lives, in the conflict with the emperor and his
administrators. Nien-han was deprived of his military
power, while his protégé Kao Ch'ing-i was executed.
P'u-lu-hu and O-lu-kuan allegedly plotted against the
emperor but he forestalled their action and killed
them.[7] Ta-lan was executed in 1139 and his scheme for
peace with the Southern Sung was dropped. Finally even
Hsi-yin could not manage to escape execution at the
hands of the emperor.[8]

The Interaction Between
Centralization and Sinicization

Tan's most important institutional reforms were the
abolition of the *po-chi-lieh* system in 1134, and the
introduction of Chinese bureaucratic machinery in 1138.
In the new government there were the Three Teachers and
the Three Dukes (*san-shih* and *san-kung*), the Three
Councils and the six ministers under the Presidential
Council. Also under the Presidential Council there was
a reorganized Bureau of Military Affairs, which was a
central government apparatus. The Censorate (*yü-shih
t'ai*) came into being in 1126 and increased its power in
1135 and 1138.[9] The Han-lin Academy (*Han-lin yüan*)
consisted mostly of Chinese members. To recruit officials Tan reinstituted the civil service examination
system in 1138. Thenceforward there were two kinds of
examinations: one on Chinese classics, and the other on
the *tz'u* poetry and *fu* prose. The Northern Chinese were
to take the former examinations, and the people in the
Yen region and Manchuria the latter. Quotas were set up

in favor of the people in the northern region, who were
trusted by the Jurchen and who usually cooperated with
them. Examinations on three levels were given in
counties, prefectures, and the capital.[10] Other Chinese
institutions and customs adopted by Tan were: calendar
(1135-37), noble titles and privileges (1138),[11] rules
of imperial audience, court dresses for officials,
emperor's robes (1139), titles for descendants of Confucius (1140), Sung music (1140), new imperial ancestral
temples (1136, 1143, and 1148), law code (1145), and
imperial guards (1141-48). Tan even offered sacrifices
in person at the Confucian temple in 1141.[12]

These reforms were closely related to the growth of
imperial authority and government power. Most of the
customs were symbols and ceremonies in the Chinese
civilization that entailed the exaltation of the emperor.[13] It should also be noted that although Tan
promoted Chinese culture, his suspicious character led
him to repress not only Jurchen generals and officials,
but also Chinese scholar-officials, in order to nip all
opposition in the bud. While the execution of a number
of recalcitrant Jurchen generals and their advisers
could be interpreted as necessary means to centralize
control, and the death of Chang Chün, a Chinese Han-lin
academician, at the very hands of Tan could be explained
as terror inflicted by an individual tyrant rather than
organized violence, these incidents nevertheless provide
a sharp contrast with the Northern Sung, under whom no
high-ranking officials had ever been punished in the
same manner. Further, the Jurchen rulers ruthlessly
suppressed Chinese officials involved in factional
struggles. In one case alone, eight officials were
executed and thirty-four were put into exile.[14] Such
intimidation naturally resulted in the total silence
of Chinese officials on state affairs.

Wan-yen Liang, the usurper of Tan, had established
his position during Tan's reign, for his father Wo-pen
was the most influential man under Tan, and his wife
was the daughter of another powerful official, Hsieh-
yeh. Liang liked Chinese classics, and it is said that
he never forgot what he read. He was fond of dress,
etiquette, and fashions of the Southern Sung. He was
proud of his knowledge of Chinese classics, and his
poems were outstanding among his contemporaries.[15]
Before usurpation of the throne he once wrote:

> Under vast waves the dragon is concealed,
> Temporarily he mingles with frogs;
> One day when he emerges,
> He will shake the world like thunder.[16]

When he was still a prince he wrote a poem on a fan for a friend:

> If the great handle of the fan were in my hands,
> Light breezes would spread all over the world.[17]

As the fourth emperor of the Chin he tried to conquer the Southern Sung and unify China. Ambitiously he wrote: "I will command a million soldiers along the West Lake, and hold my horse on the highest peak of the Wu mountain."[18]

Once he described his three wishes in life: to make all important decisions concerning his state; to conquer other countries and bring their rulers to trial; and to marry the unsurpassed beauty of the world. Above all, he accepted the basic cultural orientation and legitimation of the Confucian order, and strove for the unification of the whole of China, as if this were the only way for him to establish a legitimate Chinese dynasty.[19] Later Wu-lu exclaimed: "I consider it proper that during the late Liao dynasty the Ch'i-tan never forgot their customs. Hai-ling (Liang) learned Chinese customs; how he forgot his origins!"[20]

In national policies Liang not only followed the measures initiated by his predecessors, but also greatly accelerated the building of a centralized state. In the process Liang adopted a great number of Chinese institutions and ideas, but not without making some alterations and modifications. As usurper and champion of the Chinese culture, Liang had his reasons to increase centralized control and to curb the power of the Jurchen aristocracy. Admiration of the Chinese culture, on the one hand, stimulated Liang's ambition to set up a genuine and legitimate Chinese dynasty; fear of the conservative Jurchen aristocratic and hereditary elements such as the *meng-an* and *mou-k'e*, on the other hand, compelled him to use force to suppress opposition. The result was the transformation of the Jurchen tribal organization into a sinicized political system, with much more authority centered in the government than existed in the rule of the Northern Sung.

In order to increase centralized control, in 1150 Liang abolished the Office of the Grand Marshal and the

Mobile Presidential Council.[21] Thus the entire area of the Chin kingdom came under the direct administration of the central government. To facilitate the rule of North China, Liang moved the capital to Yen-ching in 1153. Reasons for moving the capital were several, including difficulties in controlling the whole country from its northeast corner, and economic considerations. There was a need for the Jurchen to adopt the agricultural economy of China for exacting revenues from the Chinese subjects as well as from the Jurchen tribesmen who were gradually transforming themselves into farmers. Administration of the enlarged territory called for appointment of a great number of officials in central and local governments. Transportation of the increased quantity of goods and foodstuffs from the much more productive land in North China to the rather uncultivated land around Shang-ching in Manchuria to support a large bureaucracy was inefficient and costly. Communication and transfer of official dispatches became slow, and even military control of the country was difficult. Most officials wanted the capital changed, and thus Liang decided to move Yen-ching.[22] The new city of Yen-ching with its buildings was more beautiful than Pien-ching. Liang even destroyed all the palaces in Shang-ching in 1157, showing his admiration for China and firm decision to leave the uncivilized environment forever.[23]

In 1141 the Chin had obtained supremacy over the Southern Sung and had become the center of a new international order. The first steps for Liang to establish a unified and legitimate Chinese empire were to adopt Chinese culture and institutions in order to rally the support of the Chinese. These measures included the holding of sacrificial ceremonies in the southern and northern suburbs of the capital (1149), use of the imperial carriage (1151) and a system of feudal rights (1156), and adoption of *shan-hu*, a Sung way of uttering court ceremonies (1157).[24] Palace examinations were held from 1150 onward and the Imperial Academy (*kuo-tzu chien*) was set up in 1151.[25] He ordered Confucian temples built in all prefectures and counties in 1156, thus manifesting his respect for Confucius. Above all, he lifted the ban on wearing Chinese dress in 1150, a move that marked the official end of the Jurchenizing movement launched in 1126.[26]

Following the abolition of the Mobile Presidential

Council and the Office of the Grand Marshal in 1150, Liang radically revised the organization of the bureaucracy in 1156 when he did away with the Secretarial Council and Court Council.[27] The Secretarial Council was the originator of policies and the Court Council a check on the authority of the emperor in Sui and T'ang times. Although in the Northern Sung the power of the administrative council grew considerably, the very existence of three councils ensured a relatively enlightened despotism. But Liang as an alien ruler was not restricted by Chinese tradition and could disregard checks on him. Therefore he felt free to discard whatever checks and balances existed in the Chinese political heritage, preferring a more simplified government.[28] This simplified bureaucratic system persisted until the fall of the dynasty and the three-council organization was never restored in later dynasties. It should be emphatically pointed out, therefore, that the reform of 1156 marked the climax of attempts to build a centralized despotism. Along with some other measures to be discussed, it left a remarkable imprint on Chinese political history.

As many usurpers in Chinese history had done, immediately after his enthronement Liang started to rid himself of a number of aristocrats who were a potential threat to his position. In a mass execution of several princes and their families, the lineage of Wu-ch'i-mai was exterminated, so that the predominant prestige of A-ku-ta's descendants, including Liang himself, could be secured.[29] Related to this terrorism was the corporal punishment of important officials, which seemed to be one of his techniques to establish the authority of the emperor. Although corporal punishment of minor officials had existed in China prior to the Chin period, the flogging of officials with whips and poles was much more common among the Ch'i-tan and Jurchen tribes. In the early Chin it was retained by A-ku-ta. Later it became a common punishment for misbehaving officials, Chinese as well as Jurchen, and developed into a notorious practice when Liang enjoyed watching its execution right at his court. Records show that approximately fifty persons, including prime ministers, high-ranking officials, censors, military officers, monks, a cook, and a princess were flogged at his court. Lou Yüeh, a Southern Sung envoy to the Chin, observed that neither

Chin officials nor scholars could ever avoid the punishment of beating. When Lou was en route to the Chin capital, a local official complained to him: "Although my rank is very high, I cannot be exempted from beating. What kind of life is this!" This uncivilized practice, called *t'ing-chang* later, was obviously a deliberate means to belittle and humiliate the hitherto much respected scholar-officials in Chinese society, and was followed by the Yüan and Ming rulers.[30]

There were a few censors among the officials beaten at the court of Liang, signifying that another Chinese institution was being downgraded, and the censors retreated into silence. This practice was continued by Liang's successors, both of whom flogged at least two censors. The power of the censors was thus limited, as shown in the memorial submitted by a censor in 1216: "Although our dynasty has censors, they are only sinecurists. . . . The duty of the censors includes merely supervising the officials, checking documents, and inspecting treasuries." In other words, the censor's power of remonstration with the emperor weakened. His main function seems to have been holding the administrative institutions and the high officials in check. Possessing the special privilege of having direct contact with the emperor, the censor acted as if he was the emperor's spy. Even in this respect the censors did not enjoy a monopoly, for the eunuchs also performed the same function during the later Chin period. Thus the authority of the emperor was enhanced and one of the most important functions of the censorial officials, the criticism of policies and remonstration with the emperor about his aberrations, was gradually impeded.[31]

Liang reduced hereditary forces by divesting the political and military power of certain aristocrats. The most powerful local officials were the hereditary *wan-hu* or head of ten thousand men,[32] whose office was abolished in 1151 on ground that they had "no less than several tens of thousand men under their command," and monopolized local affairs. He adjusted the *meng-an* and *mou-k'e* system by moving a few powerful *meng-an* and *mou-k'e* around Shang-ching to North China, by reassigning new *meng-an* and *mou-k'e* titles to loyal men, and by depriving those who were unreliable of titles. Further, he divided the country into fourteen routes (*lu*), each administered by a chief general officer (*tsung-kuan*),

Sinicization: 1123-61   47

which was not a hereditary position. Having been assigned land scattered among the farms of the Chinese since the time of Tan, the Jurchen *meng-an* and *mou-k'e* were thenceforth under direct control of these new officers.[33] With all these measures Liang tried to prevent Jurchen military officers from having too much local and hereditary influence.[34]

Finally, Liang also paid attention to economic unification in the state; paper money was issued in 1154, monetary bureaus were set up in 1158, and the government began to mint its own coins.[35]

The Great Migration

After the Jurchen gained control of North China, it was necessary to dispatch soldiers to strategic posts in that vast territory. In general, soldiers in the newly acquired land did farm work to feed themselves, a practice that started with Wo-li-pu's evacuation of his troops from Pien-ching in 1126, when he stationed many garrisons in Hopei.[36] In the ensuing years a great number of the Jurchen emigrated to North China, accompanying the expansion of their territory. It became a major policy to transplant the tribesmen in China during the late years of Wu-ch'i-mai. According to one Sung source, all the Jurchen had moved to China by 1133; only the emperor, his courtiers and their families, and some imperial guards remained in Manchuria. In another source it is recorded that the people moved one whole village after another to China.[37]

There seems to have been a "farmer-soldier" institution (*t'un-t'ien chün*) after 1145. Under this measure, the government assigned farming land to Jurchen, Hsi, and Ch'i-tan in North China. These immigrants worked their fields, paid few taxes, and even received clothing from the government. In case of war they took up arms and obtained extra money and rice. This institution was similar to the Chinese *t'un-t'ien*. It is worth noting that the Jurchen usually did not stay in towns, but lived in fortresses and camps among Chinese villages. Moreover, there was no intermarriage between the conquerors and the conquered.[38]

The great migration ended approximately at the time of Liang. To prevent the remnant Wan-yen clansmen around Shang-ching from rising against him, Liang moved all of them to the south. He sent officials to confiscate land illegally occupied by influential officials, Buddhist and Taoist priests, and local thugs in Hopei and Shantung, and to redistribute such land to the Jurchen.[39] The Jurchen conquerors enjoyed the fruits of victory, and their function was to control the Chinese populace, like the stationing of Manchu bannermen in China in the Ch'ing dynasty.

As a rule the Jurchen tribesmen were under the control of the *meng-an* and *mou-k'e*, who were in turn administered by the chief general officers. On the frontiers of the empire the duty of the *meng-an* was to administer military affairs, drill the soldiers, and persuade the people to engage in agriculture. As local officials, *meng-an* and *mou-k'e* performed the function of police to the Chinese. In terms of the nine-grade system, *meng-an* on the frontiers belonged to the lower fourth grade (*tsung ssu-p'in*), a position next to the chief general officer, the mayor (*fu-yin*), and the commanding prefect (*chieh-tu shih*). The *mou-k'e* was of the lower fifth grade (*tsung wu-p'in*), next to the prefect and superior to the magistrate of the county.[40]

To monopolize military power, Tan had abolished Chinese and Po-hai *meng-an* and *mou-k'e* in 1140. Thenceforth Chinese and Po-hai could not inherit *meng-an* and *mou-k'e* titles.[41] Tan further divided the *meng-an* and *mou-k'e* into three groups: the imperial lines constituted the first group, other Jurchen were in the second group, and non-Jurchen peoples belonged to the lowest group. This measure was, of course, for the purpose of concentrating military power in the hands of the Jurchen, especially the Wan-yen clansmen. Although Liang abrogated the three-group system in 1150, he ordered non-Jurchen *meng-an* and *mou-k'e* with Jurchen surnames to resume their original names, thus distinguishing the Jurchen from other peoples.[42]

One of the most important aspects of tightening Jurchen control in China was that *meng-an* and *mou-k'e* from the era of Tan became hereditary officers. At the time of Tan and Liang there were restrictions on bestowal of these titles to non-Jurchen peoples. Even the Jurchen found it difficult to get these positions, for during Tan's reign the war with the Southern Sung became stalemated, and there was little chance for the Jurchen to obtain the titles of *meng-an* and *mou-k'e* by fighting aggressive wars, as did many in earlier times. Such titles turned out to be feudalistic and were granted to the nobles rather than awarded to meritorious soldiers. According to a modern study, after Tan the government gave away few *meng-an* and *mou-k'e* titles that were not hereditary and those titles that were not hereditary became so.[43] Much evidence bears out this transition. Wan-yen Ssu-ching, who was a *mou-k'e* at the time of Wu-ch'i-mai, received the title of hereditary *mou-k'e* under Tan. Wan-yen Ho-chu got his *meng-an* at the beginning of the dynasty, but his son, Fu-shou, was able to inherit his position in 1139, and became a hereditary *meng-an*. One can find similar cases in the biographies of Tu-chi Pi-la, Wu-yen Ssu-lieh, Wu-yen Hu-sa-hün, and A-lu-pu in the *Dynastic History of the Chin*.[44] As for the principle of inheritance, usually the eldest son or grandson of a *meng-an* or *mou-k'e* inherited his post, but a second son or brother could also inherit in special cases. There were examples of inheritance of one's uncle's position or even that of other relatives.[45] The establishment of the hereditary principle naturally consolidated the power of the Jurchen aristocracy.

The Jurchen enjoyed very special privileges. It is probable that they alone could receive land from the government. The government did not distribute land to Chinese peasants; in case of relief or on other occasions, the land received by them was from 10 to 100 *mou* (about 1.37 to 13.7 acres). In contrast, 25 Jurchen as a unit could receive 4 *ch'ing* (1 *ch'ing* equals 100 *mou* or 13.7 acres) and 4 *mou*, or 404 *mou*, of farming land from the government. This practice of collective farming was a remarkable feature of the Jurchen way of life. Although the government limited the ownership of land by any person to 40 *niu-chü* (oxen unit) or 16,160 *mou*,[46] in the latter part of the dynasty many Jurchen landlords owned much more.[47]

Taxation of the Jurchen was different from that of the Chinese. The population under the control of the *meng-an* and *mou-k'e*, that is, mostly under the Jurchen, paid taxes different from those under the local government.[48] The tax paid by the Jurchen was the so-called *niu-chü* tax or *niu-t'ou* tax (oxen-unit tax), leveled on every three oxen as a unit. Land corresponding to each unit was 404 *mou*. At first the tax was a little less than 1 *tan* (picul) per unit; later the rate changed to

5 *tou* (peck, the tenth of a *tan*). For each *mou* the Jurchen only paid 1 *ko* (the tenth of a *sheng* or pint, which in turn was the tenth of a *tou*) and 2 *shao* (the tenth of a *ko*) per year. Taxation of the Chinese peasants was 53 *ko* and a bundle of *chieh* (corn or wheat stalks) per *mou* per year.[49] In other words, the tax paid by the Jurchen was a little less than 1/44 of that paid by the Chinese.

Unequal taxation was not only for upholding the privileged position of the conquerors, but for their protection and relief in case of bad harvest. Part of the foodstuffs turned in as taxation may not have been transported to the central government but kept in local storage. Evidence is that in 1125 each *mou-k'e* had to build storage for extra food from good harvests, so as to feed the poor in case of bad harvest, and that in 1163 Wu-lu ordered military posts to store food.[50]

When the Jurchen became new landlords, they began to keep slaves. Although the Jurchen abolished Liao slavery in early Chin, it was for the sake of increasing tax revenues and eliminating big Ch'i-tan landlords. The Jurchen rulers often gave slaves, cattle, horses, and money to meritorious military officers as well as the nobility. At the beginning of the dynasty, Shih-t'u-men received 500 slaves as a reward for his victory at the prefecture of Huang-lung. Wu-ch'i-mai gave 1,000 slaves and 1,000 horses and cattle to Wan-yen Wu-chu. Tan granted his father-in-law 500 slaves and 500 head of livestock. Slavery had its origin in earlier times, when the Jurchen captured the Chinese when they invaded North China, and Wu-chu moved many Chinese from there to Manchuria as slaves. Before Shih-tsung rose against King Hai-ling, he owned about ten thousand servants and slaves. Under the *mou-k'e* the number of slaves ranged from one or two to two or three hundred.[51] There were slave markets that were abolished by Shih-tsung.[52]

The result of the Jurchen migration, in short, gave rise to a new social structure in North China. The conquerors and Chinese bureaucrats, landlords, and gentry constituted the upper class. Among the commoners, the population under the control of the *meng-an* and *mou-k'e* enjoyed more privileges than others. Both the government and landlords owned slaves, whose status was fixed largely by Jurchen conquest wars. The number of slaves undobtedly exceeded that of the Northern Sung. The population of North China reached the figure of 48.5 million in 1195.[53] The population of the Jurchen in 1182 was about 6.15 million, which included 1.34 million slaves, who were actually non-Jurchen. In addition, a little less than one-third of the Jurchen still lived in Manchuria. It means that they were approximately outnumbered by the Chinese at a rate of 1 to 10, with a proportion even more in favor of the Chinese in North China. Since the Jurchen were outnumbered by the Chinese, they were mainly the recipients of Chinese influences, although at this stage there existed many barriers between the conquerors and the conquered. Such barriers naturally led to political struggles and social conflicts, which almost brought about the destruction of the Jurchen regime in 1161.[54]

5

Jurchen Bureaucracy and Political Recruitment

Characteristics of the Bureaucracy

The early Chin political structure centered upon the institution of the *po-chi-lieh*, which originally was filled by the chieftains of Jurchen tribes. After the founding of the Chin in 1115, Wan-yen A-ku-ta transformed the *po-chi-lieh* into government officials, appointing predominantly Jurchen nobles as various *po-chi-lieh*. The Jurchen nobility, especially the Wan-yen clansmen, completely controlled the government. As for local officials, the Jurchen government preserved Ch'i-tan and Chinese local functionaries to rule the newly acquired Liao and Northern Sung territories, who were, however, watched closely by Jurchen *meng-an* and *mou-k'e*, who guarded the strategic posts. Ch'i-tan and Sung governmental system (*chou-hsien*) was maintained. During the time of dualistic political practices (1115-50), some of the top local officials were given titles of prime ministers, although, as mentioned, they did not see the emperor often and only performed local official functions, like the officials of the southern region of the Liao.[1] However, they were responsible for introducing the civil service examinations and recruiting officials to fill the local posts.

Several reforms, which have been noted above, led to the formation of the Chin bureaucracy. Wan-yen Liang abolished the Court Council and the Secretarial Council, and the Presidential Council monopolized political and military affairs. Having adopted various

Sung political institutions, the Chin bureaucracy developed several characteristics of its own.[2]

First of all, due to the simplification of the political structure, the power of the emperor was greatly enhanced. He became the chief decision maker, and exercised political authority through the Presidential Council. There were no checks and balances; the censors watched the conduct of ranking officials for him. In addition, the Bureau of Palace Attendants (*chin-shih chü*) was one of the most powerful organizations in the late Chin period, and also served as the "ears and eyes" of the emperor.

The enhancement of the authority of the emperor is clearly indicated in the flogging of the high-ranking officials. The institutionalization of flogging marked the debasement of the status of the Chinese scholar-officials.

Second, the Jurchen monopolized the military authority in the state--military generals naturally were almost always Jurchen. Although there were some non-Jurchen auxiliary forces, the majority of the Chinese population was practically disarmed. The *meng-an* and *mou-k'e*, and the people administered by them, alone could bear arms. In case of war, they were drafted by the central government to organize armies. The chief general officers (*tsung-kuan*), who were always Jurchen, controlled these *meng-an* and *mou-k'e*, who in turn performed the function of police during peacetime.

There was a smooth flow of personnel between the military service and the civil service among the Jurchen. The Bureau of Military Affairs was under the Presidential Council, which insured civilian control of the military. In addition, in most cases a military command was formed when there was an emergency, and it was dissolved after the emergency. The commanders were unable to transform their armies into their own.[3] It was clearly an administrative principle devised to protect the throne against the independent power of military leaders. This principle was innovated and developed in the Northern Sung, and adopted by the Chin, notwithstanding the marked difference between the basic military organizations of the Sung and the Chin: the former employed professional armies but the latter conscripted troops from the *meng-an* and *mou-k'e*. Similar tendencies to reduce hereditary local military power and to nationalize the troops could be seen in the Yüan dynasty under Qubilai Qan.[4]

Third, there was a balance of political influence between Jurchen and non-Jurchen elements. Table 3 shows the ethnic composition of the Chin bureaucracy based upon the biographical data provided in the *Dynastic History of the Chin*.[5] The Chinese, who at first only constituted 28 percent of the ruling stratum, became increasingly important with the lapse of time. But the Chinese percentage never exceeded 50.

TABLE 3

Ethnic Composition of Chin Political Structure (in percentages)[6]

Categories	Periods			
	1115-44	1145-74	1175-1204	1205-34
Jurchen				
Imperial clansmen	50	20	19	6
Other Wan-yen	5	4	3	8
Non-Wan-yen	9	23	20	35
SUBTOTAL	64	47	42	49
Chinese	28	35	50	45
Ch'i-tan	5	7	5	4
Po-hai	3	6	3	0.7
Hsi	--	3.5	--	0.3
Others	--	1.5	--	1
TOTAL	100	100	100	100
Number of Subjects	106	192	104	246

Finally, in order to insure the balance of Jurchen and non-Jurchen elements, there was the emphasis on the inner court. In traditional Chinese political systems, there were some institutions that managed the affairs of the emperor and his family. Some important government institutions were developed from these inner court organizations. Under the conquest dynasty, this division between the outer and inner courts was especially clear, and the inner court possessed great political power. A good example is the Bureau of Palace Attendants (*chin-shih chü*). The head of the bureau had only the fifth rank in terms of the scale of officials, but he possessed much political authority. There were many other minor officials in the imperial palace, whose political prestige should not be measured by their humble status. Almost all these posts were filled by Jurchen personnel.[7] The Jurchen emphasis on the inner court was, consciously or unconsciously, for the purpose of enhancing their political power.[8]

Political Recruitment[9]

Recruitment Examinations

Most of the Chinese recruited in the early Chin were former Liao officials, who came from the Yen-Yün region (ex-Liao territories) and Liaotung regions.[10] It is evident that these people had persuaded the Jurchen conquerors to adopt the Chinese examination system.[11] The earliest examinations were held in 1123 (the first year of *T'ien-hui*, the reign title of Wu-ch'i-mai) and 1124, without regular time intervals.[12] These aimed at recruiting a large number of Chinese personnel to help rule occupied Chinese territory.

Triennial examinations were given after 1129. Before 1150 there were three levels of examinations--the magistrate examination, the district examination, and the departmental examination. The palace examination was implemented in 1150. Half of the candidates of the district examinations were enlisted to take part in the departmental examination, in which approximately one out of six candidates could pass.[13]

The subject matter of the examinations was different for the northerners and the southerners. In fact, two kinds of examinations were given: the examinations for the northerners who were from the Liaotung and Yen-Yün regions had poetry as their subject matter, while the southerners took the examination on the classics. Apparently the examinations for the northerners were easier than those for the southerners. Also, the quotas were so devised that the northerners found it easier to attain positions in the government. In the early examinations the quota for the northerners was fixed at 200, whereas that for the southerners was only 150. Thus, with the smaller area and population in the Yen-Yün and Liaotung regions, and the higher quota given them, the northerners enjoyed more privileges than the southerners. The quota was a weapon for the northerners, who were trusted by the Jurchen, to assert their political influence. The northern *chin-shih* had the advantage of being able to attain the seventh grade within 120 months after the first appointment in the office of a magistrate, but the southerners had to serve 30 additonal months.[14]

The examinations on the classics were abolished in 1151, and the government gave examinations only on poetry. The former, however, were resumed again in 1188, without specifying who should take them. It was ruled in 1190 that the subject matter would be confined to the six classics, the *Canon of Filial Piety*, the *Analects*, the *Mencius*, the *Hsüntzu*, the *Yangtzu*, and the *Laotzu*. There were also decree examinations and facilitated examinations, which were not important. The government forbade slaves, musicians, actors, and workers in the Imperial Workshops (*shao-fu chien*) to take examinations. Sons of slaves, however, were permitted to become *chin-shih* candidates. Merchants were not mentioned when those who were not qualified to take the examinations were enumerated.[15]

During the period between 1151 and 1183, the *chin-shih* enlisted by the government in triennial examinations totaled 60 to 70. After 1164 there was no limit on the *chin-shih* enlisted each time, although the average number of *chin-shih* recruited was about 500 between 1164 and 1188. The number increased to 586 in 1188, and in 1197 reached the all-time high of 925. Two years later the government limited the *chin-shih* to be recruited to 600; nevertheless 800 were recruited in 1213.[16] Table 4 summarizes the percentage distribution of Chinese officials by their respective path of recruitment.

In the first period most of the *chin-shih* came from the Liao dynasty. During the second period, the bulk of Chinese officials began to be recruited through examinations. The decline in the number of *chin-shih* recruited

TABLE 4

Percentage Distribution of Chinese
Officials by Path of Recruitment[17]

Categories	Periods			
	1115-44	1145-74	1175-1204	1205-34
Examination	40	52	90	58
Military Achievement	20	16	--	27
Miscellaneous	40	32	10	15
TOTAL	100	100	100	100
Number of Subjects	30	68	52	110

during the last period perhaps was due to the gradual disintegration of the Chin political order, while the increase in the category of military achievement indicated the growth of Chinese regional power.

Recruitment examinations did not provide the Ch'i-tan, Po-hai, and Hsi with much opportunity for participation in the government. They attained high rank mostly through protection and military achievements. Only one Ch'i-tan and five Po-hai were ever granted the *chin-shih* degree so far as the record in the *Dynastic History of the Chin* shows.[18]

During and after the *Ta-ting* (reign title of Emperor Shih-tsung) period (1161-89) recruitment through examinations became an important means for Jurchen commoners to start their political careers. The interesting aspect of these examinations is that the government designed a Jurchen examination system for the privileged minority. It was apparently easier for the Jurchen than for the Chinese to acquire the *chin-shih* degree. One Chinese *chin-shih* was enlisted from every five Chinese candidates in 1202, whereas the ratio for the Jurchen *chin-shih* was one to three. This was partly because there were only a few Jurchen who studied their language and could write essays in Jurchen. The total number of Jurchen *chin-shih* recruited, therefore, was much smaller than that of the Chinese counterpart. The number of Jurchen *chin-shih* given in each examination never exceeded 100.[19]

The establishment of the Jurchen *chin-shih* degree by Emperor Shih-tsung (Wu-lu; r. 1161-89) perhaps did not aim at creating another privileged Jurchen group over the Chinese. The first appointment of the Jurchen degree holder was generally not higher than that of the Chinese counterpart, although, as will be shown below, his promotion was generally more rapid. Shih-tsung, at any rate, perhaps wanted to show the Chinese that he would like to work out a recruitment system paralleling that of the Chinese and sharing the Chinese characteristic of fair competition.

The examination increased the opportunities for the Jurchen to acquire government posts, but did not replace the existing institutions of recruitment. In the *Dynastic History of the Chin* only forty-nine Jurchen officials with the *chin-shih* qualification are found. Nevertheless, among the *chin-shih* fourteen climbed to the ranks of prime ministers, indicating that they still exerted considerable influence on politics. Most of the Jurchen *chin-shih* seem to have come from families of nonofficial background. According to the biographies in the official history, only five *chin-shih* had official or noble family background, and one of these preferred taking the examinations to inheriting the post of *mou-k'e* from his father. It seems the examination not only provided the Jurchen with one more channel to the officialdom, but also facilitated upward social mobility. This policy was imitated by the Mongols in the Yüan dynasty and by the Manchus in the early Ch'ing.[20] Moreover, the government often appointed the *chin-shih* as censors, thus creating political struggles between the *chin-shih* and officials from other recruitment paths. It is evident that the government intended to use the *chin-shih* to balance the power of the nobles, and the Jurchen examination system indeed helped stabilize the regime to some extent in the last years of the dynasty.[21] One more point about the Jurchen *chin-shih* degree should be noted. While there is no indication in the extant sources that the Jurchen ever took Chinese examinations, it is possible that the Chinese could acquire Jurchen degrees.[22]

Bureaucracy and Political Recruitment

The Jurchen conquerors, no less than the Sung rulers, considered recruitment examinations to be an important political instrument. E. A. Kracke has examined the recruitment of the Northern Sung civil service in four categories: recruitment examinations, recruitment through transfer, recruitment through protection, and miscellaneous methods of recruitment. Pointing out that most officials were recruited through examinations, Kracke writes:

> Between 976 and 1019 there were no less than 9,323 doctoral degrees conferred, or an average of nearly 212 per annum. Between 1020 and 1057 there were 8,509, an average of nearly 851 for each of the ten examinations held during that period. This represented a yearly average of nearly 224. The annual average was apparently the highest for a period of such length in the history of the Chinese civil service until 1905.[23]

It is interesting to compare these figures with those of the Chin period. The annual average of *chin-shih* recruited between 1167 and 1234 was about two hundred. The total number of *chin-shih* of the entire period must have exceeded 16,000.[24] The number of degrees conferred in various periods of the Chin is estimated in table 5.

TABLE 5

Degrees Conferred in Chin Periods

Period	Number of examinations	Total of *chin-shih*	Average per examination	Average per annum
1123-36	10	883+	88.3	59.0
1138-49	6	1,600	266.6	133.3
1150-66	6	390	65.0	23.0
1167-87	7	3,500	500.0	166.6
1188-99	4	2,711	677.7	225.0
1200-33	12	7,400	633.3	217.6
TOTAL	45	16,484	366.3	148.5

The Chin average per annum is much greater than those

of the Ming and Ch'ing. Since the population and land area were much smaller than under the Northern Sung, it is reasonable to assert that the Chin annual average was on a par with that of the Northern Sung.[25] The importance of the degree holders, however, is diminished because the total number of government officials of the Chin seems to have exceeded that of the Northern Sung. There were 10,499 officials, including 4,705 Jurchen and 6,794 Chinese, in 1193, and the figure reached the all-time high of 47,000 in 1207. The latter figure was much greater than that of early Northern Sung.[26]

These facts may have given rise to the belief during the Yüan dynasty that the employment of the Chinese literati brought about the destruction of the Chin (*Chin i ju wang*). The reason was perhaps that the indoctrination in Confucianism and literature hampered Jurchen martial spirit.[27]

Although the Jurchen never rid themselves of the feeling they were a privileged minority, there were a few who did believe in the advantages of employing both Chinese and Jurchen *chin-shih* during the Chin period. Wan-yen Shou-chen, a minister, commented in 1191:

> Concerning the channel through which government offices of our dynasty were filled, talent came mostly from the conferring of the *chin-shih*. The warders of various bureaus ordinarily could not attain ranks in the government; since the beginning of the *Ta-ting* they have been employed. There were few, however, that could be used. Recently more *chin-shih* degrees have been conferred, and it would be proper to increase the number still further.

And it was because of his recommendation that the limit on the *chin-shih* recruited was lifted. Shih-tsung was especially pleased with the good quality of the Jurchen *chin-shih*.[28] He ordered the appointment of Chinese as well as Jurchen *chin-shih* as assistant secretaries (*ling-shih*) and their promotion to regional commandants and finance commissioners in the future.[29] It was an established policy during his reign to employ both Chinese and Jurchen *chin-shih* as censors, for they made better officials than those who relied upon birthright to fix their life status.[30] According to Wang Yün, all the ranks from the clerks to the prime ministers were filled with *chin-shih* during the peaceful days of the reign of Chang-tsung.[31]

Yüan Hao-wen, the great poet and writer of late

Bureaucracy and Political Recruitment

Chin and early Yüan, however, was highly critical of the Chin recruitment policy. In addition to the estimation that "four out of ten officials came from the ranks of the protected sons,"[32] Yüan evaluated the Chin utilization of Chinese literati in the following words:

> Most of those who occupied these positions [of ministers] were imperial clansmen, relatives of the empresses, and Jurchen tribesmen with military merit and those who participated in decision-making in the inner circle of the government. Less important were the great families of the north [*Huang-hsi*]. Still less important were the *chin-shih*. The use of the so-called *chin-shih* was specifically for the purpose of showing fairness to the people and earning their confidence. Thus power was distributed by a comparison of people's respective favors, and the rulers possessed different feelings toward different peoples.[33]

It is possible that Yüan Hao-wen was critical of the Chin recruitment policy both because it was collapsing rapidly in the last years of the dynasty, and because, as a Confucian scholar, he was disappointed with the dualistic practices.

Protection, Hereditary Selection, and Transfer from the Military Service

Although the Jurchen put much emphasis on the recruitment examinations, political recruitment of the Chin was also marked by the even more important policy of inducting Jurchen manpower into political roles on the basis of particularistic criteria. This policy resulted in a careful balance between Jurchen and non-Jurchen elements in the government throughout the dynasty. The chief censors, for example, were half Jurchen and half Chinese.[34]

There were three channels through which the Jurchen attained government posts: protection, hereditary selection, and transfer from the military service. As mentioned, in the middle of the dynasty, Jurchen examinations were also implemented.

It was ruled in 1154 that there would be no limit on the number of personnel nominated for entrance into the civil service by officials from the seventh grade and up. During the *Ta-ting* period, an official of the seventh grade could only "protect" (*yin*) one person. During the reign of Chang-tsung (r. 1189-1208), an official of the sixth grade could "protect" as many as six. This clearly indicates the growth of the influence of the elite with official and noble background.[35]

Closely related to protection is hereditary selection. Wittfogel has distinguished hereditary selection from protection. The former, according to him, was a characteristic institution of a relatively simple tribal state, giving members of a specific family a claim over generations to a specific office or class of offices.[36] In the Chin period, it seems that sons of imperial clansmen could enter into the palace service without being "protected." Sons of Jurchen commoners, who were obviously not "protected," were also eligible to be selected as imperial guardsmen.[37] It is unclear how many sons and relatives of Jurchen officials were similarly selected as imperial guardsmen, and various chiefs and warders of the palace service. There is reason to believe they could receive such appointments either through protection or through hereditary selection. In the latter case, talent became a factor to be considered. All these could be considered as hereditary selection in the broad sense. The inheritance of hereditary *meng-an* and *mou-k'e*, it should be noted, is similar to the Liao practice of hereditary selection.

The palace service included a number of offices occupied by the imperial clansmen, sons of high-ranking officials, and some Jurchen commoners. These offices were seemingly unimportant, but they had the advantage of being close to the throne. During the *Ta-ting* period the government tended to use those who at first served as imperial guards and local officials, and it was a standard practice that these guards could be promoted to positions of the fifth grade within ten years.[38] There is even one case indicating that an imperial clansman attained the post of minister from the position of imperial guardsman within ten years.[39]

The Office of Palace Corps Supervisor (*tien-ch'ien tu-tien-chien ssu*) and the Department of Court Etiquette (*hsüan-hui-yüan*) provided the Jurchen with a number of minor posts, in addition to the posts of imperial guards. These included various chiefs of palace service (*feng-yü*) and warders (*chih-hou*). The Bureau of Palace Attendants (*chin-shih chü*) was one of the most powerful organizations under the Office of Palace Corps Supervisor, which exerted important influence on politics in the late Chin period.[40]

No less important than the above offices as starting appointments are the *meng-an* and *mou-k'e*. The *meng-an* and *mou-k'e*, the basic military units of the Chin, gradually evolved into units of the entire Jurchen social, political, and economic system. When the conquest wars against the Sung were over, *meng-an* and *mou-k'e* titles were given to nobles and important officials as hereditary titles that carried special privileges.[41] The hereditary *meng-an* and *mou-k'e* usually guarded the strategic posts in the empire, but were also eligible to be appointed as local officials.[42] In fact, having inherited the titles, the Jurchen became at least members of the privileged class and were more likely than others to be assigned additional posts. Unlike the titular positions that generally corresponded to the functional offices, the *meng-an* and *mou-k'e* titles were not included in any governmental honorary scales. Even when a *meng-an* was promoted to the rank of minister and acquired a high titular position, he still held the title of *meng-an* and enjoyed the pertinent privileges. Furthermore, all the Jurchen officials, and occasionally a few non-Jurchen, were eligible to receive the titles of hereditary *meng-an* and *mou-k'e* as a special favor from the emperor, or as a reward.[43]

Transfer from the miltary service to the civil service was frequent. Since the Jurchen monopolized military affairs, transfer from the military to the civil service was an important path for them to attain high posts in the government. In the military, Jurchen could easily accumulate merits. For example, Wan-yen Shuang was a hereditary *meng-an*. Having served as commanding prefect, prefect, defense commander (*liu-shou*), and Palace cavalry and infantry commander-in-chief (*tien-ch'ien ma-pu-chün tu-chih-hui-shih*), he was appointed director of the Imperial Library. When imperial clansmen reached adulthood, the government often granted them high-ranking titular positions. A good example is the career of Wan-yen Wen, who was at first a hereditary *mou-k'e*, and also received the title of "general" of the third grade. Later he was transferred to the civil service and became director of the Imperial Library.[44] These examples illustrate the lack of professionalism in Chin administration.

From the brief survey above, it is clear that the recruitment of Jurchen officials relied upon the practices of protection, hereditary selection, and transfer from the military service. It should be noted that hereditary selection was similar to that of the Liao in the sense that officials were selected from an ethnic group, especially from the Wan-yen and other noble clans, but these clans did not monopolize the important posts in the civil service.[45] Protection in the Chin, like the Liao precedent, further ensured the control of the regime by the Jurchen.

Table 6 shows the percentage distribution of Jurchen officials according to their paths of recruitment.

TABLE 6

Percentage Distribution of Jurchen Officials By Channels of Recruitment[46]

	1115-44	1145-74	1175-1204	1205-34
Examination	--	1	5	37
School	--	2	7	--
Sponsorship and Clerical Service	--	7	--	3
Military Achievement	38	19	5	9
Protection and Hereditary Selection	48.5	41	65	43
Hereditary *Meng-an* and *Mou-k'e*	13.5	30	18	8
Subtotal	62	71	83	51
TOTAL	100	100	100	100
Number of Subjects	66	90	43	104
Information unavailable	2	2	1	16

In the *Dynastic History of the Chin* there is a passage describing the dualistic character of recruitment in the dynasty: officials in the civil service came mainly from the *chin-shih* examinations, and those in the military service were drawn from men with military achievements.⁴⁷ There is not, however, such a clear-cut dichotomy. It is proper to say that the Jurchen provided the government with military officers whereas the Chinese, together with the Jurchen, managed civil affairs. The division of officials according to their means of recruitment was along their ethnic origins--the Jurchen often started their careers by serving in the inner court (*nei-ch'ao*), that is, the palace service, whereas the Chinese mainly worked in the outer court (*wai-ch'ao*). This division also points to the existence of remnant tribal heritage throughout the dynasty.⁴⁸

Ethnic Status and Promotion

A brief sketch of promotion practices in the Chin political system reflects the nature of Chin recruitment, for the entrance method is an important factor affecting promotion.

Like the practices in the Sung dynasty, the advancement of Chin officials was based upon merit and seniority. The Ministry of Personnel kept files of all the officials and evaluated their merit. It adopted in 1204 T'ang rules of merit rating, called "Four Merits and Seventeen Mosts."⁴⁹ A promotion sequence was carefully devised to measure the seniority aspect of the officials. Thirty months constituted a term (*jen*) for civil servants of the third grade and below. For each term there was a merit rating.⁵⁰

Usually a *chin-shih* degree holder's first appointment was a civil aide position in a prefecture or a county. According to the rules of 1153, for the southern *chin-shih* it was possible to attain the sixth grade after 120 months, while for the northerners it took only 90 months. The unequal treatment was eliminated in 1156.⁵¹ During the reign of Shih-tsung the *chin-shih* should serve four terms to obtain the post of magistrate. It took 180 months to attain the sixth grade, and more than 40 years to reach the rank of prefect (*tz'u-shih*, fifth grade).⁵² For a Jurchen palace chief (*feng-yü*) or an imperial guard (*hu-wei*), however, it was possible to advance to the sixth grade as soon as he had completed the required 150 months in the palace service according to the rules of 1157, and the tenure was even reduced to 120 months in 1162.[53] This was due to the existence of a Jurchen promotion practice called "rapid promotion sequence" (*ch'ao-ch'ien ko*).[54] A preliminary survey of the careers of Jurchen palace chiefs, imperial guards, *chin-shih*, and Chinese officials with the *chin-shih* qualification yields the following results (the number of years is the average tenure required to attain the posts of ministers, usually the assistant civil councilor or *ts'an-chih cheng-shih*).[55]

```
            Jurchen chin-shih.................21 years
            Jurchen imperial guards
              and palace chiefs................22 years
            Chinese chin-shih..................31 years
```

It is apparent that the Jurchen had greater advancement and attained high posts earlier than the Chinese. Among the Jurchen *chin-shih*, there is only one case in which an official had served in various posts for thirty years before receiving the appointment of minister. Some of the palace chiefs (*feng-yü*) could enter into the palace service very early. One case has it that a certain Jurchen served as *feng-yü* when he was a child of only five or six years of age. Some of the officials were kept in the service longer than required for they were too young to take more important jobs.[56] Officials in this category generally enjoyed the advantage of being able to serve in the military, and thus they could advance rapidly by accumulating military merits.[57] As for the Chinese *chin-shih*, they had to climb the official ladder slowly; rarely did they advance to the ranks of ministers within twenty years.[58] The Jurchen in general stayed in high-ranking posts longer and accumulated more seniority than the Chinese.[59]

Conclusion

As pointed out by Wittfogel in his study of Liao public offices, protection, which assumed unusual importance in the Liao, manifested itself in all post-Liao conquest societies of China. With regard to the Chin, Wittfogel cited Yüan Hao-wen, indicating that 40 percent of the officials came from the ranks of the protected sons.[60] Although the findings in the present study do not verify Yüan's assertion as far as officials of the higher strata are concerned (for what Yüan described was the situation toward the end of the dynasty), hereditary selection and protection together did contribute to the attainment of most leading political roles in the bureaucracy by Jurchen personnel throughout the dynasty. In addition to proving the obvious, however, this study has emphasized that the conquerors did appreciate the advantages of adopting the Chinese civil service examinations and thus the establishment of a rationalized recruitment policy. The foreign conquerors were not devoid of an antagonistic attitude toward their fellow tribesmen who acquired various privileges through birthright. The continuous employment of personnel solely upon particularistic criteria would not only result in the limitation of the reservoir of talent, and the deterioration of the quality of the officials, but also alienate the majority of the ruled, and thereby bring about the decline of the political system. The implementation of the Jurchen *chin-shih* degree bears witness to this attitude, and the rulers' efforts to deal with the political dilemma.[61]

The Chin recruitment policy is similar to the Liao in its employment of particularistic criteria for the selection of Jurchen officials. A salient feature of the recruitment policy is that there was a division between the civil officials and the military personnel. Occasionally, Chinese military officers did advance to the ranks in the civil service, but the Jurchen were frequently transferred from the military to the civil service. Another feature is the induction of Jurchen into the palace service. The practice is similar to the appointment of Mongol tribesmen as *kesig* (*ch'üeh-hsüeh*) in the Mongol empire.[62] Consequently the inner court possessed much political power. Yet the Jurchen put much more emphasis than did the Ch'i-tan and the Mongols on the examinations as a major path to the officialdom.[63] The combined practices of recruitment examinations, protection, hereditary selection, and transfer from the military maintained a precarious balance between the Jurchen and the Chinese in the bureaucracy. Recruitment procedures based upon both particularistic and universalistic criteria clearly demonstrate the dualistic character of Chin recruitment policy.

6

The Jurchen Movement for Revival

There was a movement of revitalization in the mid-Chin period,[1] a movement aimed at the recovery of Jurchen culture, and the conditional adoption of Chinese elements. In addition to the defeat in the Battle of Ts'ai-shih in 1161, which threatened the Jurchen rule in North China, it seemed that the Jurchen culture would be unable to survive the intensified and accelerated drives of Tan and Liang to sinicization. How the Jurchen met these sociopolitical crises and reacted against the encroachment of Chinese culture makes a fascinating story.

Ever since the establishment of the Southern Sung, incessant warfare characterized its relations with the Chin. The southern dynasty in time managed to stabilize its position in South China, and the war gradually developed into a stalemate. While the southerners were unable to recover the lost territories in the north, the Jurchen likewise failed to conquer the south. They finally reached a peace settlement in 1141, making the Southern Sung a tributary state of the Chin. The demarcation line between them was settled from the Huai River in the east to Ta-san Pass, Shensi, in the west.[2]

Peace lasted for twenty years. During this period, the Jurchen consolidated their rule in North China, while the Chinese civilization in the south entered into another golden age. The ambitious Chin ruler Wan-yen Liang, however, tried to reunify the Middle Kingdom. His major motive to conquer the Southern Sung may have been that he desired to establish a legitimate Chinese dynasty, accepting the Chinese ideal of "whoever reunifies China secures legitimacy."[3] He personally commanded an army of about five hundred thousand men to invade the south in 1161.[4] Fortunately for the southern state, Liang failed. The superior Sung navy and the high morale of soldiers under the command of Yü Yün-wen prevented Liang from crossing the Yangtze River. A revolt broke out in Liang's army that cost him his life.

The influence of the famous Battle of Ts'ai-shih of 1161 was profound. The Chinese victory, indeed, bolstered up the morale of the southerners, stabilized the southern dynasty, and ensured the continuous existence and development of the Chinese and therefore "orthodox" tradition. The battle so depressed the Jurchen that thenceforth they never made any other serious attempt to reunify China. The new peace settlement of 1165 maintained the division of China until the Mongol invasions and conquests. The Southern Sung and Chin treated each other on equal terms, although the former still paid annual tribute to the latter.[5] East Asia enjoyed a long period of peace and prosperity.

Background

The fifth emperor of Chin, whose posthumous title is Shih-tsung, had the Jurchen name of Wu-lu, and two Chinese names.[6] He was a grandson of A-ku-ta, and his father Tsung-fu was a meritorious general in early Chin. Because Wu-lu was only twelve years old at the time of Tsung-fu's death, his mother became the most influential person in his family. This woman was a descendant of highly sinicized Po-hai gentry in Liaoyang, Manchuria, where the Chinese had assimilated the Po-hai during the Liao dynasty. After Tsung-fu died, the widow rejected the Jurchen custom of levirate and entered a nunnery.[7] She taught Wu-lu with "just and righteous methods." To glorify her, the son reconstructed a temple to her memory after her death. The clan of this Po-hai lady also helped Wu-lu a great deal in his rise to power. Li Shih, Wu-lu's maternal uncle, held influential posts during Wu-lu's reign, and Wu-lu took his daughter as an imperial consort.[8] Probably owing to his mother and her clansmen, Wu-lu received a good Chinese education. He was able to read

Chinese classics, and to discuss Chinese history with his ministers. In other words, he demonstrated a knowledge of Chinese classics as good as that of Chinese emperors.

Another person having important influence on Wu-lu was his wife (née Wu-lin-ta). It was she who advised Wu-lu to be patient and pretend to be loyal to Liang for the purpose of maintaining Wu-lu's power. Liang admired her and called her to his inner court in 1151, but she committed suicide on her way there. The tragic incident resulted in a deadly feud between Wu-lu and Liang. He never made any woman empress after he became ruler of the Chin.[9]

When Liang crossed the Huai River in 1161 to invade the Southern Sung, he sent agents to exterminate many of his relatives, including Wu-lu, thus forcing Wu-lu to rebel against Liang. Among the most enthusiastic supporters of Wu-lu was, of course, his uncle Li Shih.

Discontent and dissatisfaction among the Jurchen population contributed to Wu-lu's success. Liang's preparation for conquest had tyrannized the people, for he severely punished any person opposing his grandiose plan of unifying China and his ruthless amassion of manpower and resources for his adventure. In spite of his oppressive measures there were uprisings, and many soldiers deserted Liang's expeditionary army. Taking advantage of this general unrest, Wu-lu rose in Liaoyang, and readily became the new ruler, without fighting against Liang, who was murdered not long after Wu-lu's rebellion.

Wu-lu's ascendancy may have represented the reaction of the remnant conservative forces against Liang's policy of centralization and wholesale sinicization. Liang's reorganization of many *meng-an* and *mou-k'e* had provoked great confusion and discontent among the aristocrats who either lost their positions or were degraded. The first Jurchen military officer to support Wu-lu was Wan-yen Mou-yen, who suffered from Liang's abrogation of the position of *wan-hu*, or head of ten thousand men, in 1151 and lost his job. There were other displaced Jurchen officers who went to Wu-lu's camp following Liang's drastic changes of the *meng-an* and *mou-k'e* system.[10] Furthermore, as a result of Liang's work of centralization, most Jurchen nobles lost their military as well as political power. Many princes and military men rebelled mainly because of Liang's increasing pressure on them, which was the result of Liang's methods for establishment of a central Chinese state.[11] Wu-lu's rise was also for the protection of both his life and privileges. It is interesting that Wu-lu as a cousin of Liang still possessed many privileges in Liang's last years. When Liang was mobilizing manpower and resources in 1161, for example, Wu-lu did not send a single servant nor any horses to take part in the campaign against the Southern Sung, though at the time he owned thousands of servants and livestock. Evidently the remaining forces of the imperial clansmen were still powerful.[12]

Having become emperor, Shih-tsung reversed Liang's plan to unify China and sinicize the Jurchen. Shih-tsung's Jurchen conservatism had two origins. For one, simply because of his personal bitterness against Liang he was in opposition to many of Liang's measures. For another, he employed and protected Jurchen conservatives in order to counter Liang's policy of wholesale sinicization, for he often attributed Liang's defeat to his abandonment of Jurchen customs and institutions. He lamented in 1173 that since Liang moved the capital to Yen-ching the people had forgotten their customs. He worried about disastrous consequences in the future and wanted to save Jurchen society from disintegration. On another occasion he criticized Liang for forgetting his origins because he learned Chinese customs. Shih-tsung believed there would be no foreign menace to the country if the Jurchen could keep their old way of life.[13]

For Shih-tsung, to recover the traditional Jurchen culture was the best way to maintain the Jurchen regime in China. He preferred a simple and sincere Jurchen culture to the complicated Chinese culture that corroded the Jurchen way of life. He disliked the luxurious manners and fashions of Liang's time. He was pleased to claim in 1173 that the customs of the people were more "natural and honest" than in the previous period.[14]

Shih-tsung, opposed to ethnic integration, made efforts to uphold the position of the Jurchen among other ethnic groups. He once blamed a Jurchen official, T'ang-kua An-li, for his suggestion that the Chinese and the Jurchen should be treated as members of the same family, and for his imitation of Chinese customs. Shih-tsung pointed out that the Jurchen, the Chinese, and the Ch'i-tan did not belong to the same family, because when he ascended the throne he could only rally the support of the Jurchen, not the Chinese and the Ch'i-tan, who even rose against the Jurchen. He had reservations about the loyalty of the Yen Chinese because of their trickiness and their shifting allegiance. The Yen people, according to Shih-tsung, would collaborate with the Ch'i-tan, the Chinese, and the Jurchen for the purpose of obtaining security, so that they retained prosperity in spite of recurrent calamities. The southerners were more respectable; they were straightforward and would risk their lives to admonish their sovereign.[15]

But Shih-tsung was by no means a narrow-minded ruler who only cared about the well-being of his own tribesmen. Although he would promote the illiterate Jurchen imperial guardsmen to higher positions, he severely punished the corrupt ones and criticized Jurchen ministers' favoritism towards their own people.[16]

Nor was Shih-tsung entirely opposed to the Chinese culture. Once he even identified good old Jurchen customs with the ancient Chinese way of life. He said that Chinese classics had been valuable for teaching the people for many generations, but he questioned the advantage of merely reading the classics if one could not put what he learned into practice. Jurchen customs, he contended, were "the purest and most honest." Though people could not read in pre-Chin times, their way of life came into being naturally, and the basic ideas were not different from those recorded in ancient Chinese classics.[17] The immediate motive for Shih-tsung's efforts to recover the old tradition may have been his perception of the decadence and demoralization of the Jurchen people. It was difficult for many Jurchen to accommodate the political, economic, and social changes, and they suffered from the corrosive effects of the Chinese civilization.

What were the socioeconomic changes in Jurchen society after the people migrated southward into North China? Not only could they attain high positions in the government and enjoy many political and economic privileges, but they also received different treatment from the Chinese in other respects. In legal affairs, because of their privileged position and their relations to powerful officials and noble families, the common Jurchen always benefited. Shih-tsung once had to prohibit powerful families (mostly Jurchen) to pull strings to defeat the Chinese in legal disputes and incidence of

Jurchen conniving with officials are many. The big
families in the prefecture of Shuo (now in Shansi)
monopolized legal affairs and changed their rate of
taxation.[18] The hereditary *meng-an* Liaotung were
"prodigal and did unlawful things." Local officials of
Shou-chang county in Hopei could not handle affairs of
those unruly "hereditary officials," that is, hereditary
meng-an and *mou-k'e*. In Shensi *meng-an* and *mou-k'e*
oppressed the poor and even kidnapped Chinese women at
will. Hereditary *meng-an* and *mou-k'e* often made and
sold alcoholic liquors and smuggled salt unlawfully.[19]
In general, in the words of contemporary officials:
"In every route the *meng-an* and *mou-k'e* disturbed the
people, for their jobs were hereditary and they were not
afraid of anybody."[20]

Furthermore, powerful and wealthy Jurchen gradually
became big landlords. Not only did the government assign much land to the Jurchen, but a number of landowners were able to acquire large estates. A report from
the prefecture of Hsing (the present Hsing-t'ai, Hopei)
told of powerful families occupying state-owned farm
land and lands not under cultivation but otherwise productive. The poor owned bad land but paid heavy taxes.
Before the *Ta-ting* (Shih-tsung's reign title) period
A-li owned 14,000 *mou* of land in Shantung, and in the
early *Ta-ting* period the government granted A-li's
family another 10,000 *mou*. Shih-tsung had to confiscate
A-li's holdings in Shantung in 1180.[21] In the following
year some people reported that powerful families often
seized others' estates. Shih-tsung commented:

> The former Assistant Civil Councilor, Na-ho Ch'un-nien,
> seized more than 800 *ch'ing* of land. I am also informed
> that land in Shansi has been mostly seized by powerful
> men; one single person from each family owns as much as
> 30 *ch'ing*. As a result the common people have no land to
> till and are compelled to move to poor soil under the Yin
> mountains. How can they manage to sustain themselves?[22]

He ruled that whoever seized government land over 10
ch'ing would have extra holdings confiscated and redistributed to the poor. Relatives of Na-ho and other
officials totaling 70 households possessed extra land
of about 3,000 *ch'ing* that was confiscated and redistributed. Shih-tsung further ruled in 1181 that from
then on whenever imperial lines moved to a new place
and were given new land, they could no longer retain

their original holdings. The government punished six county magistrates and many royal retainers the next year, for they illegally occupied government land for their masters. Many princes, princesses, and powerful families acquired land by illegal means and leased it to tenants.[23]

These are mainly examples of seizure of government land. In extant sources one can hardly find clear evidence of illegal seizure of estates belonging to the Chinese commoners. The reason may have been that influential people did not have to do such things, for the government had many ways to take the estates from the common people. Early in 1177 Shih-tsung decided to give fertile land to the Jurchen, for he reasoned that when they moved into China, they always received bad farming land.[24] The government confiscated untilled land and land illegally acquired by the common people and granted them to some "officials and people" as pasture.[25] When the government distributed confiscated land in Shantung to the Jurchen in 1181, Shih-tsung said that such land could be taken from the people legally, for they could not provide enough evidence to claim it. This indicates an important aspect of the campaign to confiscate land. Many places bearing such names as Queen's Village, Prince's Estate, Great Wall, Swallow's Town, and so on, owned by the common people for hundreds of years, were taken by the government on the ground that these names indicated government ownership. Thus wherever the Jurchen went, the government always took good care of them and assigned them new holdings.[26]

Accompanying the rise of the big landlords was of course tenantry. Since *meng-an* and *mou-k'e* did not like to do farm work, they often leased their land to others, particularly Chinese peasants. Powerful families seized government land and employed tenants. They also had a number of slaves to do farm work for them. Statistics in the *Dynastic History of the Chin* reveal details of land ownership by the Jurchen. There were 615,624 households under control of *meng-an* and *mou-k'e* in 1182, and the population was 6,158,636, consisting of 4,812,669 nobles and commoners and 1,345,967 slaves. They owned 1,690,380 *ch'ing* of land; that means 2.7 *ch'ing* per household. But imperial lines and powerful generals differed from the common Jurchen. There were only 170 such families, including a Jurchen population of 982 and 27,880 slaves. These families owned about 3,684 *ch'ing*. An average household of Jurchen nobility, therefore, owned 22 *ch'ing* of land and 160 slaves.[27]

The Jurchen were deeply involved in the Chinese society and in such an environment maladjustment was inevitable. A number of the people loved luxury and became bankrupt; some others were demoralized, lost identity, and turned out to be parasites. Although the Jurchen as a whole owned more land and enjoyed more privileges than non-Jurchen peoples, the general tendency of their life in China was a decline into poverty and a loss of martial spirit.[28]

Shih-tsung was keenly aware of his tribesmen's love of luxury. He once said they were holding good jobs and did not know the hardships of earning a living. When some imperial clansmen could not work, Shih-tsung kept them as sinecurists. He observed in 1180 that many *meng-an* and *mou-k'e* were so overbearing and prodigal that they did not work nor did they let their family members farm, leasing land to the Chinese instead. The rich loved fine dresses, big banquets, and exciting games, while the poor admired the rich and tried hard to imitate them.[29]

The Jurchen's poverty and laziness were serious problems of the time. Government agricultural inspectors reported in 1181 that many Jurchen were addicted to alcohol and leased their land; some lost their holdings and became paupers. Because most were not big landowners, they could collect little rent and their life was harsh. In Shantung and Hopei many Jurchen lived among the Chinese and many became unemployed vagrants. Jurchen impoverishment is evidenced by the large amount of relief work Shih-tsung did for his own people during the *Ta-ting* period.[30]

Most Jurchen lost their martial spirit. Shih-tsung criticized them for not practicing shooting and riding, and not joining the army. Even some of the imperial guards failed to master archery. The emperor was alarmed when in 1170 his guards could not match Sung envoys in an archery contest held at a banquet. He warned his ministers in 1186 that the Southern Sung Chinese were training their soldiers very hard, while the Jurchen were so lazy that they neglected military drill.[31]

The Movement

The Ch'i-tan rebellions and Southern Sung invasions that shook the Jurchen regime in North China in the early 1160s impelled Shih-tsung to begin his nativistic movement by improving the martial spirit, with the emphasis on hunting, with was the foundation of Jurchen military maneuvers.[32] He made hunting an annual royal activity in 1162, and from that year until 1188 the emperor went hunting almost every autumn and winter. Besides frequenting areas around Yen-ching, he often traveled to the "Spring River" (*ch'un-shui*), usually in northern Hopei. Sometimes he spent the summer at Chin-lien ch'uan (now north of Chan-yüan, Chahar), where he also hunted; as a rule he devoted at least one month a year to hunting.[33] Other activities included shooting willow wands and playing ball. The purpose of hunting was military exercise. When a Chinese official advised Shih-tsung to stop hunting in 1168 he refused, on the grounds that it was for military practice, and that he had to set an example. His ancestors had established the state by military force, he said, and posterity in time of peace should not forget it.[34]

Another lifelong task for Shih-tsung's revival of indigenous Jurchen culture was the promotion of the Jurchen language. Altaic in origin, the Jurchen language did not have writing before A-ku-ta, and Ch'i-tan script was used instead. In 1119, A-ku-ta ordered Hsi-yin to create a new script that followed the Ch'i-tan pattern in using Chinese characters. Tan further made the "small characters" (*Nü-chen hsiao-tzu*) in 1138.[35] Though language schools were set up as early as 1125,[36] Chinese studies were popular during the reign of Liang, who made no attempt to promote Jurchen learning. Shortly after Shih-tsung ascended the throne in 1161, he published the Jurchen version of the *Book of History* (*Shang-shu*), and chose 3,000 men from the Jurchen population to study their language. Then he offered the Jurchen *chin-shih* degree in 1173. The same year the government set up at the capital the Jurchen Imperial Academy (*Nü-chen kuo-tzu-hsüeh*), and established local schools in all the routes (*lu*). Jurchen learning was flourishing by 1180.[37] It seems the purpose of the Jurchen examination system was more to promote Jurchen learning than to channel fresh blood

Jurchen Movement for Revival 77

into the officialdom. Most Jurchen *chin-shih* became teachers of the language and Chinese classics in translation during Shih-tsung's reign.

Shih-tsung made a few attempts at restoration of ancient Jurchen customs in 1173. He admonished the people not to forget their customs, and revealed his intention to visit Shang-ching. He told the heir apparent and other princes that because they had learned the Chinese way of life since childhood they did not know the unadulterated Jurchen customs and practices. Some could not speak Jurchen, and according to Shih-tsung this was "forgetting their origins." He prohibited translation of Jurchen names into Chinese, and restored the name Hui-ning for Shang-ching.[38]

Shih-tsung advanced the Jurchen learning campaign in 1174 by forcing the imperial guards to learn Jurchen and forbidding them to speak Chinese. Later he ordered those who were to inherit *meng-an* and *mou-k'e* titles to learn Jurchen. When Shih-tsung bestowed the title of prince on his eldest grandson Chin in 1185, the young man conversed with him in Jurchen at the court. Shih-tsung was deeply moved. When the Jurchen made statements to the government, officials were ordered to talk to them in Jurchen.[39]

A measure related to learning language was translation of Chinese classics, a project initiated by the government in 1164.[40] By the end of the *Ta-ting* period three of the Five Classics (the *Book of History*, the *Book of Changes*, and *Spring and Autumn Annals*) were available in Jurchen. Other Chinese works translated in the same period were the *Confucian Analects*, the *Mencius*, the *Lao-tzu*, the *Yang-tzu*, the *Wen-chung-tzu*, the *Liu-tzu* (*Hsin-lun*), the *Canon of Filial Piety*, the *Historical Records*, *Dynastic History of the T'ang*, *New Dynastic History of the T'ang*, *Important Policies of the* Chen-kuan *Period* (*Chen-kuan cheng-yao*), and *Pai-shih ts'e-lin*. Shih-tsung maintained that the translation project was to acquaint the Jurchen with basic virtues. The government in 1183 issued to the imperial guards one thousand copies of the *Canon of Filial Piety*. These translated works were also studied by Jurchen students in preparation for Jurchen examinations.[41]

Shih-tsung banned the wearing of silk by servants and slaves, seeking to prevent Chinese clothes from becoming too popular. Finally in 1188 he prohibited the Jurchen to wear Chinese clothes.[42]

An important measure introduced in Shih-tsung's last years was reassignment of land to the Jurchen. To discourage fraternizing between Jurchen and Chinese peasants, he earlier had made the alien minority live in groups among the Chinese majority.[43] The purpose was also to redistribute land to the commoners and to eliminate the concentration of land in the hands of a few big landlords. The measure sought more efficient farming for the Jurchen, who had been accustomed to cooperate with one another in such work since primitive times.[44] The ultimate goal was to improve Jurchen living conditions as well as to avoid demoralization and assimilation by the Chinese culture.

Another of Shih-tsung's revival measures was the appointment of more Jurchen officials in the government, a policy reversing Liang's employment regulations. Whereas Liang divested the aristocracy of power, Shih-tsung filled his government with more Jurchen. He had twenty-two Jurchen ministers, fourteen Chinese, two Po-hai, and two Ch'i-tan. Most of the Jurchen officials (fifteen of them), however, were not from the imperial clan.[45]

Shih-tsung paid much attention to the implementation of ancient Chinese as well as Jurchen ceremonies. He revived the traditional ceremonies at the Confucian Temple in 1174.[46] Instead of adopting T'ang and Sung precedents, he restored ancient Chinese ceremonies concerning the worship of the Heaven.[47] An interesting innovation was the ceremony of offering sacrifices to the Ch'ang-pai Mountain in 1172, in which the god of the mountain was invested with the title of "The Efficacious State Constructing God" (*Hsing-kuo ling-ying chu*).[48] This was a combination of the Chinese practice of investing the gods of famous mountains and rivers and the Jurchen respect for their mother country. Ceremonies held to worship the Heaven in Chinese festivals are another indication of Sino-Jurchen synthesis.[49]

Shih-tsung's visit to Shang-ching in 1184-85 strikingly illustrates his admiration of ancient Jurchen culture and his longing for his home country. Staying there for a year he frequently enjoyed hunting, dancing, and chatting with native people. At the farewell banquet the old emperor sang a Jurchen song, and was so deeply moved that he wept.[50] Before leaving he ordered three *meng-an* to move to Shang-ching to defend the city as well as to make it a center of Jurchen culture. He lamented the disappearance of old customs, and appealed for restoration of primitive ways.[51]

Related to the revival movement is Shih-tsung's fiscal policy. He emphasized economic reconstruction in order to better the life of the Jurchen.[52] His policy was to enrich the country by introducing a property tax, called "property money" (*wu-li ch'ien*).[53] The government sent commissioners to investigate the property of all households, including those of the nobility, and assess the property tax accordingly.[54] The tax sought to limit the growth of influential Chinese families, to prevent big Jurchen families from further expanding their power, and also to help the poor. The measure was unsuccessful; contemporary officials and traditional historians unanimously criticized it severely. The major cause of its failure may have been that the commissioners were corrupt and often assessed the tax irresponsibly.[55]

The Failure of the Movement

Most of the measures inaugurated by Shih-tsung were carried out effectively during his lifetime, but on the whole the movement was far from successful. Ostensibly he was against many of Liang's sinicization measures, but he did not alter Chinese institutions introduced by his predecessors. Shih-tsung continued Liang's efforts at centralizing power by eliminating opposition, appointing loyal men as *meng-an* and *mou-k'e*, setting up a Chinese heir apparent practice, making hereditary the succession to *meng-an* and *mou-k'e*, and putting new *meng-an* and *mou-k'e* under more powerful state control. His only important political policy was to preserve key government positions for the Jurchen, for he distrusted the Chinese and Ch'i-tan.[56]

The difficulties Shih-tsung encountered in making hunting popular reveal the inadequacy of his planning and the superficiality of his policies. Hunting remained a royal practice. Because all Jurchen commoners engaged in farming, they could hardly have time to leave their fields for hunting, even if able to afford a vacation. It is doubtful that there was any space for hunting on their farming land. Shih-tsung once said that because there was no hunting ground even on the borderlands the Jurchen could not master the arts of shooting and riding. Ironically, he had helped to create such a situation, for shortly after he became emperor, he accepted suggestions to reduce hunting grounds so as to give more land to the peasants. He also granted the people some pasturage to cultivate.[57]

Some measures were incompatible with hunting. He often sent agricultural advisers (*ch'üan-nung shih*) to encourage and assist those who did not like farming (these people were presumably Jurchen). Such commissioners, recorded in the *Dynastic History of the Chin*, were not few, but there were no commissioners sent to propagate the importance of hunting.[58] Once when Shih-tsung went hunting near Shang-ching, he ordered a peasant negligent in farming punished. Further, Shih-tsung was interested in agriculture, often going to inspect crops in the suburbs of Yen-ching, just as traditional Chinese emperors had customarily done. He said that because he had held many posts before his accession to the throne, he understood the affairs of the countryside and difficulties in farming. The government required in 1174 that peasants not leave their fields from the second to the eighth month of the year; meanwhile they were not allowed to hold feasts and drinking parties.[59] All these measures sought to maintain the Jurchen as farmers. It is interesting that the more the people remained on their farms, the less they could practice hunting and war and clearly these measures were effective in making the Jurchen tend their land and crops.

Another difficulty was to keep Jurchen a living language. Despite efforts to establish a system of Jurchen learning and recruitment of Jurchen officials through examinations given in Jurchen, the plans did not work out. The fundamental weakness of Shih-tsung's language policy lay in translation of Chinese classics. The Jurchen lacked their own folk literature and they had to rely on Chinese books. Shih-tsung tried to identify old Jurchen customs with those in ancient China, and believed that the Jurchen could learn virtue from Chinese classics. He did not realize that such learning only led the people to accept Chinese ideas of virtue and ethics. For example, pre-Chin Jurchen warriors did not respect the aged, but Shih-tsung distributed the *Canon of Filial Piety* to the imperial guards, teaching them to love their parents and to worship their ancestors. Translations of Chinese works filled the Jurchen mind with more and more Chinese ideas and customs, and learning the Chinese classics was one of the most effective ways to transform the Jurchen population unwittingly, indeed contrary to Shih-tsung's intentions, into Chinese.

The Jurchen language was gradually dying out and many Jurchen may have doubted the practicality of using it, for no book was originally written in Jurchen. Only a few people were able to master the mother tongue, and to the majority Chinese may have been more convenient.[60] Even Shih-tsung himself was not sure of the practical value of his native language, because, as he once said, it was "inferior to Chinese," and could not match Ch'i-tan. He was afraid that posterity might criticize his stubbornness in forcing the people to use the "inferior" language.[61]

The most striking weakness of the revival movement hence was lack of systematic planning and consistency. There were many contradictions in Shih-tsung's ideas and practices, besides the language-learning campaign. Sometimes he would reprove an official who bowed in Chinese fashion; on other occasions he would punish a peasant who failed to cultivate his farm.[62] He never punished anybody who failed to hunt. To bow in Jurchen fashion, compared with forcing the Jurchen to become peasants like the Chinese, and to study Chinese classics, was a superficial attempt to preserve Jurchen customs. Shih-tsung's opinions and discussions about politics and economics impress one as identical with what a typical Chinese emperor might say. As an old Jurchen leader, Shih-tsung had reminiscences of his ancestors' primitive ways, but as a ruler in China he admired good Chinese emperors. He even tried to match Emperor Kuang-wu of the Han dynasty and Emperor T'ai-tsung of the T'ang in their good deeds. He often reminded his sons and ministers not to forget the old way of life, but he also admonished them to practice Chinese virtues. He encouraged his people to assimilate what was admirable in the Chinese civilization, and his efforts greatly furthered the adoption of the Chinese culture. Above all, his diligence in fostering the people's livelihood and his love of peace ironically earned him the fame of a typical Chinese emperor. Popularly and traditionally his era was called a "miniature of Yao and Shun," the sage kings of ancient China.[63] The rule of Shih-tsung was described by contemporaries as "restoration" (*chung-hsing*), not in the sense of restoring Jurchen customs but a political restoration in which emphasis was on the learning of Chinese classics.[64] Indeed during the *Ta-ting* period there was great improvement in education. The first duty to be performed whenever an official took his post was to visit the local Confucian temple. At all levels of local government civil service examinations were held to enlist scholars. Imperial clansmen and relatives, as well as ranking officials in the central government, were appointed as local officials who "upheld the five human relationships, refined the customs, and promoted public morals."[65] In addition to the establishment of the Jurchen Imperial Academy (Nü-chen kuo-tzu-chien), local schools for both Chinese and Jurchen were installed and education was widespread.[66]

In conclusion, the movement for revival in the late twelfth century was an effort made by a self-conscious alien ruler to seek identity for his people, and to prevent the minority from being assimilated by the Chinese majority. To the Jurchen it was a far-sighted task to maintain and strengthen their ruling position in China. In assessing the success and failure of the movement, one should note especially two interesting aspects of it. First, Shih-tsung apparently had tried to secure an equilibrium between two contending cultures: Jurchen and Chinese. He seems to have been able to achieve this by emphasizing the preservation of the Jurchen culture and by improving the wealth of the state. As a consequence the Jurchen were able to defend themselves successfully against the Southern Sung. That emperor Hsiao-tsung of the Sung (r. 1162-89) could no longer find opportunity to overthrow the northern kingdom after his disastrous defeat in 1164 testifies to Shih-tsung's achievement. Second, Shih-tsung seems to have striven to diminish the conservative forces--the aristocrats and officials who had been seizing land since 1161. One of the ways to restrain the growing Jurchen influence was to carry out financial reforms. Property taxation aimed at collecting equitable taxes from all the subjects in the state; the restriction on landowners' encroachments on small holdings benefited the free farmers. Another was the establishment of the Jurchen examination system, which not only was a measure to promote Jurchen culture, but also purported to recruit new Jurchen personnel in order to diminish the power of the Jurchen aristocrats. Nevertheless, the Jurchen examination system was not institutionalized long enough to channel more Jurchen commoners into the officialdom to broaden the base of the government.[67] This failure perhaps was one of the factors that ultimately alienated many social groups, Chinese as well as Jurchen, from the existing political framework.

The movement for the restoration of Jurchen culture thus was only a temporary success. Shih-tsung could not make fundamental changes in Chinese institutions, which took root firmly in the state. Torn between the fading Jurchen way and the dominating Chinese culture, he could do little to alter the present situation and his choices were limited. The nativistic movement was unable to halt the trend of the time, and the Jurchen were prisoners of Chinese tradition, with no alternative but to bow before its demands.

7

From Prosperity to Decline

In order to comprehend the sinicization of the Jurchen in the early thirteenth century one must evaluate the whole process of sociocultural change. One should not merely look at one phase of the process--for example, the phase when under Emperor Shih-tsung the Jurchen were able to maintain and even recover their customs-- and then assert that the Jurchen generally could preserve their ethnic and cultural identity. Only when analyzing the situation near or after the end of the dynasty can one see the whole picture and discern various forces at work during the transformation in the twelfth century.[1]

The Reign of Chang-tsung

By the end of the twelfth century the Jurchen rulers had adopted the Chinese practice of primogeniture. Shih-tsung's successor was his grandson, Chin or Ma-ta-ko (1168-1208), whose posthumous title is Chang-tsung. Shih-tsung's eldest son and heir apparent, Prince Yün-kung, died in 1185 at the age of forty. Following the Chinese principle of primogeniture, Shih-tsung made Yün-kung's son, Chin, the heir apparent.[2] Chin had received a Chinese education, and was able to maintain the Chin kingdom in prosperity. To strengthen the position of the emperorship, Chin strictly controlled members of the imperial family, and even rid himself of two uncles who were allegedly extremely ambitious.[3] As for fiscal policy, Chang-tsung continued to finance the government with the property tax. On the local administrative level, increased control of the people is indicated in harsh punishment of the guilty. Some officials fastened a knife on the end of a stick, with which they often beat criminals and even suspects to death.[4] Meanwhile, in the field of justice, he promulgated the famous *T'ai-ho* legal code, largely based on the T'ang code.[5]

The *T'ai-ho lü* was the only complete legal code compiled and practiced between the T'ang and the Ming periods.[6] It also marked the apogee of legal sinicization in the Chin.[7] The Chin code in general followed that of the T'ang, with minor modifications, some of which concern the Jurchen whose customs were different from those of the Chinese. Thus the Jurchen did not have to live with their grandparents and parents in the same household and share the common property.[8] They were also allowed to preserve the old custom of collateral inheritance.[9] In general, punishment for people who violated the social order was more severe than in the T'ang, a reflection of the conquerors' emphasis on the maintenance of law and order by legal enforcement and by the employment of Confucian morality.[10]

In foreign relations, there was a war against the Southern Sung in 1206, when the Southern Sung prime minister Han T'o-chou took the advice of a few militant officials, including the famous poet Hsin Ch'i-chi, and launched an ambitious northern expedition to recover North China. Chang-tsung met the challenge and defeated the Sung army, demanding an indemnity, territory, and Han T'o-chou's head as guarantee for future peace.[11] Unable to continue the fighting, the southern state met his terms.

Maintaining the old Jurchen customs, Chang-tsung encouraged intensive use of the Jurchen language, forbade the wearing of Chinese clothes, and practiced Jurchen rituals. He punished those who did not perform the Jurchen kowtow ceremony.[12] During his reign there was the compilation of the *Ta Chin chi-li* or *Compendium of Ceremonies of the Great Chin*,[13] and the implementation of the "Jurchen wedding ceremony." He also ordered the *meng-an* and *mou-k'e* who wanted to take the *chin-shih* examination to take the test on archery.

However, he was not as enthusiastic as his grandfather about recovering the Jurchen way of life. He seems to have understood that sinicization had gone on during Shih-tsung's reign, notwithstanding the revival movement. The last stronghold of Jurchen culture, his grandfather the Emperor Shih-tsung, fell in 1189. There were no more ways to prevent the Jurchen from learning Chinese customs; they could not avoid becoming Chinese. Although Chang-tsung insisted on the use of Jurchen kowtow ceremony at his court, he permitted the people to follow Chinese funeral practices. Despite the compilation of the *Ta Chin chi-li*, which may have included many Jurchen practices, he performed T'ang and Sung court rituals in 1194. Further, he established Confucian temples in all prefectures and counties, a continuation of King Hai-ling's work of building local temples for the ancient sage.[14]

The change in attitude and values at the time of Chang-tsung clearly appeared in hunting. While Shih-tsung liked to hunt several times a year as military training, Chang-tsung conceived of hunting as recreation during vacation. The Jurchen in general no longer thought of hunting as having a military function.[15] The emperor did not hunt as often as did his grandfather, nor did he travel far to hunt.[16] Once when he intended to take a hunting trip to Chahar, many courtiers memorialized him not to do so, for the traditional Chinese reason that it was dangerous for an emperor to ride in the wilderness, and that it also was detrimental to the economy of the state.[17] A few advisers evidently had shown their sinicized attitude toward this problem.[18]

Furthermore, from the discussions on the *te-yün*, or the dynastic virtue and element of the Chin during the reigns of Chang-tsung and Hsüan-tsung, it is clear that the rulers and their officials considered their dynasty as having assumed the position of a legitimate Chinese dynasty. This marked another step taken by the Chin rulers to identify their dynasty with China. The dynastic element theory was an ancient Chinese tradition according to which a dynasty should choose to adopt one of the five elements: fire, water, earth, wood, and metal. The dynasty recognized the magic power of the adopted element and observed the relevant ritual ceremonies and practices, such as the color of the dynastic flags and vestments and the date for winter sacrifice.[19] Ever since Wu-ch'i-mai started the military campaigns against the Sung, the Jurchen had repeatedly claimed that what they did to the Chinese dynasty was for the purpose of "consoling the people and punishing the rebellious" (*tiao-min fa-tsui*). The Chin became the leading state of East Asia during the reign of Tan, who established the "ruler-subject" relationship with the Southern Sung emperor. According to the treaty of 1141 the Southern Sung sent annual tribute to the Chin, addressing the latter as "your superior state."[20]

King Hai-ling tried to reunify the whole of China but failed. His successors did not attempt reunification, but concentrated on legitimizing their state. When Shih-tsung resumed the peaceful relationship with the Sung, his endeavor was extolled by Chin writers as "the people of the Ch'u begged for peace," and "the people of distant places came to submit."[21] When Shih-tsung implemented Chinese ritual ceremonies and music at his court, he was praised for restoring the institutions of the ancient sage kings and following the way of the Chou dynasty. Shih-tsung claimed that "my country defeated the Liao and the Sung and occupied the legitimate position under Heaven," even calling the neighboring states barbarians.[22]

Although there were many auspicious omens at the time of the founding of the dynasty, there had been no discussions on them until the reign of Chang-tsung. From 1193 to 1216, discussions on the dynastic virtue and element were held six times. During the reign of Chang-tsung, three views on the dynastic element were put forward. Those who propounded the recognition of the element of metal generally based their argument on the omens relating to gold when the state was founded and proposed that the Chin, according to the "production" scheme of the Five Elements theory, should succeed the T'ang, because the T'ang element earth would produce metal. Moreover, the Chin should follow the native tradition related to metal, not paying special attention to the Five Elements theory. Others suggested the recognition of the element wood, which was produced by water, the element of the Liao. Still others insisted on succeeding the Sung element fire, considering that the element earth should be recognized. Chang-tsung and his officials reached the decision in 1202, making the element earth the symbol of the state.[23]

In 1214 during the reign of Hsüan-tsung, there was another discussion of the problem. In order not to succeed the Sung, some officials pointed out that the Sung choice of the fire element was a mistake. They proposed that the Chin should be a successor state of the T'ang instead of the Sung, so that the auspicious element for the Chin should be metal, the element produced by the T'ang earth element. In so doing, these officials refused to recognize the position of the Sung in history, and claimed the sole legitimacy for the Chin after the fall of the T'ang, bypassing and overpowering the Five Dynasties, the Liao, and the Sung. It should be noted that in the discussion there was an important opinion put forth by Jurchen officials, who also wanted to correct the mistake of the Sung, replace fire with earth for the Sung, and make metal the dynastic element of the Chin in succession to the Sung. The interesting point about this argument is that these officials of Jurchen origin asserted that their dynasty had acquired legitimacy for more than eighty years, and that "all the four barbarians were submissive; the six points [the world] shared the same customs."[24] Certainly their claim aimed to show the Chinese as well as Jurchen subjects that the Jurchen rulership in China had long been legitimately established, and that all other states, including the Southern Sung, were subordinate to the Chin. Inasmuch as they suggested the change of the representative element of the nonexistent Northern Sung, they did not give much value to that state they destroyed. These arguments were, however, rejected by Emperor Hsüan-tsung. The last attempt to change the dynastic element was made in 1216 by a certain official Wang Kuai, who upheld the element fire, and proposed to build a temple for the ancient Yellow Emperor.[25] This proposal was again rejected.

The choice of the dynastic element was an important political issue during the reign of Chang-tsung. Chao Ping-wen, a famous scholar-official of the late Chin, attributed it to Chang-tsung as one of his major achievements: "The virtue of earth was amplified so that the Central Plain was unified."[26] Clearly the issue served the purpose of propaganda. The attempt of

some Jurchen officials in 1214 to alter the dynastic
virtue of the Sung to fit into their own view demonstrates their belief in the traditional connection
between gold and the rise of their ancestors. But
Chang-tsung's adoption of the earth element and Hsüantsung's confidence in it unmistakably point to the Jurchen abandonment of their ethnocentric standpoint. The
whole event thus could be considered as a Jurchen effort
to identify their state with the traditional Chinese
dynasty.

The Decline and Fall of the Chin

As described earlier, in both central and local
governments the Chinese became more important in the
latter half of the twelfth century than before. Chinese
intellectuals found that the gate to success was the
examination system, firmly established in mid-century.
Chinese officials were allowed to enjoy equitable treatment in promotion and in receiving awards.[27] The ban
on Sino-Jurchen intermarriage was also lifted in 1191.[28]
Yet many intellectuals gradually realized the examination system was by no means a perfect institution, and
came to detest it as corrupting. In the last thirty
years of the dynasty quite a few people attained high
posts without academic degrees, emerging from such
positions as *ling-shih* or assistant secretaries. Hence
the power of the lower echelons of the bureaucracy
increased at the expense of the prestige and influence
of scholar-officials who had passed the civil service
examinations.[29] During the reign of Chang-tsung the
most powerful persons in the central government were
his Chinese consort, her brothers, and a Chinese prime
minister who had started his career with a certificate
for *ching-t'ung*, a degree awarded to young students of
a few classics.[30] Perhaps the rulers were trying to
ally themselves with these lower bureaucrats in order
to diminish the power of the scholar-officials. In
addition, after 1214 when the capital was moved to
Pien-ching, the government became increasingly corrupt
and the Jurchen became parasites living on revenues
collected from the Chinese. All these conditions
alienated the Chinese from the dynasty.

As the Chinese drifted away from the offices on
the central government level, on the local level they

assumed much political and military power. Owing to
the lack of military strength during the campaign in
1206 against the Southern Sung, the Chin army had to
enlist a great number of Ch'i-tan (mainly the "cha"
乣 army) and Chinese soldiers. Many Chinese became
meng-an and *mou-k'e*.[31] The government even appointed
a *chin-shih*, Liu Ts'ung-i, and a literary man, Liu
Yüan-kuei, who was sixty years old, as *ch'ien-hu* (the
Chinese term for *meng-an*).[32]

To avoid a Mongol invasion of the region north of
the Yellow River in the early thirteenth century, the
Chin government in 1214 moved to Pien-ching, the old
Sung capital, just south of the Yellow River. Soon
the Mongols devastated territories north of the Yellow
River, and the government lost control of them completely. The court tried to recruit influential Chinese local leaders and ruffians to defend the kingdom,
rewarding them with *meng-an*, *mou-k'e* and even *wan-hu*
(head of ten thousand men) titles and privileges.[33]
Many of these positions were hereditary, given to
meritorious soldiers during wartime.[34] For example,
the emperor issued an edict in 1223, announcing that
anyone able to capture a rebellious Na-ho Liu-ko, who
occupied the prefecture of I (now Lin-i), was to be
awarded the position of hereditary *mou-k'e*.[35]

The last attempt of the Chin government to maintain the territories north of the Yellow River was to
appoint the "Nine Dukes" and "Ten Princes," who were
the most powerful local Chinese leaders in these regions until the Mongols conquered North China.[36]
Some of these Chinese warlords were authorized to
organize a *hsing-t'ai* or Mobile Presidential Council
in their respective domains. The Mongols did the same
when they invaded North China. This practice gradually
developed into the provincial system of the Yüan
dynasty.[37]

In the last several decades of the dynasty there
was a general economic decline. The corrupt Jurchen
nobility seized government transportation ships, and
exacted levies from merchants. They refined and sold
salt, and brewed alcoholic liquor illegally. Extravagant high officials and military men enjoyed fine food,
clothes, and carriages.[38]

Especially serious was the situation of unequal
land distribution. Important officials often took

farm land illegally.³⁹ Many members of the imperial family were presumptuous; even when Emperor Chang-tsung heard that the high official Wan-yen K'uan had seized other people's land, he did not say a word against this powerful dignitary.⁴⁰ Rather than deter such confiscation of Chinese peasant land, the government usually helped. After the Jurchen moved their capital to Pien-ching, more than 420,000 Jurchen *chün-hu* or military households under administration of *meng-an* and *mou-k'e* migrated to the south. The government was unable to provide them with land to till, and these *chün-hu* became a great burden to the Chinese peasants.⁴¹

The morale of the Jurchen soldiers during this time was at a low ebb, the military administration was inefficient and disorderly, and the officers corrupt. Although the *chün-hu* had both salary and land, they were men who "neither till the land nor fight."⁴² In case of war, only two out of every ten officers dared take up arms.⁴³ A Chinese official criticized Jurchen officers and soldiers bitterly, alleging that "military officers always have been hereditary. They have been arrogant and lazy since their childhood. Unable to bear hardships, they are cowards. How can we rely on them?"⁴⁴

Soldiers were few, officers many. A *mou-k'e* only commanded twenty-five to thirty men and four *mou-k'e* formed a *ch'ien-hu* or *meng-an*.⁴⁵ Because of the bad morale of Jurchen soldiers, irregular troops took the place of drafted men. The best-known troops at the end of the dynasty were the *chung-hsiao chün* or "loyal and filial troops," who were courageous but had no discipline.⁴⁶

Another military problem was lack of horses, in addition to poor weapons and equipment. I-la Fu-seng reported in 1218 that the east was full of bandits, government troops were few, and there was no cavalry. Pa-hu-lu in 1222 reported cavalry were so scarce that local governments could not catch bandits.⁴⁷ The last Chin ruler lamented that the reason for the Mongol victory over the Jurchen was that the former could employ horses to upset the latter.⁴⁸ No wonder, then, the regime collapsed in 1234, under conditions similar to the fall of the Northern Sung in 1127.⁴⁹

"The Employment of the Chinese Literati Destroyed the Chin"

The decline of the Chin was vividly described by Liu Ch'i, who also presented his views on the rise and fall of the dynasty, and the causes for the fall.[50] Liu Ch'i attributed the collapse of the Chin mainly to the rulers' inability to achieve complete sinicization. What the last rulers adopted was the "polished phraseology" of literature (*tz'u-chang*), not the principles of the classics that would provide guidance for the protection of the state and the people. They employed petty bureaucrats and dismissed the scholar-officials. They discriminated against the Chinese in employment and even Chinese prime ministers could not participate in the processes of decision making.[51] Thus the foundations (*ken-pen*) of the state were not stable, and Chinese scholar-officials were alienated.

Yüan Hao-wen agreed with Liu Ch'i's observation on the position of the Chinese. Yüan stated that most important positions in the government were occupied by the Jurchen, and that the civil service examinations were intended to deal fairly with the people and earn their confidence.[52] Some other scholars in the Yüan period shared Liu's opinion that the Chin scholars did not probe into the essential principles of the classics. Yang Huan pointed out that after the Ming-ch'ang period (1190-95) the scholarship of the literati was ornate (*hua*), not realistic (*shih*).[53] Su T'ien-chüeh lamented that the literati only memorized "polished phraseology" during a hundred years of the Chin period.[54]

The compilers of the *Dynastic History of the Chin* presented conflicting views on the sinicization of the Jurchen. On one hand, they stated that although the Chin, like the Liao, utilized military power to establish the state, it differed from the Liao in its ability to install better institutions, for the Jurchen also employed literary culture (*wen*). On the other hand, they attributed the decline of the Chin state to the adoption of the complicated literary culture of the Sung, and of the harsh policies of the Liao.[55]

Contemporaneous views did not, however, blame Aitsung, the last ruler, for the collapse of the dynasty. Although Liu Ch'i described political, economic, and military causes contributing to weakening of the state, he did not depict Ai-tsung as a "bad last ruler." Wang O, who had served at the court of Ai-tsung, and who was afraid that the deeds of the last ruler would perish, wrote the chronology of Ai-tsung, entitled *Ju-nan i-shih*. In this chronicle Wang O recorded Ai-tsung's efforts to reconstruct the state and praised his courage in fighting for the state until the end.[56] Moreover, Ai-tsung respected Confucian scholars, dismissed corrupt bureaucrats, and invited scholars to give lectures on the *Shang-shu* (Book of History), *Chen-kuan cheng-yao*, *Tzu-chih t'ung-chien*, among others, in the I-cheng yüan, or Bureau for Improving State Affairs.[57]

When Qubilai Qan asked Chang Te-hui in 1247 whether the utilization of Chinese scholar-officials was responsible for the fall of the Chin, Chang replied that the scholar-officials constituted less than 40 percent of the total number of officials and were employed as clerks, judges, and accountants, and that the Jurchen military men and aristocrats made all the important decisions on state affairs. Therefore the Chinese scholars should not bear the responsibility.[58]

Indeed, Chinese scholars in the Yüan dynasty in general favored sinicization. The employment of Chinese officials was not detrimental but beneficial to the Chin. They cited the examples of the Chin and other alien dynasties that adopted Confucianism, to convince the Mongol rulers of the importance of sinicization. In 1260 Hao Ching submitted a memorial to Qubilai Qan that the Jurchen adopted Liao and Sung institutions and consulted Chinese officials about the rule of China, so that during the reign of Shih-tsung the empire was peaceful, with proper institutions and pure and honest customs. Since the Mongol empire was larger and the population was greater than those of the Han and T'ang, Hao Ching contended, even if the empire could not match the Han and T'ang, she could at least achieve the rule of Yüan Wei and the Chin.[59] In a memorial submitted in 1266, Hsü Heng compared the achievements of alien dynasties and reached the conclusion that the Wei, the Liao, and the Chin, which adopted Chinese institutions, enjoyed longer rule in China than those that did not. He argued for the necessity of sinicization, and persuaded Qubilai Qan to adopt Chinese institutions despite objections from Mongol aristocrats.[60]

In short, to most Chinese scholars at the end of the Chin and during the Yüan period, sinicization was not a cause of the decline of the Chin; on the contrary, it was a necessity. From the point of view of historical hindsight, the alienation of Chinese and Ch'i-tan officials from the Jurchen, and their defection to the Mongols and the Southern Sung, constituted a major cause of the destruction of the dynasty.[61] External causes such as the Mongol military power, too great for the Jurchen to resist, also may have been decisive in bringing the Chin to an end.[62]

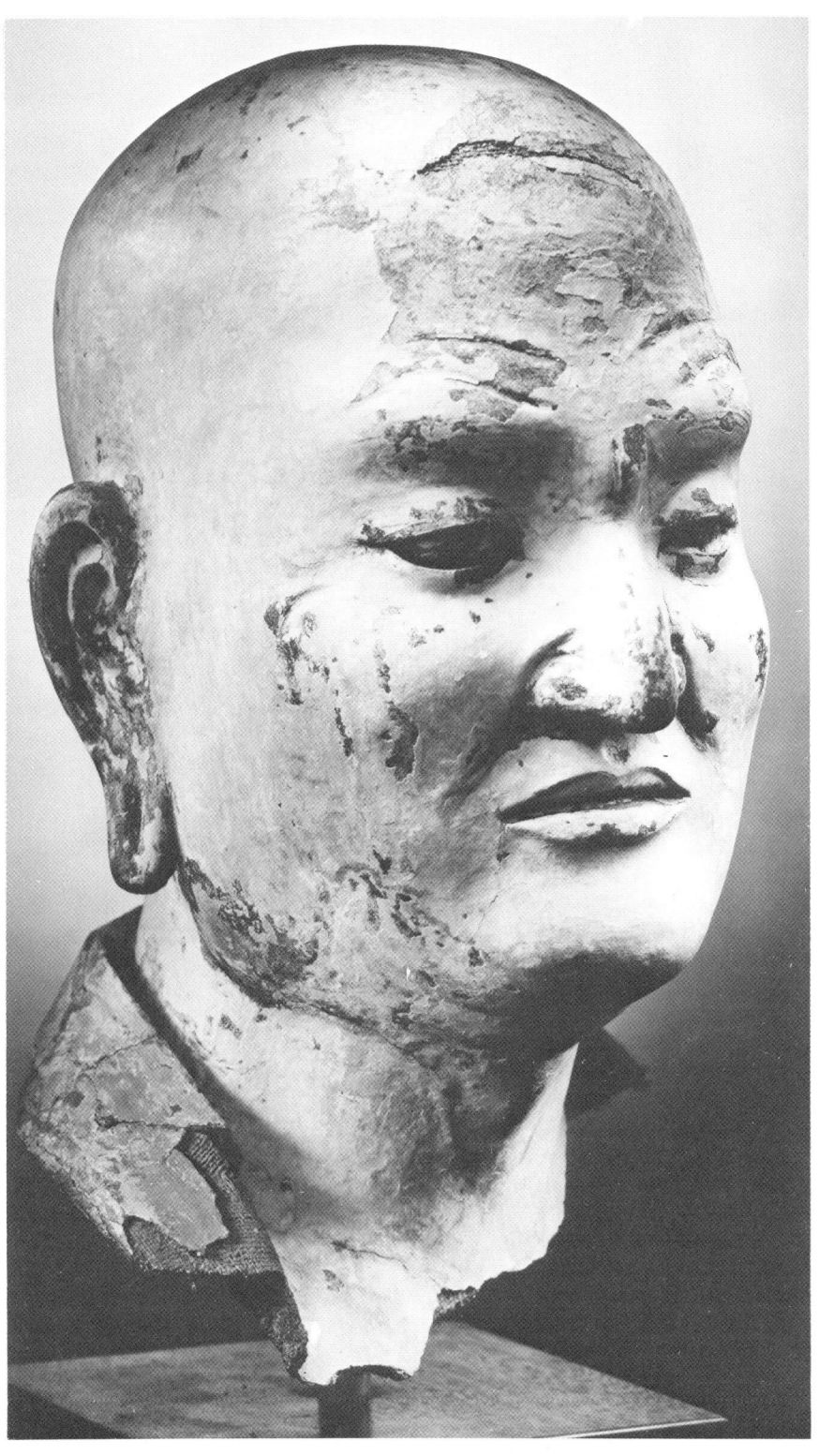

Chin Buddhist art. Head of a lohan, dry lacquer
(*Nelson Gallery--Atkins Museum, Kansas City, Missouri. Nelson Fund*)

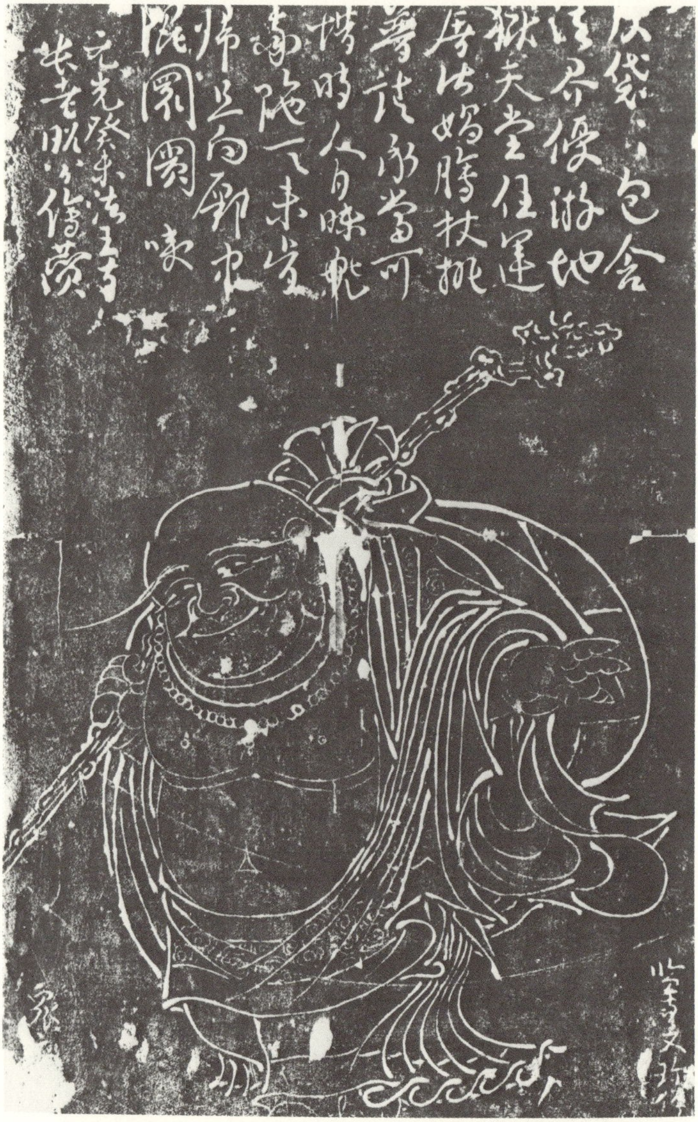

Chin Buddhist art. Lohan with sack (*Courtesy of the Institute of History and Philology, Academia Sinica, Taipei*)

Coins of the Chin (*From the author's collection*)

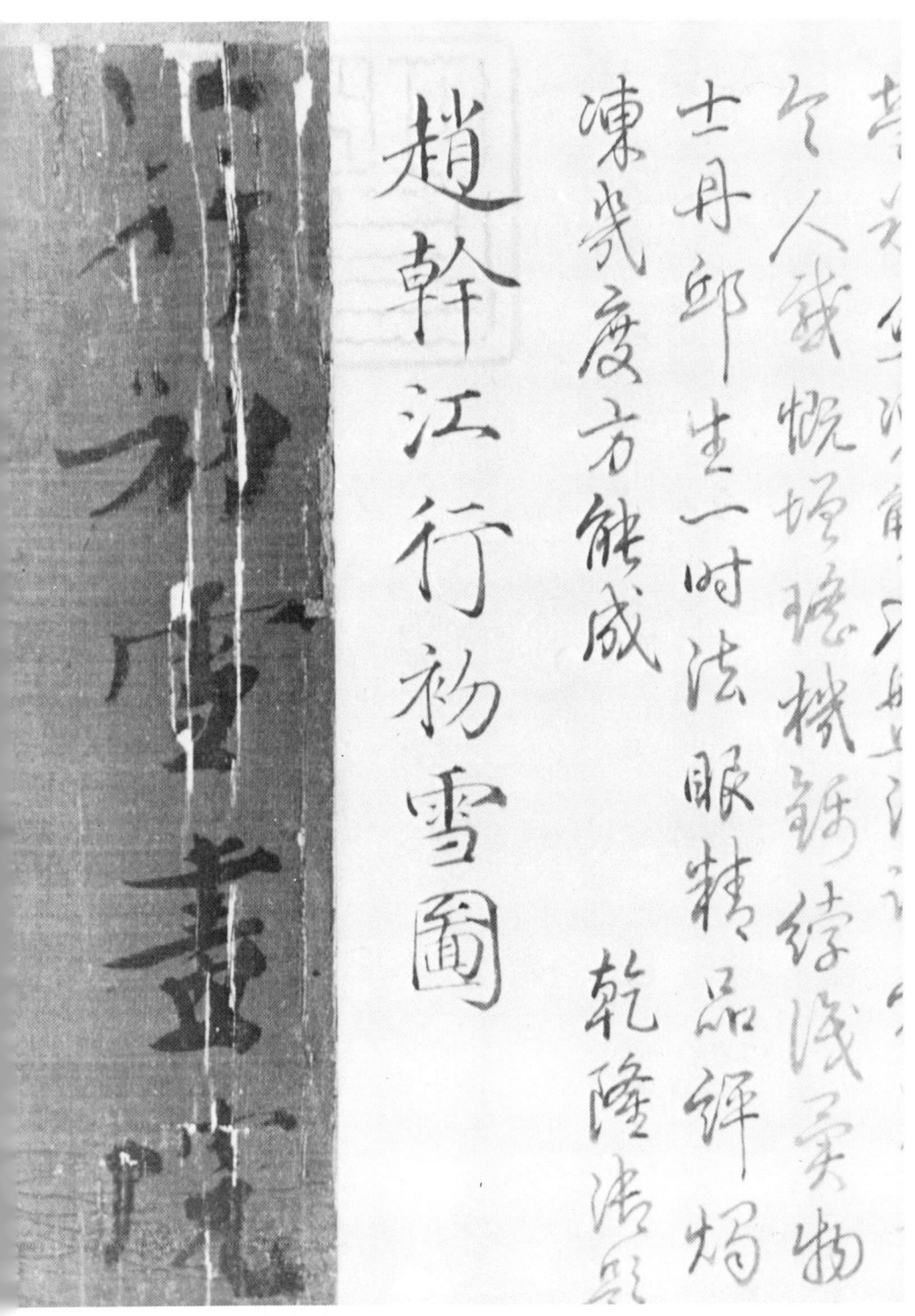

Calligraphy of Emperor Chang-tsung (*Courtesy of the National Palace Museum, Taipei*)

Scroll of the Tripitaka in the Kuang-sheng-ssu, Chao-ch'eng, Shansi (*Courtesy of the Institute of History and Philology, Academia Sinica, Taipei*)

8

Several Aspects of Sinicization in the Early Thirteenth Century

Intermarriage and Change of Surnames

When the Jurchen conquerors banned intermarriage between their people and the Chinese in North China is not clear, but the ban was lifted in 1191 by Emperor Chang-tsung.[1] However, the two peoples had already practiced intermarriage much earlier. In fact it was a royal custom to take Chinese girls into the palace of the Jurchen rulers,[2] and some of them became imperial consorts. Shih-tsung had a favorite with the maiden name of Li, who bore Yün-chi, later Prince Wei and ruler of Chin from 1209-13. Shih-tsung's eldest son and father of Emperor Chang-tsung, Yün-kung, also had a Chinese consort, née Li, who was the mother of Wan-yen Hsün. Hsün was later Emperor Hsüan-tsung (r. 1213-23), who also took Chinese concubines. One of these, née Wang, was the mother of the last Chin emperor (r. 1224-34).[3] Clearly all the emperors of the late Chin dynasty had some Chinese blood running in their veins.

It was not solely a royal prerogative to violate the marriage law; Jurchen officials also practiced intermarriage very early. Wan-yen Hsi-yin, the chief shaman of the Jurchen state before its conquest of the Northern Sung and one of the most important officials in the early Chin period, arranged his son's marriage to a Chinese girl whose surname was Li.[4] Wan-yen Hsi-nei, an obscure official, took a Chinese wife in 1161, thirty years before the lifting of the ban on intermarriage.[5] Another example is Yen Ting-chi (1126-93), whose daughter married a Jurchen, T'u-tan Ch'üan.[6]

It seems that after a long period of Sino-Jurchen cooperation and the sinicization of the Jurchen, the ban on intermarriage was no longer in effect at the time of Chang-tsung. Furthermore, Chinese influence became more and more important in the ruling circles, compelling Chang-tsung to take action to abolish the obsolete law. Chang-tsung had received a good Chinese education, and perhaps because of this he upset the Jurchen practice of always having Jurchen women as empresses by taking a Chinese slave girl as an imperial favorite in 1194, intending to make her empress. Although Chang-tsung did not succeed in doing so, he nevertheless compromised with his stubborn subordinates and made the girl his first imperial consort, whose status was just beneath that of the empress.[7]

In the late Chin dynasty intermarriage between the Jurchen and Chinese became even more common than during the reign of Chang-tsung. I have found thirteen cases of Jurchen men having Chinese wives and eighteen cases of Chinese taking Jurchen wives.[8] By far the most important and interesting case of Sino-Jurchen intermarriage is that of the Shih family in Yung-ch'ing, Hopei.[9] Due to the local power and wealth enjoyed by the Shih family, it played a significant role in Hopei in the last years of the Chin dynasty. After the evacuation of the Jurchen from the area north of the Yellow River, local thugs and strong men had to organize self-defense units to protect their families and properties against bandits and undisciplined soldiers. It was natural that the weak would seek protection under the strong. Under these circumstances a rich and generous man by the name of Shih Lun protected scholars and set up food storages to feed the poor. Shih Lun was also the founder of a self-defense society called the Purity and Happiness Society (*Ch'ing-lo she*) in North China, which had forty branches. All 1,000 members of the society worshipped Lun's portrait after he died. When the Mongols invaded North China, one of their tactics of pacification was to recruit local self-defense units to form a native army. In 1213 Muqali, Činggis Qan's able general responsible for the conquest of North China, enlisted Lun's great grandson T'ien-ni, who reorganized the best members of the Purity and Happiness

Aspects of Sinicization

Army.[10] The chaotic situation in North China after the Jurchen retreat led many remnant Jurchen families to establish relationships with the powerful native families in order to survive. One of the most effective means to establish such an alliance with the Chinese naturally was intermarriage. The marital genealogy of the Shih family therefore reveals interesting facts in this respect.

This most prominent member of the Shih family was Shih T'ien-tse (1201-74), who attained the post of prime minister during the early Yüan, and was one of only two Chinese who ever held this post. Extant epitaphs disclose that this man had four wives, including two Jurchen, who gave him eight sons and seven daughters. He also had sixteen grandsons and thirteen granddaughters.[11] An examination of the epitaphs of members of the Shih family and a genealogy yields enough sources to reestablish the structure of the family, as well as its marital relations to the Jurchen and Mongols. Table 7 is an illustration of these details.

TABLE 7
The Shih Family[12]

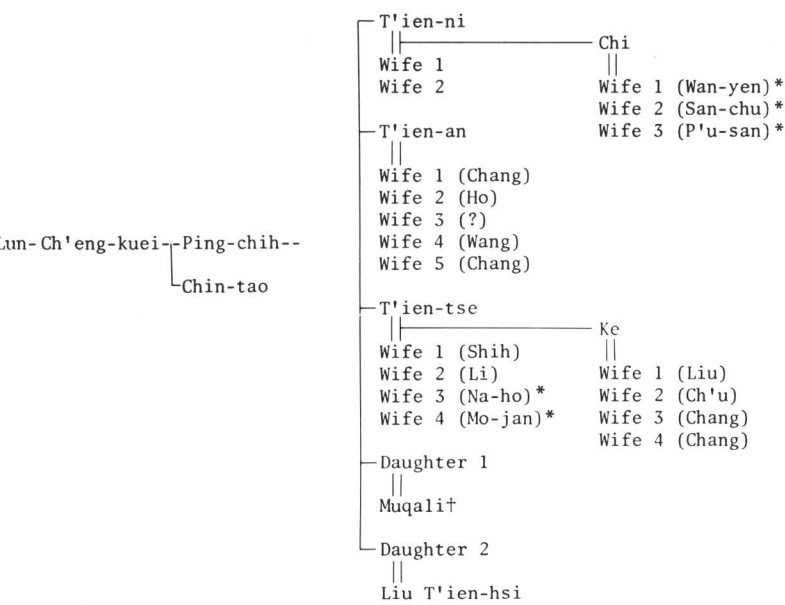

*Jurchen
†Mongol

From the reconstruction above, one may reach the following conclusion. First, the equality of the Jurchen and Chinese in North China by the end of the Chin dynasty is revealed by the Chinese practice of taking Jurchen women as concubines. Second, the case of the Shih family shows the extent to which the peoples in North China were mingled, and the degree of the assimilation of the Jurchen by the Chinese.

Another aspect of sinicization was adoption of Chinese surnames by the Jurchen. At the end of the Chin dynasty, T'ao Tsung-i noted, every Jurchen surname had its Chinese counterpart.[13] In fact during the Liao period a few Jurchen already had Chinese surnames, and one account traced the practice back to the T'ang period.[14] The ancestors of an eminent Jurchen, Ch'ih-chan Hui, who became a subject of the Ch'i-tan during the Liao, once adopted Chang as their last name, and at the end of the Chin period, Ch'ih-chan Hui's descendants again used Chang as their surname. Sung accounts referred to pre-Chin Wan-yen men as having the Chinese name Wang.[15] In the early Chin some Jurchen adopted Kao as their last name.[16] During the reigns of Shih-tsung and Chang-tsung, edicts forbade the Jurchen to change their surnames into Chinese, indicating the popularity of such practice.[17]

To secure help from non-Jurchen peoples, the Chin rulers often gave Jurchen surnames, Wan-yen and some others, to them. This had been an old Chinese practice, and the Jurchen were not slow to follow it. When the Jurchen were prosperous and had control of their subjects, they once ordered these non-Jurchen on whom Jurchen names had been conferred to resume their original names, but in the last years of the dynasty the Jurchen frequently had to grant their surnames to the non-Jurchen to secure their loyalty or enlist allies.[18]

Literature and Art

The Jurchen achievement in Chinese literature and art is another indicator of sinicization. During the trying period of Jurchen cultural restoration, although Shih-tsung promoted Jurchen learning, many Jurchen still took keen interest in Chinese classics and literature. They did not endeavor to create their own literature and style of painting. In the *Dynastic History of the Chin* there is a Jurchen song composed by Shih-tsung, but from the lyric in classical Chinese one could find no trace of the original Jurchen style.[19]

Among the emperors, Hsi-tsung (Tan) was the first to take an interest in Chinese learning, whereas Hailing (Liang) was good at poetry and painting.[20] Shih-tsung was interested in Chinese music, and his grandson Chang-tsung was the best among Jurchen rulers at Chinese literature, painting, and calligraphy.[21] In the imperial household, Shih-tsung's eldest son Yün-kung had a good Chinese education and liked to discuss Chinese classics with literary figures of the time.[22] As a painter he specialized in ink bamboos and horses.[23] Among Shih-tsung's other sons, Yün-kung 允功 also received an excellent Chinese education, and Yün-ch'eng, a poet, loved Chinese literature. Yün-ch'eng never treated literary men arrogantly, and adopted the Chinese style *Lo-shan chü-shih* or "scholar fond of good deeds." His collected works, like those of other Jurchen scholars, unfortunately no longer exist.[24]

After Wan-yen Chin became emperor (Chang-tsung), the atmosphere was more favorable to Chinese literature and art. A poet, painter, and calligrapher, Chin contributed greatly to book collecting,[25] and his personal library of first-rate calligraphy and painting exceeded 550 pieces.[26] His calligraphy was an imitation of the style of Sung Hui-tsung.[27]

Another grandson of Shih-tsung and a son of Yün-kung, Shou, was by far the most famous Jurchen literary figure. He befriended eminent contemporary Chinese scholars such as Chao Ping-wen, Yang Yün-i, Lei Yüan, and above all, Yüan Hao-wen, the most celebrated writer of the time. Shou was a gifted poet, and produced a poetry collection, most of which has disappeared.[28] He possessed a huge library, and was a talented painter, following the tradition of Su Shih and Huang T'ing-chien.[29] His ink bamboo painting was not as good as that of Wang T'ing-yün, but it had its own style.[30] It should be noted that many Jurchen scholar-painters liked ink bamboo painting, a predilection markedly different from the Ch'i-tan preference for deer and battle scenes.[31] Wan-yen Shou enjoyed reading and studying Ssu-ma Kuang's *Tzu-chih t'ung-chien* (Comprehensive Mirror for Aid in Government) and in his old age he liked Ch'an Buddhism.[32]

Wan-yen Shou was not the only Jurchen scholar who patronized Chinese writers and artists. Another example is Po-chu-lu Hsiao-chung, who owned an estate in the country of Yeh (掖), and frequently entertained guests. Taoist priests, Buddhist monks, scholars, and poets enjoyed wine and tea, wrote poems, and played *wei-ch'i* (*go* in Japanese), and music at his parties.[33]

In the last thirty years of the Chin dynasty, there were a number of noted Jurchen scholars, such as Wan-yen Pi, Wan-yen Shou-chen, Chu-hu Yün-shou, and Wan-yen Ch'eng-hui. Wan-yen Ch'eng-hui reportedly hung pictures of great Northern Sung scholars Ssu-ma Kuang and Su Shih in his room, saying, "I am a student of Ssu-ma and a friend of Su." A certain Mu-jan of Ta-ming was especially good at the *Book of Changes*. A few scholars were *meng-an* and *mou-k'e*, such as Chu-hu Chü, Wu-lin-ta Shuang, Wan-yen Hsieh-lieh, Chia-ku Te-ku, and Wu-lin-ta Su.[34]

T'u-tan I, a well-known Jurchen statesman in the *Ta-ting* period (1161-89), acquired his Jurchen *chin-shih* degree in 1169, and appointed many men of letters to government service, some of whom later became high officials. He believed the learning of the literati should be founded on benevolence and righteousness, among other virtues. His essays on learning and the *tao* or the way were inscribed on stone tablets in the National University (t'ai-hsüeh).[35] Local officials such as Wu-yen Kung-jui, who loved to study, passed the *chin-shih* examination, and as a prefect Wu-yen "persuaded the people to cultivate their crops, build schools, esteem filial piety, and distinguish between the young and the old; within a year the customs were changed."[36] Another prefect, whose last name was Wan-yen, appointed two Jurchen and a Chinese to build the prefectural school, and hired a Jurchen and a Chinese as teachers.[37]

It has been noted that men like Wan-yen Shou and Po-chu-lu Hsiao-chung made friends with the Chinese literati. This development in social integration continued in the early Yüan. Among the friends of Wang Yün, the famous Yüan writer, there were Wan-yen Meng-yang and Wu-ku-lun Chen; the former had a collection of more than one thousand volumes of ancient Chinese books. Hsü An-shang, another Yüan writer, had Ho-shih-lieh Chao-hsing as his best friend and they were like brothers.[38]

There were also Ch'i-tan scholars. Yeh-lü Lü, father of the great Yüan statesman Ch'u-ts'ai, wrote fifteen *chüan* of collected works.³⁹ Shih-mo Shih-chi was an outstanding poet, and other noted scholars included I-la Mai-nu and I-la Nien-ho. Yeh-lü Hao-jan was a famous painter.⁴⁰

The most important contributions to Chin literature, historiography, and philosophy were made by Chinese scholars. To go into the details of their literary achievements is beyond the scope of this study. Suffice it here to say that during the Chin most writers followed the traditions of Su Shih and Huang T'ing-chien of the Northern Sung.⁴¹ It was only after the Southern Crossing (*nan-tu*) that there appeared a literary renaissance. It involved a return to ancient prose styles, archaic (*ku*) and unusual (*ch'i*), which were represented by Chao Ping-wen and Li Ch'un-fu, respectively.⁴²

Chin writers, including a few Jurchen, paid more attention than did the Ch'i-tan to the writing of history. Although Chin official historians did not complete the writing of the dynastic history of the Liao, they compiled ten sets of the "veritable records" of Chin emperors.⁴³ Other historical works include: Wan-yen Po-ti, *Chung-hsing shih-chi* (History of the restoration); Yang Yün-i and others, *Hsü tzu-chih t'ung-chien* (A continuation of the *Tzu-chih t'ung-chien*); and A-li-ho-man, *Pen-ch'ao p'u-tieh* (Imperial genealogy of the Chin).⁴⁴ In addition to the translation of Chinese historical works, the Jurchen also translated other books into Jurchen.⁴⁵

The Chin published more books than previous alien dynasties. The Imperial Academy (kuo-tzu chien) and the Academy of Letters (hung-wen yüan) with the duties of collating and translating the classics and histories, together published over thirty works in Chinese and fifteen in Jurchen.⁴⁶ In P'ing-shui (in Shansi), Sung-chou, and Chieh-shih, publishing flourished.⁴⁷ Of the 7,000 volumes of the Tripitaka published in Hsieh-chou (in Shansi), 4,957 are still kept in the Kuang-shen Buddhist temple in Chao-ch'eng. Some publications are comparable to the best of the Sung in workmanship.⁴⁸ Chin publications are mostly in classics and history, in addition to collected works, poems, encyclopedias, and dictionaries written by Chin scholars.⁴⁹

The most important development in literature was the rise of vernacular literature in late Chin. The

Yüan drama, with its origins in both Northern and Southern Sung, was acquiring its characteristic form during the last years of the Chin and the early years of the Yüan. The Chin rulers showed much interest in music, dance, and variety shows, and there were performances of drama in the imperial palace. It is said that Chang Hsing-chien, a censor of the court of Chang-tsung, wrote thirty-five pieces of *chiao-fang ch'iang-tzu*.[50] Tung Chieh-yüan, another Chin scholar and a contemporary of Chang-tsung, wrote the famous *Hsi-hsiang* or "The West Chamber," a *chu-kung-tiao*. *Hsi-hsiang* was unquestionably the greatest vernacular work produced in the Chin period, and it has been acclaimed as the single most important contribution of Chin literature. The Liu Chih-yüan *chu-kung-tiao* perhaps could be dated even earlier than the Tung *Hsi-hsiang*. T'ao Tsung-i recorded 690 titles of Chin *yüan-pen* (variety shows).[51] Although the *yüan-pen* did not have value for posterity, it nevertheless paved the way for the development of Yüan drama.[52] In fact, all eminent Yüan dramatists came from Hopei and Shantung, the central area of the Chin kingdom, and grew up in the combined Sung-Chin tradition.[53]

Why did drama flourish in the Yüan dynasty? An explanation traditionally given is that under the Mongol rule for several decades the civil service examinations were suspended, and Chinese scholars had little access to high official positions. They sought escape from reality in a world of literary entertainment enjoyed even by the Mongol ruling class. Such a trend was already discernible in the late Chin, when, as mentioned, individuals having higher degrees could not always find government positions owing to corrupt examinations and other channels to the officialdom.[54] According to this view, dramatists such as Kuan Han-ch'ing, Tu shan-fu, and Pai P'u were all minor bureaucrats whose main interest was writing popular poetry and drama.[55] After the Jurchen and the Chinese had mingled, the people could not understand the classical literature produced by the scholars, and preferred vernacular works based on their everyday experience.[56]

A more recent work based on research into the social background and families of a few important dramatists, however, reveals that while it is true that the Yüan conquest diminished the literati's opportunity in the civil service, it was mainly the change in ethics and the shift in taste of both the literati and the common people that brought about the creation of the Yüan drama.[57] Moreover, Kuan Han-ch'ing and Pai P'u were not bureaucrats in the Chin. Most of the important writers were not commoners but were from literati or government official families.[58] This is one aspect of the intellectual ferment in which scholars and writers chose to express a variety of new ideas through different literary forms.

Before analyzing this intellectual ferment in the late Chin, I shall comment briefly on the sculpture and architecture of the period.[59] In sculpture, the Chin and the Yüan followed the tradition of the Liao and the Sung. The Buddhist sculpture in the Yüan is lively and narrative, a style corresponding to the development in drama in the Chin-Yüan periods.[60] Similarly, in the production of china, there were also some innovations brought about by alien rule.[61] More important is the contribution in architecture. The palaces and buildings in the Chin capital laid the foundation for the Yüan construction of the great Ta-tu (Peking). A few architectural ideas were followed in Yüan and Ming times;[62] these, however, await further research.

Intellectual Ferment and Religion

With the stress on substance in literature, a few Chin writers began to offer new explanations of classics and history after the Southern Crossing. Two points merit discussion, for they are related to the Jurchen rule.

First, although the Chin scholars inherited Northern Sung literary and philosophical tradition, they were by no means completely confined to that tradition. After the Southern Crossing, the Chin government was considerably weakened and could no longer exercise effective control over the people. Nor could they rally the support of the literati, who began to explore the meaning of classics, history, and philosophy, without concentrating on the study of limited materials in order to pass the civil service examinations.

Wang Jo-hsü wrote provocative essays on the classics and history. He criticized the Ch'eng brothers and Wang An-shih of the Northern Sung, and Chang Chiu-ch'eng, Chang Shih, Lin Chih-ch'i, and above all, Chu Hsi of the Southern Sung. He was, for example, disappointed in Chu Hsi's commentaries on the Four Books, pointing out that Chu did not even know the meaning of *hsin* (信). He severely attacked Ssu-ma Ch'ien in his *Shih-chi pien-huo* (Clarification of doubts in the *Historical Records*), accusing the ancient historian of committing such grave mistakes and misjudgments in the work that he should have been sentenced to death. He also condemned Ssu-ma Kuang for his attempt to cover up Ts'ao Ts'ao's crimes in usurping the Han throne.[63] Neither did Wang Jo-hsü agree with the policy of the founder of the Sung dynasty to reunify China. He wrote:

> The universe does not belong to any single individual. The occupation of various areas and the demarcation of state lines should be tolerated. The small serves the big; the big protects the small. Every country does its best. Since the Three Dynasties the guilty have been punished and the innocent pardoned. There is no reason why every country should be destroyed and unification achieved.[64]

This argument is very important for it is the reverse of the opinion of Northern Sung Confucianists, including Su Shih, that the universe should always be unified. Evidently the Chin scholars were free to express their ideas opposing the Sung tradition. Wang Jo-hsü's argument also reflects the political situation of the time, the coexistence of the Southern Sung and the Chin.

Chao Ping-wen, another influential scholar in the late Chin, interpreted history with benevolence and righteousness as its foundation. There were cases of rulers who did not possess the virtue of benevolence yet were able to obtain control of the world, but, he asserted, these rulers were never able to maintain the ruling positions for generations. He praised the rulers who were broad-minded enough to share the world with others, and censured those who waged wars against others. He was against the Han scholar-official Chia I, who attempted to "change the institutions, to eliminate the dukes, and attack the barbarians outside." He even suggested that the name Shu Han be rectified as Han, for Liu Pei and Chu-ku Liang were willing to share the world with others, but other rulers of the time did not think that way. Although Shu Han only occupied a

Aspects of Sinicization

corner of the universe, Chao argued, it was still China, for according to the *Book of History*, "when the dukes adopt barbarian institutions, they are barbarians; when the barbarians enter into China, they are sinicized." It is interesting that Chao justified the rule of sinicized barbarians, obviously no longer considering the Jurchen as barbarians. He not only recognized the Jurchen as Chinese, but also went so far as to compare the Southern Sung Chinese with the "barbarians of the Huai" (*Huai-i*) and the "barbarians of the island" (*tao-i*). He described the political fiasco of King Wei-shao (r. 1209-13), which brought about the Mongol invasions and the decline of Chinese customs (*Hua-feng pu-ching*). In Chao's view the Chinese and the Jurchen undoubtedly shared the same civilized customs.[65]

Second, in the late Chin there emerged a theory that combined the doctrines of Confucianism, Buddhism, and Taoism, a theory propounded by the philosopher Li Ch'un-fu (Li P'ing-shan).[66] Li's thinking underwent three stages: before thirty he was a Confucianist, but after thirty he turned from Confucianism to Taoism, and from Taoism to Buddhism. He stated that after he studied Buddhism, there was nothing else to be learned. He realized that "the Buddha is sage, but the sage is not Buddha; there is Chinese knowledge in the West, but there is no Western knowledge in China."[67] Liu Ch'i noted that Li Ch'un-fu argued that the Neo-Confucianists in the Northern Sung stole principles from Buddhism, so that he was severely attacked by the Confucianists of his time. But Li remained unconvinced.[68] Li wrote 217 pieces of commentaries of Neo-Confucian statements on Buddhism in which he criticized Sung scholars such as Chou Tun-i, Ssu-ma Kuang, Chang Tsai, the Ch'eng brothers, Hsieh Liang-tso, Liu An-shih, Chiang Min-piao, Yang Shih, Chang Shih, Lü Tsu-ch'ien, and Chu Hsi, and eloquently defended Buddhism, identifying Buddhist and Taoist principles with those of Confucianism. It was the first systematic attempt in Chinese history to combine and promote the "*tao* of the three sages."[69] Li Ch'un-fu was not alone, however, in being enthusiastic about Buddhism. According to Liu Ch'i, Chao Ping-wen also indulged in Buddhism, but he was afraid of incurring attacks from the Confucianists, such as those on Li Ch'un-fu, and tried to earn the reputation of upholding Confucian teachings. Therefore when he revised his collected works in his old age, he deleted all the essays relating to Buddhism and Taoism. When Liu Ch'i discussed Chao's inconsistent behavior with Wang Jo-hsü, Wang said, "this old man is doing what we call 'to secrete the head and leave the tail showing.'"[70]

In short, Li Ch'un-fu's efforts to combine Confucian, Buddhist, and Taoist teachings in philosophical thinking demonstrate the extent to which the literati departed from the Confucian way of Sung thinkers. Li Ch'un-fu's *hsin-hsüeh* or idealistic thinking exerted influence on the *tao-hsüeh* in later times and he probably was the most important thinker of the Chin.[71] A parallel development could be found in the eclecticism of Ch'üan-chen Taoism.

The people in the late Chin inclined to simple and popular religious sects. The most important was the polytheistic and ascetic Ch'üan-chen sect of Taoism. In the early Chin many Jurchen turned from shamanism to Buddhism, but Buddhism never had been as popular among the Jurchen as among the Ch'i-tan during the Liao dynasty. The Chin government at first relieved the Buddhist monasteries of control over the *erh-shui* (double-taxed) households, so that the monasteries could no longer collect taxes from these households, thereby increasing the government's income. The turmoil in the early 1160s gave rise to financial problems, and the government encouraged the sale of licenses to people who desired to become monks and nuns and planned to build temples. In this way the government did raise money, but in the long run the increase in the number of tax-exempt monks, nuns, and Taoist priests was detrimental to finance.[72]

The rise of the Ch'üan-chen sect initiated a reform movement in Taoism, when the existing Buddhist and Taoist sects were degenerating.[73] There were elements of enthusiasm on the part of many Chinese who had grievances against the Jurchen rule and tried to find relief in religion.[74] The founder of the Ch'üan-chen sect, Wang Che, perhaps at first intended to rebel against the Jurchen,[75] but after a long period of meditation in what he called the "tomb of the living dead," he initiated the Taoist reform in the 1160s, a reform that combined Buddhist, Confucian, and Taoist elements and emphasized asceticism and simple faith.[76] There were two other new Taoist sects in North China during the Chin: the Ta-tao and the T'ai-i.[77] Similar reforms were also launched by some Buddhists, led by Hsing-hsiu or *Wan-sung lao-jen* (The old man of ten thousand pine trees), whose followers included the famous Buddhist-scholar Li Ch'un-fu, and the great scholar-administrator of the early Yüan, Yeh-lü Ch'u-ts'ai. Shih-tsung, Chang-tsung, and many royal family members also believed in Buddhism and Taoism.[78] Wang Ch'u-i and Ch'iu Ch'u-chi, Wang Che's disciples, were summoned by Shih-tsung to his inner palace to preach. Later Shih-tsung requested Wang's presence on his deathbed.[79] Although Chang-tsung once forbade the preaching of the Ch'üan-chen and a few other religious orders because they deluded and caused disorder among the people, he was converted by the Ch'üan-chen later, and made Wang Ch'u-i live in Yen-ching for a year.[80] The Taoist priests associated themselves with Chinese and Jurchen scholars and officials. Ch'iu Ch'u-chi wrote poems and *tz'u* for such Jurchen dignitaries as Shih-tsung, the wife of a prince, the prefect of the Western Capital, the sister of a prime minister, a general, a *meng-an*, a defense prefect, and a commoner who was to take his civil service examination.[81] Wan-yen Shou was a friend of Wang Ch'u-i, and wrote a biography of Wang Che.[82] It is unnecessary to relate here the details of the famous meeting between Činggis Qan and Ch'iu Ch'u-chi and its importance to the maintenance of law and order in early Yüan China.[83]

Many Jurchen believed in various sects of Taoism. There was a Jurchen master who was in charge of the Ch'üan-chen church at Ch'ien-yang in the prefecture of Lung.[84] Chang-tsung highly respected the T'ai-i sect, founded in the late 1140s. Qubilai Qan once summoned a T'ai-i high priest to preach in Qarakulem. The Tai-i Taoism may have been very popular among the Jurchen, for a Jurchen priest named Wan-yen Chih-ning was almost selected as the third high priest of the sect. It is interesting to note here that a Jurchen, Wan-yen Te-ming, did become the Ch'üan-chen high priest in the Yüan.[85]

Relations with the Southern Sung

An important channel of cultural diffusion between

the Sung and Chin was the exchange of diplomatic missions. Some of the Sung envoys sent to the Chin were detained and made teachers or political advisers. One of them, Hung Hao, wrote about the political and military situation in the Chin, in addition to describing Jurchen customs. After the peace of 1141, there was the regular exchange of envoys for celebrating the new year and the birthday of emperors. These envoys were required to report on the details of their mission, and sometimes they did intelligence work. Thus on the eve of the war of 1161, a few Southern Sung diplomats reported on the activities of Chin mobilization. Shih I-sheng, a Chin envoy, brought with him a painter who drew a map of Hangchow. The diplomats were permitted to talk to local officials, to visit religious temples, and to watch the famous tides at the Hangchow Bay.[86] There were banquets and various recreational activities to entertain these guests.

The envoys presented gifts from their governments and smuggled goods. Smuggling was very prevalent, so much so that the minor missions in the diplomatic service often took place under false pretenses by merchants. Sung envoys usually had connections with Chin officials that facilitated trade. The Sung government repeatedly issued orders forbidding smuggling by diplomats.[87]

This trade, however, was only a small part of the large-scale smuggling between the two states. The two governments monopolized their trade, carried out at specific posts. Imports from the south were tea, spices, drugs, silk, cotton, coins, cattle, and rice. The last three items were forbidden to be exported by the Sung government, but large amounts of these commodities were smuggled out. Exports from the Chin to the Sung included hides, pearls, ginseng, silk, and horses. Although the Chin government banned the export of horses, smuggling went on. In international trade the Sung government enjoyed an export surplus and consequently an influx of much silver. Besides the merchants, many personnel in the diplomatic missions, officials in the border areas, and military officers engaged in smuggling.[88] A few officials in Hangchow were also involved.[89]

The contraband trade in horses from the north improved the strength of the Southern Sung army, and

Aspects of Sinicization

in turn the Chin learned navigation skills from the southerners. Some Southern Sung generals and officers defected to the Chin, providing valuable military information and shipbuilding techniques.[90] With the assistance of these experts King Hai-ling (Liang) was able to build a huge fleet to invade the south in 1161. There were also a few Jurchen military men, mostly Ch'i-tan, who went to the Sung.[91] During the last few decades of the Chin, a great number of rebels in the north cooperated with the Southern Sung until the end of the Chin.

Not only soldiers but scholars changed sides. The most famous instance occurred during the war of 1161, when many Chinese rose against the Jurchen in North China and a few of them established contacts with the southerners. One of the rebellious groups in Hopei sent a representative, Hsin Ch'i-chi, to the Southern Sung, requesting military and financial assistance.[92] Revolts in the north were unsuccessful, and Hsin settled down in South China, becoming one of the celebrated poets of the Sung period.

One of the effects of the Mongol invasions in the late Chin was the lack of books and teachers in North China. It was said that to the north of the Huai River there was no full set of books.[93] To facilitate Chinese learning Southern Sung scholars were brought to the north to serve as teachers.[94] It is assumed that after the fall of both the Chin and the Sung scholars and works in the south were brought to the north to revitalize scholarship there.[95] Before the Mongol invasions, however, the situation was different. The philosophy of Chu Hsi, among others, was not unknown in the north. Wang Jo-hsü and Li Ch'un-fu, as mentioned, read all the philosophical works of the south. The teachings of the school of the Cheng brothers, Ch'eng I and Ch'eng Hao, were also carried on in North China.[96] Books were exchanged between the Sung and the Chin, despite government orders to ban the sale of certain books in the border markets.[97] The memorials of Sung Hui-tsung submitted to Chin emperors were published and sold in these markets, together with such other books as Ssu-ma Kuang's commentaries on the *Book of Changes*.[98] Books were also sent to the Chin by the Sung government as gifts.[99] It is, then, not surprising that Wang Jo-hsü (1174-1243) read Hung Mai's

(1123-1202) *Jung-chai sui-pi*, for Wang was born much later than Hung. But Hung Mai also read Wang's criticisms of classics and histories. Hung's *I-chien chih* was available in the north, and Yüan Hao-wen wrote a supplement to it. The supplement was then brought to the south.[100]

It seems that Southern Sung culture exerted more influence on the Chin than the other way around. King Hai-ling admired the dress, etiquette, and culture of the Southern Sung. Some of his courtiers persuaded him to invade the southern state to obtain its wealth and share in its advanced culture. Hai-ling adopted some southern etiquette, and, as mentioned, tried to become a Chinese emperor and rule the whole Middle Kingdom. After he lifted the ban on wearing Chinese dress, many Jurchen took an interest in the fashions of the Southern Sung. Shih-tsung forbade his people to wear Chinese clothes, and Chang-tsung twice reiterated this ban.[101]

The diffusion of culture, however, was by no means one way. There was considerable mutual influence between the Chin and the Sung in drama.[102] The southerners also appreciated Jurchen fashions, music, and certain customs. They imitated the purple dress, called "barbarian purple," of Jurchen diplomats.[103] Jurchen fashions and music were so popular in the south that in the memorials of a few officials the threat of "barbarization" of China was repeatedly pointed out.[104] The Sung government banned the wearing of Jurchen clothes in 1163,[105] and all the barbarian clothes were banned later. "Barbarian" (*hu*) music and dance were also banned in 1161 and 1163. Jurchen musical instruments and other products such as "Nien-han"s pigtail" (*Nien-han fa-so*), perhaps a Jurchen wig, were for sale in Hangchow.[106]

9

Conclusion

Barbarian invasions, and the dynasties set up by them in China, formed a constant factor in premodern Chinese history. In the long centuries of barbarian invasions and conquests the Chinese people have been able to resist their inroads quite successfully, if one considers that the defenders' military power often could not match that of the mobile nomads and seminomads. In this respect only the lengthy history of the Byzantine Empire parallels the Chinese achievement. However, since 1453 the Byzantines have ceased to exist, while in East Asia the Chinese have sustained continuous barbarian attacks and rule. Until the modern period it was the aliens rather than the Chinese who could not preserve their cultural and ethnic identity.

Only twice did aliens conquer the whole of China. In the first instance, the Mongols refused to accept the Chinese way of life, and this is probably one of the reasons they did not maintain their power in China very long. In the second case the Manchus ruled the Chinese much longer, but only after they adopted the Chinese culture and achieved a Sino-Manchu synthesis.[1] In the days when there were no national feelings in the modern sense, and when the Chinese believed in their ability to assimilate barbarian elements, they accepted alien rule time and again. The Jurchen and Manchus eventually did transform themselves into Chinese, and after their dynasties vanished they ceased to be a distinguishable ethnic and cultural group in China.[2]

They serve as the best examples of China's conditional acceptance of alien rulers and her assimilation of them.

A few observations on the sociocultural change of the Jurchen in the twelfth century are in order. Natural environment and human ecology in the Jurchen homeland conditioned their development. Their use of the horse enabled them to become the first people from Manchuria to establish a dynasty in China. But it is my contention that originally they were not true nomads, but lived a sedentary life in the Sungari region. Their large-scale use of horses parallels the acquisition of these animals from the Spaniards by the Indians of the great plains of North America and of the pampas and Patagonia in South America.[3] The Jurchen were much more successful than the Indians, for the latter had to confront enemies who possessed firearms and were superior in military organization. The combined effect of a sedentary existence and horse breeding was an important contributory factor in the Jurchen conquest first of Manchuria and later of North China. Precisely because they were not a nomadic people, different from the nomadic Ch'i-tan and Mongols, they were mentally as well as socially inclined to become full-time farmers after they entered China.

To rule the heterogeneous population in the early period of the dynasty (1115-50), the Jurchen practiced a political dualism. It was an imitation of the Ch'i-tan example--they used Jurchen institutions to rule the Jurchen, and Chinese bureaucratic apparatus to govern the Chinese. This policy later developed along a different line from that of the Ch'i-tan and changed in nature. At first the Jurchen rulers seemingly lacked the ambition to occupy both Manchuria and North China; they set up puppet regimes in North China as buffer states. Powerful generals in North China also imposed a feudal control on the Chinese subjects, establishing their respective spheres of influence. Nevertheless a feudal system did not materialize and the dualistic rule turned out to be a transitional organization, facilitating the central authority's takeover of North China. In terms of acculturation of the Jurchen, the period of dualistic rule was also transitional, from limited to wholesale adoption of Chinese elements.

Once having passed from the primary stage of conquest and becoming settled in North China, the rulers

Conclusion

strove for stability and security. They found it convenient to retain the Chinese economic organization in order to secure manpower and material resources. The new regime created many privileges for the *meng-an* and *mou-k'e*, who garrisoned strategic posts. Politically the rulers suffered a great deal from decentralization during the period of dualistic rule. The issue of the succession to the throne and the problem of the expansion of power by the ambitious military generals forced the administrators to adopt Chinese institutions to consolidate their position. Stabilization of their rule accompanied sinicization, for they had to learn the Chinese way of governing. After a long period of political conflicts, which occurred between the central government and local regions and among contenders for the throne, the central authority was eventually established on Chinese models and the problem of succession was solved by adopting the Chinese practice of hereditary primogeniture.

The career of Wan-yen Liang (King Hai-ling) is an interesting illustration of this process. He ruthlessly curbed the growth of Jurchen aristocratic power and tightened control of the Chinese as well as Jurchen population. Although the Jurchen had already adopted the civil service examination system to draw administrative staff from the Chinese, it was Liang who effectively employed the system to secure support from the Chinese elite, to legitimize his dynasty, to diminish the power of the aristocracy, and to accomplish a transformation of the "familistic" dynasty to a patrimonial bureaucratic state.[4] He seems to have recognized that in order to perpetuate Jurchen rule the state could not base itself on the acquisition of "booty" and on the distribution of immediate gains to its founders and supporters. It was at the time of Tan and Liang, in short, that the state resulting from conquest became rationalized to form permanent structures.

The sinicization of the Jurchen by 1161 had gone so far that the revival movement in the late twelfth century was doomed. There are a few remarkable aspects of the movement. For one, Wu-lu (Shih-tsung) was able to stabilize Jurchen rule after the crisis of 1161. For another, Wu-lu tried very hard to maintain an equilibrium between different sets of forces: Chinese and Jurchen, commoners and aristocrats. One of the failures of the movement was that it could not halt the tendency toward the deterioration of Jurchen morale and the continuation of sinicization. The people gave up hunting, fishing, and fighting, lived on revenues collected from the Chinese peasants, and neither worked nor fought. Mingling with the vast sedentary Chinese populace, they suffered from the strains of social change and lost their fighting spirit. Another failure was that the preservation of the special position of the Jurchen aristocrats eventually alienated the Chinese elite from the regime. Wu-lu was caught in a basic dilemma posed by contradictory interests of Jurchen and Chinese elite, and by the need for maintaining a precarious balance between Jurchen and Chinese cultural elements. In the latter problem he tried to steer a course between the two cultures and was quite successful during his lifetime. After him, however, the equilibrium was broken. His successors resorted to more proscriptive policies to maintain the special position of the ruling stratum, thus continuously alienating the Chinese elite.

The Jurchen experienced a thorough sociocultural change near the end of the twelfth century. Their dynasty almost evolved into a traditional one, possessing Chinese characteristics. Politically the Chin state followed Chinese central and local government organizations, recruiting the scholar-gentry by the civil service examinations, and ruling their subjects with Confucian ethics and modified T'ang legal codes. Economically the Jurchen took over the agrarian, landholding bases and participated in the newly adopted agricultural society. But harvests were not the only source of wealth. Like the Chinese, these foreign rulers also maintained the Chinese monetary system with all their financing practices, such as monopolies of salt and iron and collection of the property tax.

In the processes of sociocultural change the Chinese patterns prevailed. The Jurchen spoke Chinese, adopted Chinese surnames and clothes, arranged Sino-Jurchen marriages, and raised children according to Chinese norms and educational ideas. They were converted to Buddhism and Taoism, and enjoyed the Chinese vernacular literature. The implementation of the Jurchen *chin-shih* examination gave rise to a group of Jurchen scholar-officials who were trained in Chinese

Conclusion

classics and statecraft. Together with some *meng-an* and *mou-k'e*, they took part in Chinese literary, artistic, and social activities. There was little prejudice and discrimination against the Chinese and vice versa, as indicated in the cases of Sino-Jurchen intermarriage, and in the social relations of Wan-yen Shou.[5] Militarily the *meng-an* and *mou-k'e* institution deteriorated, and soon was on the brink of a breakdown. At the turn of the century the Chin state began to rely on Chinese and other non-Jurchen for defense against Mongol and Southern Sung invasions. Surprisingly, the Jurchen suffered from the same military difficulties as did the Northern Sung Chinese a century earlier-- lack of martial spirit, shortage of regular troops, a desperate need for horses. In short, it need not surprise us that when the Mongols conquered North China, they treated the Ch'i-tan, the Jurchen, and the Chinese as one people--the people of the Han (*Han-jen*).[6]

How many and what customs and practices did the Jurchen retain at the end of their dynasty? The answer is difficult, for lack of data. Perhaps the paucity of sources is because not much of the Jurchen way of life remained. The Jurchen rulers kept alive a few rituals such as *shao-fan* for mourning the dead until the end of the dynasty, but it was only a royal practice.[7] Remnants of the *meng-an* and *mou-k'e* in the form of *ch'ien-hu* and *pai-hu* existed in Yüan times, but the system was intentionally retained by the Mongols. A few Jurchen tribes in Manchuria still used the language down to the Ming dynasty, as evidenced in Jurchen letters accompanying tributes to China.[8]

All this does not mean that the Jurchen did not leave any sociocultural imprint on Chinese civilization, for indeed they did. There were many ways in which cultural borrowings and syntheses between the Chinese and the Jurchen enriched and modified the Chinese civilization. In literature, drama flourished in the Chin and Yüan, both dynasties of conquest, and exerted a large influence on the vernacular literature. The literary and intellectual achievements in the Chin, though generally following the traditions of the Northern Sung, did have their own characteristics such as a critical spirit and an attempt to synthesize Confucian, Taoist, and Buddhist elements. In government, the three "barbarian" dynasties--the Ch'i-tan, the Jurchen, and the Mongol--perhaps accelerated the trend towards a more centralized government than those of the T'ang and the Sung. The Chin-Yüan periods saw a remarkable growth of power of the central government, and the trend continued in the era of Ming-Ch'ing. The tendency is visible in the Presidential Council's (*shang-shu sheng*) monopoly of state affairs, the growth of the prototype of the provincial system, and the degradation of the scholar-officials, all of which survived the downfall of the Chin and thrived and grew thereafter.

The rule of Shih-tsung was imitated by early Ch'ing monarchs, especially T'ai-tsung (Abahai), who implemented many Chinese institutions, but also tried to preserve Manchu power.[9] Militarily there are similarities between the Jurchen *meng-an mou-k'e* and the Manchu Banners. Both were military garrisoning forces as well as socioeconomic units, maintaining solidarity of the tribal structure and power. The employment and organization of Chinese army units also had counterparts in the Yüan and the Ch'ing. Socially the Ch'i-tan and Jurchen rule in North China influenced the marriage customs--sororate and levirate were fairly common during the Yüan. The Ming rulers had to impose harsh punishments on those who violated traditional Chinese customs. Barbarian influence was also found in clothing.[10] The origin of the remarkable regimentation of the population under the Mongols--the classification of the households along ethnic and professional lines--could also be traced to the Chin period.[11]

From the experience of the Ch'i-tan and the Jurchen rule in China, in general, the Mongols and Manchus learned that it was possible for them to establish a regime in China so long as they adopted the Chinese models of government and adjusted themselves to the Chinese way of life. One should also mention the Japanese attempts in modern times to establish their rule in Manchuria and China, which, in certain respects, such as sponsoring puppet governments, followed the patterns of alien conquests in the past. In order to preserve their ethnic and cultural identity, however, the Mongols and the Manchus devised various measures to prevent the erosive effect of sinicization on their tribesmen. An important measure was the retainment of

Conclusion

reservoirs of their own cultures in their homeland, in Mongolia and Manchuria respectively, which were closed to Chinese immigrants and hence exclusive to the penetration of the Chinese culture.[12] On the part of the Chinese, the experience in dealing with the foreigners in the past has conditioned their response to the West. The importance of Sino-barbarian relations has persisted into modern times, for in the nineteenth and twentieth centuries Western inroads replaced barbarian invasions.

The Chin left a rich heritage in literature and art, and exerted considerable influence on political as well as intellectual developments. The alien conquerors undoubtedly harmed China at the initial stage of military conquests. Although the Jurchen adapted themselves to the Chinese society and culture, in the long run perhaps their rule diminished the initiative of the Chinese people. In order to reduce to the minimum their chance of organizing independent political and economic forces, the Jurchen controlled the activities of the most vigorous groups such as the scholar-officials and the merchants, both in politics and in other fields.[13] They suppressed the scholar-officials who ventured into opposition, and made others obedient instruments of the highly centralized imperial court. Thus the development of some central aspects of Chinese civilization more or less stagnated under the long period of successive alien administrations, and the consequences for China of alien rule were profound.

Appendix

EMPERORS OF THE CHIN DYNASTY

Jurchen Name	Chinese Name	Posthumous title	Reign Period
A-ku-ta	Min	T'ai-tsu	1115-1123
Wu-ch'i-mai	Sheng	T'ai-tsung	1123-1135
Ho-la	Tan	Hsi-tsung	1135-1149
Ti-ku-nai	Liang	Hai-ling Wang	1149-1161
Wu-lu	Pao, Yung	Shih-tsung	1161-1189
Ma-ta-ko	Ching	Chang-tsung	1189-1208
---	Yung-chi	Wei-shao Wang	1208-1213
Wu-tu-pu	Hsün	Hsüan-tsung	1213-1223
Ning-chia-su	Shou-hsü	Ai-tsung	1223-1234

Abbreviations

BIHP	*Bulletin of the Institute of History and Philology, Academia Sinica*
ch.	chapter or *chüan* in Chinese books
CS	*Chin-shih* 金史
CWT	*Chin-wen tsui* 金文最
HCSL	*History of Chinese Society: Liao (907-1125)*
HNC	*Hu-nan i-lao chi* 滹南遺老集
HNYL	*Chien-yen i-lai hsi-nien yao-lu* 建炎以來繫年要錄
ISC	*I-shan hsien-sheng wen-chi* 遺山先生文集
KCC	*Kuei-ch'ien chih* 歸潛志
KCS	*Kinchōshi kenkyū* 金朝史研究
KS	*Kŏryo sa* 高麗史
KSKK(1)	*Kinshi kenkyū*, Vol. 1 *Kindai Joshin shakai no kenkyū* 金史研究一

KSKK(2)	Kinshi kenkyū, Vol. 2 Kindai seiji seido no kenkyū 金史研究二
KSKK(3)	Kinshi kenkyū, Vol. 3 Kindai seiji shakai no kenkyū 金史研究三
LS	Liao-shih 遼史
MAC	Mu-an chi 牧庵集
SCPM	San-ch'ao pei-meng hui-pien 三朝北盟會編
SKCS	Ssu-k'u ch'üan-shu chen-pen 四庫全書珍本
SMCW	Sung-mo chi-wen 松漠紀聞
SPTK	Ssu-pu ts'ung-k'an 四部叢刊
SS	Sung-shih 宋史
TCKC	Ta-chin-kuo chih 大金國志

Notes

Introduction

1. Ch'ien Mu describes China in terms of a melting pot in his "Sung i-hsia Chung-kuo wen-hua chih ch'ü-shih" [Trends of Chinese cultural development since the Sung], *Ssu-hsiang yü Shih-tai*, no. 31 (1944), pp. 18-28. Yao Ts'ung-wu formulates his theory of the four periods of amalgamation of the Chinese people and the peoples of the frontiers in his "Kuo-shih k'uo-ta mien-yen ti i-ko k'an-fa" [A view of the historical development of China], in *Tung-pei-shih lun-ts'ung* [Collected essays on the history of the Northeast], 1: 1-26. For a discussion of the problem of the periodization of Chinese history, which is relevant to Sino-foreign relationship, see Ch'un-shu Chang, "The Periodization of Chinese History," BIHP, 45, pt. 1 (1973): 157-79. For Communist views, see David M. Farquhar, "Chinese Communist Assessments of a Foreign Conquest Dynasty," in *History in Communist China*, ed. Albert Feuerwerker, pp. 175-88.

2. Owen Lattimore, *Inner Asian Frontiers of China* (the Beacon Press ed., 1962, is used here). See also his *Studies in Frontier History: Collected Papers, 1928-1958*; Wolfram Eberhard, *Conquerors and Rulers: Social Forces in Medieval China*, pp. 27-28, 58, and chaps. 5, 6.

3. Karl A. Wittfogel and Feng Chia-sheng, *History of Chinese Society: Liao (907-1125)*, pp. 20, 219-25, 4-14. The quotation is from his *Oriental Despotism: A Comparative Study of Total Power*, p. 326.

4. Mary C. Wright, *The Last Stand of Chinese Conservatism: The Tung-chih Restoration, 1862-1874*, pp. 51-56; Lien-sheng Yang's review of the work of Wittfogel and Feng, in *Harvard Journal of Asiatic Studies* 13 (1950): 217-18, 219;

Tsuda's article is "Ryō no seido no nijū taikei" [Dualistic structure in Liao institutions], *Mansen chiri rekishi kenkyū hōkoku* 5 (1918): 131-226; "Liao-tai ssu-shih na-po k'ao wu-p'ien" [Nat-pat: the seasonal life of the Khitan grand khans], *BIHP* 10 (1942): 223-347.

5. See the writings of Shimada Masao, especially his *Pei ya-chou shih* [History of North Asia]; Fujieda Akira, *Seifuku ōchō* [Conquest dynasties]; Tamura Jitsuzō, *Chūgoku seifuku ōchō no kenkyū* [Studies on the conquest dynasties in China]; T'ao Chin-sheng [Jing-shen Tao], *Pien-chiang-shih yen-chiu chi: Sung Chin shih-ch'i* [Studies on Chinese frontier history: the Sung and Chin periods], pp. 1-3; Otagi Matsuo, *Ajia no seifuku ōchō* [The conquest dynasties in Asia].

6. Edwin O. Reischauer and John K. Fairbank, *East Asia: The Great Tradition*, pp. 259-61; John K. Fairbank, ed., *The Chinese World Order: Traditional China's Foreign Relations*. For a general discussion of the theories on China's relations with the non-Chinese peoples, see T'ao, *Pien-chiang-shih yen-chiu chi*, pp. 16-23.

7. Wittfogel also makes this distinction in *HCSL*, p. 25.

8. *Histoire de l'empire de Kin ou empire d'Or*; Hok-lam Chan, *The Historiography of the Chin Dynasty: Three Studies*; Susan Bush, *The Chinese Literati on Painting: Su Shih (1037-1101) to Tung Ch'i-ch'ang*; Stephen H. West, "Studies in Chin Dynasty (1115-1234) Literature," (Ph.D. diss., University of Michigan, 1972); Dagmar Thiele, *Der Abschluss eines Vertrages: Diplomatie zwischen Sung--und Chin--Dynastie 1117-1123*; Jutta Rall, *Die vier grossen Medizinschulen der Mongolenzeit: Stand un Entwicklung der chinesischen Medizin in der Chin--und Yüan-- zeit*, Munich East Asian Studies, vol. 7, 1970; also M. V. Vorob'ev's studies mentioned in François Aubin, "Travaux et tendences de la sinologie Sovietique recente," *T'oung Pao*, 58 (1-5) (1972): 170-71. There is a brief description of the Chin Dynastic History Project in *Sung Studies Newsletter*, no. 3 (1971), pp. 36-37.

9. See their works listed in the bibliography.

10. Sung Wen-ping, "Nü-chen han-hua k'ao-lüeh" [A brief study of the sinicization of the Jurchen], in *Sui-T'ang shih-tai hsi-yü-jen hua-hua k'ao* [The sinicization of westerners in the Sui and T'ang periods], Ho Chien-min, ed., pp. 172-94; Yao Ts'ung-wu, "Nü-chen han-hua ti fen-hsi" [An analysis of the sinicization of the Jurchen], *Ta-lu tsa-chih* 6, no. 3 (1953): 91-103.

11. Francis R. Allen, *Socio-cultural Dynamics: An Introduction to Social Change*, p. 43.

12. According to Robert Redfield, Ralph Linton, and

Melville J. Herskovits, "Memorandum on the Study of Acculturation," *American Anthropologist* 38 (1936): 149-52, "Acculturation is to be distinguished from . . . *assimilation*, which is at times a phase of acculturation." Ralph Beals also remarks that, "in the case of a wholly acculturated individual, clearly the acculturative process has terminated and we are speaking of a condition. Moreover, it is difficult to see how this differs from sociological use of the term 'assimilation.'" See his article "Acculturation," in *Anthropology Today: Selections*, ed., Sol Tax, p. 381. Cf. also Melville J. Herskovits, *Acculturation: The Study of Culture Contact*; Milton M. Gordon, *Assimilation in American Life: The Role of Race, Religion, and National Origins*, pp. 62-66.

13. Anthony C. Wallace, *Culture and Personality*, p. 163.

14. James W. Vander Zanden defines assimilation as "a process whereby groups with diverse ways of thinking, feeling, and acting become fused together in a social unity and a common culture," in *American Minority Relations: The Sociology of Race and Ethnic Groups*, p. 298. It includes change in both society and culture, and he states that the term is an inclusive concept that may entail both acculturation and integration. But his definition does not take into consideration the distinction between the cultures involved in the process of acculturation. Ralph Beals points out that "assimilation is that form of acculturation which results in groups of individuals wholly replacing their original culture by another (as opposed to groups reformulating a 'mixed' culture)." See Beals, "Acculturation," p. 382.

15. Beals, "Acculturation," p. 390; Allen, *Sociocultural Dynamics*, chaps. 10-12; Robert T. LaPiere, *Social Change*, chaps. 4-6.

Chapter 1

1. *LS*, ch. 1, p. 1b; for discussions of the name Jurchen (*Nü-chen*), see Han Ju-lin, "Nüchen i-ming k'ao" [A study of the name Nü-chen], *Studia Serica*, no. 3 (1942), pp. 1-11; Henry Serruys, *Sino-Jürced Relations during the Yung-lo Period 1403-1424*, p. vii, n. 1. The second word of Nü-chen was taboo because it was in the given name, Tsung-chen, who was Emperor Hsing-tsung of the Liao dynasty. See also Wilhelm Grube, *Die Sprache und Schrift der Jurcen*, pp. 18 and 91. Also Yamaji Hiroaki, *Joshingo kai* [A Jucen-Japanese-English Glossary], p. 64. "Jurched" and "Jürced"

are Mongol pronunciations. "Jurchen" has been the most common usage in Western literature. An example is *HCSL*, p. 7 and passim.

2. For Su-shen tribute to China, see *Kuo-yü* (*SPTK* ed.), *ch*. 5, pp. 14b-15a.

3. Hung Hao (1088-1155) was probably the first writer to have identified the Jurchen with the Su-shen and Mo-ho; see *SMCW*, *ch*. 1, p. 1a. The work was completed in the period 1142-49 (because in the *SMCW* Hung mentioned a young man who "is now in his twenties," and who became the fourth emperor of the Chin, Hai-ling [1122-61], enthroned in 1149). See also *SCPM*, *ch*. 3, p. 1a. Hsü Meng-hsin compiled *SCPM* in 1194, according to Ch'en Lo-su, "San-ch'ao pei-meng hui-pien k'ao" [On the *San-ch'ao pei-meng hui-pien*], *BIHP* 6, no. 2 (1936): 198. There is the same assertion in *CS*, *ch*. 1, p. 1a. The authors compiled the *CS* in 1337-39. Ch'en Shou in the *Wei-chih* [Dynastic history of the Wei], *ch*. 30, p. 19a, identified the I-lou with the Su-shen. Liu Chieh considers that the I-lou and Kao-ko-li (Kororyo) originated from the Fu-yü. See his "Hao-t'ai-wang pei k'ao-shih," [A study of the Hao t'ai-wang tablet], *Kuo-hsüeh lun-ts'ung* 2, no. 1 (1929): 17-18. The Mo-ho were called Wu-chi in the Northern Wei dynasty (386-534). The people occupied an area from Korea to the lower Amur and Sungari Rivers. See Wei Cheng and others, *Sui-shu* [Dynastic history of the Sui], *ch*. 81, pp. 8b-10a; Liu Hsü and others, *T'ang-shu* [Dynastic history of the T'ang], *ch*. 199, pt. 2, pp. 10b-11a. The kingdom of Po-hai was established by a branch of the Mo-ho, the Su-mo Mo-ho, in present Kirin in 712, being destroyed by the Ch'i-tan in 926. See *T'ang-shu*, *ch*. 199, pt. 2, pp. 11b-13a; *Hsin T'ang-shu* [New history of the T'ang], *ch*. 219, p. 8b by Ou-yang Hsiu. According to Wittfogel and Feng, the Ch'i-tan belonged to a proto-Mongol tribal complex; see *HCSL*, p. 22.

4. Modern examples are: *HCSL*, pp. 94-95; A. V. Smolyak, "Certain Questions on the Early History of the Ethnic Groups Inhabiting the Amur River Valley and the Maritime Province," *Studies in Siberian Ethnogenesis*, ed. Henry N. Michael, pp. 62-72; Ling Ch'un-sheng, *Sung-hua-chiang hsia-yu ti ho-che tsu* [The Goldi tribe], pp. 1-49; V. I. Jochelson, *Peoples of Asiatic Russia*; A. P. Okladnikov, "Ancient Cultures and Ethnic Relations on the Pacific Coast of Northern Asia," in *Proceedings of the Thirty-second International Congress of Americanists* (Copenhagen: Munskgaard, 1956), p. 550.

5. See Kwang-chih Chang, "Neolithic Cultures of the Sungari Valley, Manchuria," *Southwestern Journal of Anthropology* 17 (1961): 70-71; also his *The Archaeology of Ancient China*, pp. 166-67; Cheng Te-kun, *Archaeology in China*, vol.1,

Prehistory of China, pp. 135-36. In a recent article, Kwang-chih Chang distinguishes four major cultural traditions in Manchuria: the culture of North China, the culture of the steppes of eastern Mongolia, the culture of the lakes and forests in the North, and the ocean cultural tradition. See Chang Kwang-chih, "Tung-pei ti shih-ch'ien wen-hua" [The Prehistoric cultures of the Northeast], *Chung-kuo shang shang-ku shih (tai-ting kao)* [Draft of ancient history of China], ed., Chung-kuo shang-ku-shih pien-chi wei-yüan-hui, 2: 398.

6. L. Shrenk first used the term "Paleo-Asiatics" to describe the pre-Tungus population in Siberia and Manchuria. See M. G. Levin, *Ethnic Origins of the Peoples of Northeastern Asia*, p. 109; A. P. Okladnikov, *Ancient Population of Siberia and Its Cultures*, pp. 31-32; M. G. Levin and L. P. Potapov, *The Peoples of Siberia*, pp. 691-92, and 101-3; Levin, *Ethnic Origins*, p. 105. A present example of these people is the Nivkhi of the lower Amur and Sakkalin (Levin and Potapov, *Siberia*, pp. 767-87).

7. Exactly when the people were formed is not clear. Okladnikov speculates that they originated in the second millennium B.C.; P. Schmidt thinks that the Tungus moved into Manchuria very late, in the first millennium A.D. (see Levin, *Ethnic Origins*, pp. 163-64; Okladnikov, *Ancient Population*, pp. 29, 31-32).

8. Levin, *Ethnic Origins*, pp. 171-86 and pp. 162-71 for a summary of different theories concerning the origins of the Tungus; also his *Siberia*, pp. 101-3, 622-23; and "Anthropologicheskiye tiry Sibiri i Dalnego Vostoka: K probleme etnogeneza narodov Severnoy Azii" [Physical types of Siberia and the Far East: Contributions to the problem of the ethnic origin of the peoples of northern Asia], *Sovetskaya etnografiya*, no. 2 (Moscow-Leningrad, 1950), pp. 53-64. The Tungusic-Manchu language has close relationship to the Turkic and Mongolic languages. See Levin, *Siberia*, p. 2; P. Schmidt, "The Language of the Oroches," *Acta Universitatis Lativiensis*, 17 (Riga, 1928): 21-22; especially Nicholas Poppe, *Introduction to Altaic Linguistics*, pp. 24-33.

9. Ling Ch'un-sheng, *Sung-hua-chiang hsia-yu ti ho-che tsu*, pp. 33, 34, 45-49; Levin, *Ethnic Origins*, p. 164; Liu Chieh, "Hao-t'ai-wang pei k'ao-shih," pp. 17-18; Ts'ao T'ing-chieh, *Tung-san-sheng-yü-ti t'u-shuo* [Maps and explanations of the geography of the Three Eastern Provinces], p. 26.

10. For example, see Wen Ch'ung-i, "Hui-mo min-tsu wen-hua chi ch'i shih-liao" [A study of the culture and source material of the Hui-mo tribe], *Bulletin of the Institute of Ethnology, Academia Sinica* 5 (1958): 115-214.

11. Chia Lan-po and Yen Yin, "Hsi-t'uan-shan jen-ku ti yen-chiu pao-kao" [A report on the human bones of Hsi-t'uan-shan], *K'ao-ku hsüeh-pao*, no. 2 (1963), pp. 101-9; Tung-pei k'ao-ku fa-chüeh t'uan, "Chi-lin Hsi-t'uan-shan shih-kuan-mu fa-chüeh pao-kao" [Excavations of cist tombs at Hsi-t'uan-shan, Kirin], *K'ao-ku hsüeh-pao*, no. 1 (1964), pp. 29-49. Other characteristics found in the remains are: the undecorated brown sandy ware, the *hu* vase with horizontal handles, and the long crescent-shaped stone knife. Remains of this type seem to be confined in a definite area, extending northward to Teh-hui, southward to Huai-teh, eastward to Changchun, and westward to Hua-tien. Cf. also Chang Kwang-chih, "Tung-pei ti shih-ch'ien wen-hua," in *Chung-kuo shang-ku shih* 1: 407-8, in which he considers that the prehistoric inhabitants in Kirin seem to have belonged to the Su-shen and I-lou groups.

12. For pig raising see notes 26 and 27 below; Ch'en Shou, *Wei-chih*, ch. 30, pp. 18b-19a.

13. *SMCW*, ch. 1, p. 1a.

14. *SCPM*, ch. 3, p. 1a; *TCKC*, ch. 22, p. 2a.

15. *CS*, ch. 1, p. 1a.

16. *KS*, pp. 91 and 184; Ogawa Hiroto, "Sanjubu joshin ni tsuite" [On the thirty Jurchen tribes], *Tōyō Gakuhō* 24, no. 4 (1937): 561-601; *KS*, pp. 103, 104, 111, 129.

17. Hsüeh Chu-cheng, *Chiu Wu-tai-shih* [Old dynastic history of the Five Dynasties], ch. 32, pp. 7a and 14b; *LS*, ch. 2, p. 6b; ch. 3, p. 2a. The Mo-ho sent tribute Ch'i-tan again in 937 (*LS*, ch. 4, p. 1b); Serruys, *Sino-Jürced Relations*, p. 31, for the example of the Mongols.

18. *SCPM*, ch. 3, p. 2. The center of the "savage Jurchen" was the middle and upper Sungari.

19. Chung Pang-chih, "Hsüan-ho i-ssu feng-shih hsing-ch'eng-lu" [Report of the mission of the year I-ssu (1125) of the Hsüan-ho period], included in Ch'en Lo-su, "San-ch'ao pei-meng hui-pien k'ao," *BIHP* 6, no. 2 (1936): 275; *CS*, ch. 71, p. 8a; *KS*, p. 134.

20. Chi-lin-sheng po-wu-kuan, "Chi-lin T'a-hu-ch'eng tiao-ch'a chien-chi" [Archaeological investigation at T'a-hu, Kirin], *Kaogu*, no. 1 (1964), p. 47; Hei-lung-chiang po-wu-kuan, "Hei-lung-chiang la-lin-ho yu-an k'ao-ku tiao-ch'a" [Archaeological investigation of the Lalin River banks], *Kaogu*, no. 12 (1964), pp. 603-6; *SCPM*, ch. 3, pp. 2a, 4a; ch. 4, p. 13a; ch. 71, p. 6a; Chung Pang-chih, "Hsüan-ho i-ssu feng-shih hsing-ch'eng-lu," p. 275; *CS*, ch. 65, p. 6a; ch. 73, p. 9a; *CS*, ch. 36, p. 1a; ch. 73, p. 1b; *SCPM*, ch. 244, p. 1a.

21. *SCPM*, ch. 3. p. 3a; Chung Pang-chih. "Hsüan-ho i-ssu feng-shih hsing-ch'eng-lu," pp. 274, 275, 276-77;

CS, *ch*. 67, pp. 11a-12a.

22. Chung Pang-chih, "Hsüan-ho i-ssu . . .", pp. 275-78; *SCPM*, *ch*. 4, p. 13a; Chung Pang-chih said that the people scattered around and bred their stocks; see p. 277. That, however, describes the situation in early twelfth century when the people possessed a great number of horses.

23. Ch'en Hsiang-wei, "Chi-lin Huai-te Ch'in-chia-t'un ku-ch'eng tiao-ch'a chi" [Archaeological investigation of an old town in Kirin], *Kaogu*, no. 2 (1964), p. 81; Hei-lung-chiang po-wu-kuan, "Hei-lung-chiang La-lin-ho yu-an k'ao-ku tiao-ch'a," pp. 604-5; Chi-lin-sheng po-wu-kuan, "Chi-lin T'a-hu-ch'eng tiao-ch'a chien-chi," p. 48; only some coins found in the T'a-hu-ch'eng site belong to early Chin and early Southern Sung.

24. See chap. 4, pages 47 to 48, below.

25. *SCPM*, *ch*. 3, p. 3a; *TCKC*, *ch*. 39, p. 1a. For the use of it in earlier times, see *T'ang-shu*, *ch*. 199, p. 1b; *Hsin T'ang-shu*, *ch*. 220, p. 1b; also Ku Yen-wu, *Jih-chih-lu chi-shih* [Notes of knowledge accumulated daily], *ch*. 28, p. 659. The Goldi in modern times still used it. See Torii Ryuzō, "Chin Shang-ching-ch'eng chi ch'i wen-hua" [Shang-ching of Chin dynasty], *Yen-ching Journal of Chinese Studies*, no. 35 (1948), pp. 190-91; *SCPM*, *ch*. 4, p. 14a.

26. *SCPM*, *ch*. 3, p. 2a. Chung Pang-chih, "Hsüan-ho i-ssu . . .," p. 275, and *SCPM*, *ch*. 4, p. 12a, record that the people had pork in their dishes. It was the custom of the Paleo-Asiatics. See Okladnikov, *Ancient Population*, p. 55. According to Chang Kwang-chih, "Neolithic Cultures," p. 70, pig raising and agriculture came from the Yellow River culture. The people in Shang-ching presented 20,000 pigs to the government annually until 1185; see *CS*, *ch*. 24, p. 2b.

27. E. H. Parker, *A Thousand Years of the Tartars*, pp. 83-84, 150; Shiratori Kurakichi, "Tōko minzoku kō" [On the Tung-hu people], *Shigaku Zasshi*, no. 21 (1910), pp. 369-93. But G. M. Vasilevichi and A. V. Smolyak still think the origin of the word is unclear. See Levin, *Siberia*, p. 621.

28. *CS*, *ch*. 66, pp. 1b-2a; *ch*. 1, pp. 2a, 3a.

29. The P'u-kan River is perhaps the present Mutan River, and the Hai-ku River is the present Hai-ku-le, near A-ch'eng. See Ts'ao T'ing-chieh, *Tung-san-sheng yü-ti t'u-shuo*, pp. 10-12. Cf. Feng Chia-sheng, "Ch'i-tan ming-hao-k'ao-shih" [The origin of the name Ch'i-tan], *Yen-ching Journal of Chinese Studies*, no. 13 (1933), p. 26.

30. *CS*, *ch*. 1, p. 3a says that the Wan-yen clan lived on the An-ch'u-hu River, which is the present A-shih River. According to *Chin-shih yü-chieh* (in *Liao Chin Yüan san-shih yü-chieh* [Dictionary of Liao, Chin, and Yüan Histories]),

ch. 3, p. 1, "An-ch'u-hu" equals "anc'un" ᡥᠠᠰᡥᠠ in Manchu, meaning "earring." But in Jurchen, "an-c'un-wen" 外 土 means "gold" (Grube, *Die Sprache und Schrift der Jucen*, pp. 30, 79, 90). Further, *CS, ch.* 24, p. 1b, asserts that the name of Chin derived from the An-ch'u-hu River. Another assertion in the same work (*ch.* 2, pp. 8ab) that it came directly from "gold" is inaccurate. Cf. Ts'ao T'ing-chieh, *Tung-san-sheng yü-ti t'u-shuo*, pp. 10-12; Feng Chia-sheng, "Ch'i-tan ming-hao k'ao-shih," p. 26; Torii, "Chin shang-ching," pp. 129-34, 164; and Han Ju-lin, "Nü-chen i-ming k'ao", pp. 5-8.

31. *SCPM, ch.* 4, pp. 11a-14a, *ch.* 244, pp. 8a-9a; *TCKC, ch.* 36, pp. 3ab; Hsü Sung, ed., *Sung-hui-yao chi-kao* [Collected drafts on government institutions of the Sung dynasty], p. 7712.

32. Ou-yang Hsiu, *Wu-tai shih-chi* [Historical records of the Five Dynasties], *ch.* 73, p. 8b; *SCPM, ch.* 3, p. 3a. Cf. also *TCKC, ch.* 39, p. 1a. It was still practiced by the Tungus in modern times. See Levin, *Siberia*, pp. 626-27, for the Evenks and p. 752 for the Orochi.

33. The Jurchen, like the Ch'i-tan, also went to different places to hunt in accordance with different seasons. Cf. Yao Ts'ung-wu, "Chin-ch'ao Shang-ching shih-ch'i ti Nü-chen wen-hua yü ch'ien-yen i-hou ti chuan-pien" [The Jurchen culture in the period when Shang-ching was the capital of the Chin and the change after the capital was moved to Yen-ching], in *Tung-pei-shih lun-ts'ung* [Collected essays on the history of the Northeast], 2: 31-64.

34. See chap. 2 below.

35. *CS, ch.* 44, p. 2a; Lü I-hao, *Chung-mu chi, ch.* 1, p. 11a. The *po-chin* or *po-chi-lieh* was *baile* in Manchu Ch'ing. Cf. Ikeuchi Hiroshi, "Kin no kenkoku izen ni okeru kangashi no kunsho no shōgō ni tsuite" [On the titles of the Wan-yen chieftains before the Chin], *Tōyō Gakuhō* 20, no. 1 (1932): 129; Ch'en Shu, "Cha-chün k'ao-shih ch'u-kao" [First draft of a study of the Cha-chün], *BIHP*, 20, no. 2 (1949): 296. *SCPM, ch.* 3, p. 5a says that the *po-chi-lieh* was equivalent to the *tsung-kuan* or general officer in China. This term has been reconstructed as *bogile*. See Karl H. Menges, "Problemata Etymologica," in *Studia Sino-Altaica 10: Festchrift für Erich Haenisch sum 80*, pp. 130-40; also Herbert Franke's review of *KSKK (2)* in *T'oung Pao*, 57, no. 5 (1971): 322 ff. The term *mou-k'e* has been generally interpreted as "hundred." See *SCPM, ch.* 3, p. 5a; *ch.* 244, p. 8a. However, its meaning is still unclear. In Jurchen, the word for "hundred" is *tanggo* 勺 . See Grube, *Sprache der Jucen*, pp. 35, 54, 100. In Manchu, *mukun* ᠮᡠᡴᡡᠨ means "clan" or "tribe" (*tsu*). See *Chin-shih yü-chieh, ch.*

6. pp. 1ab. Cf. also *KSKK* (1), p. 114.

36. *CS, ch.* 2, p. 7b; *ch.* 44, pp. 2ab. A household or *hu* 戶 means a soldier and his family; *SCPM, ch.* 244, p. 8a; *CS, ch.* 44, p. 2a; *SCPM, ch.* 3, p. 7a; *ch.* 244, p. 8a, states that at the beginning all the foot soldiers were not Jurchen but drafted from the Ch'i-tan, Hsi, and Chinese.

37. Ou-yang Hsiu, *Wu-tai shih-chi, ch.* 73, p. 8b, records that the people did not have permanent houses; Ma K'uo also saw many Jurchen tents (*SCPM, ch.* 4, p. 14a). The tents may have been their summer abode, as in modern times many Tungusic people had different dwellings in winter and in summer. See Levin, *Siberia,* pp. 637-38, for the Evenks, p. 702 for the Nanays, p. 753 for the Orochi, and p. 763 for the Oroks. Or, concerning Ma K'uo's account, in early twelfth century the Jurchen possessed a great many horses and became much more mobile than before; thus they might stay in their tents for a longer time. An example of current historians who think of the Jurchen as nomads is Franz Michael, *The Origin of Manchu Rule in China,* p. 15.

38. *LS, ch.* 116, p. 49a; *CS, ch.* 2, p. 9a. Cf. also *TCKC, ch.* 39, p. 1b. *SCPM, ch.* 3, *TCKC, ch.* 39, *Wu-tai shih-chi, ch.* 73, and *CS, ch.* 1 provide the information in this section.

39. For Ch'i-tan *she-liu* see *LS, ch.* 49, "se-se i"; for Jurchen practice see *SCPM, ch.* 3, p. 4b. In the ritual, sacrifice was offered to the heaven and an archery contest was held. For the diffusion of Buddhism see p. 13.

40. *SCPM, ch.* 3, p. 4a; *ch.* 4, p. 13a; *SMCW, ch.* 1, p. 8a; *TCKC, ch.* 39, p. 1b; Ou-yang Hsiu, *Wu-tai shih-chi, ch.* 73, p. 8b; *SCPM, ch.* 3, p. 3a; for Jurchen eating habits and recipes, see Herbert Franke, "Chinese Texts on the Jurchen: A Translation of the Jurchen Monograph in the *San-ch'ao pei-meng hui-pien,*" *Zentralasiatische Studien* 9 (1975): 172-77 (Appendix II, "Jurchen Food Recipes"). For Jurchen drinking habits, see also Herbert Franke, "A Note on Wine under the Chin Dynasty," *Zentralasiatische Studien* 8 (1974): 241 ff.

41. *SCPM, ch.* 3, p. 2a. According to *KS,* p. 234, they already had weavers in 1101. Their native products included cloth. See *SCPM, ch.* 3, p. 3a; *LS, ch.* 60, p. 3b. They cultivated silkworms. See A. P. Okladnikov, *The Soviet Far East in Antiquity,* p. 267. Okladnikov's archaelogical finds are up-to-date. His chapter on the Jurchen state, however, is largely based upon a Russian translation of the *Dynastic History of the Chin.* Since there are a number of mistakes concerning the origin, the history, and some Jurchen customs (e.g., the capital of the Northern Sung was mistaken for Lo-yang; see p. 216. Wei Shao-wang was a

Chin emperor, not a daughter of the emperor given to Činggis Qan; see p. 234), I generally do not cite this part of his work.

42. *SCPM*, *ch*. 3, pp. 3a-4a; cf. *TCKC*, *ch*. 39, p. 2a.

43. *SCPM*, *ch*. 3, p. 4a. According to Chung Pang-chih, "Hsüan-ho i-ssu feng-shih hsing-ch'eng-lu," p. 271, the Jurchen did not use pottery but lacquer.

44. *CS*, *ch*. 1, p. 5a; *SCPM*, *ch*. 18, p. 4a. Both sources record that at the time of Sui-k'o (ca. early eleventh century) iron casting was introduced to the people. They used iron weapons as early as 1018. See *KS*, pp. 98, 150. By 1115 they already had the profession of iron casting. See *CS*, *ch*. 67, pp. 5ab. *TCKC*, *ch*. 13, pp. 1b-2a, records that iron came from the Tartars; Ou-yang Hsiu, *Wu-tai shih-chi*, *ch*. 73, p. 8b; *SCPM*, *ch*. 3, p. 3a; *ch*. 18, p. 4a; *SMCW*, *ch*. 2, p. 3a.

45. *CS*, *ch*. 67, p. 11a; *ch*. 64, p. 11a; *ch*. 120, p. 14b; *ch*. 67, p. 5a; *ch*. 120, p. 1b.

46. The name of the Yeh-lan District was after the Yeh-lan River, which is near the present Mutan River. See Tsuda Sokichi, "Kindai hokuhen kō" [An investigation of the northern borders of the Chin], *Mansen chiri rekishi kenkyū hōkoku* (Tokyo), no. 4 (1918), p. 197; also Torii, "Chin shang-ching," p. 149, nn. 2, 3, and pp. 198-99.

47. See p. 7, above.

48. *SCPM*, *ch*. 3, pp. 1a, 3a; *ch*. 166, p. 5a; *ch*. 244, p. 7a; also *CS*, *ch*. 44, p. 2a; *ch*. 46, p. 5b.

49. *SCPM*, *ch*. 186, p. 5a; *ch*. 3, p. 3a.

50. E.g., the Jurchen looted the Ch'i-tan, capturing Ch'i-tan people, cattle, and horses in 973. See *LS*, *ch*. 8, p. 3b. In their raid of 1064 the Jurchen captured Koryŏ people. See *KS*, p. 172.

51. *CS*, *ch*. 67, pp. 3a, 12a.

52. *SCPM*, *ch*. 3, p. 6a; also *TCKC*, *ch*. 39, p. 1b; *ch*. 36, pp. 1b-2a.

53. *SCPM*, *ch*. 3, p. 6a. Flogging with sand bags was another Jurchen punishment. See *SCPM*, *ch*. 3, p. 6a; *ch*. 244, p. 9a.

54. The Jurchen, following Ch'i-tan practice, called their chieftain *t'ai-shih* or grand preceptor. See *CS*, *ch*. 1, p. 5a; also Ikeuchi Hiroshi, "Kin no kenkoku izen no okeru kanganshi no kunsho no shōgō ni tsuite," p. 111.

55. *CS*, *ch*. 55, pp. 1ab. After 1115 central government officials were generally called *po-chi-lieh* and tribal chieftains were still *po-chin*. For the *po-chi-lieh* system see *KSKK* (2), pp. 73-162; also Mikami Tsugio, "Joshinjin no hatten to Kinsho no kansei" [The progress of the Jurchen and the government organization in early Chin], *Rekishigaku*

kenkyū (Old), 4, no. 3 (1935): 277-85.
  56. *SCPM*, *ch*. 3, p. 7a; *ch*. 244, pp. 8a-b; *CS*, *ch*. 70, p. 2b.
  57. *SCPM*, *ch*. 3, p. 6a. In a crisis in 985, the Jurchen asked the Sung to help them by sending a message carved in wood. See *KS*, p. 70; *SS*, *ch*. 246, p. 4a; *CS*, *ch*. 73, p. 8a.
  58. *SCPM*, *ch*. 3, p. 3a. Examples of levirate are: *CS*, *ch*. 73, p. 10a; *ch*. 5, p. 5b; *ch*. 64, p. 1b; *HNYL*, *ch*. 84, p. 16a. For marriage customs, see *SCPM*, *ch*. 3, p. 4a; *TCKC*, *ch*. 39, p. 3a; *SMCW*, *ch*. 1, pp. 8a-b. In *TCKC*, *ch*. 39, p. 2b, there is a detailed description of bride price, the wedding ceremony, and the custom of temporary matrilocal residence.
  59. The succession of chieftainship in pre- and early Chin was among brothers. See *CS*, *ch*. 1 and chapter 2, below.
  60. Okladnikov (*Ancient Population*, p. 29) believes that shamanism originated from the Baikal region. Cf. Torii, "Chin shang-ching," pp. 171-74, for a description of Jurchen shamanism. Chinese accounts refer to it as *wu* or witchcraft. See *SCPM*, *ch*. 3, pp. 5a, 10a; *ch*. 65, pp. 3a-4b; *CS*, *ch*. 73, p. 13b; *ch*. 65, pp. 3a-4b. Cf. also *TCKC*, *ch*. 39, p. 1b.
  61. *SCPM*, *ch*. 3, p. 5a; *ch*. 98, p. 13a. It was also a Mongol practice; see Wang Kuo-wei, *Meng-ta pei-lu chien-cheng* [Annotated *Meng-ta pei-lu*], in *Wang-chung-k'o-kung i-shu*, ser. 3 (1927), p. 1b.
  62. *SCPM*, *ch*. 3, p. 11a; *TCKC*, *ch*. 27, p. 4a; *CS*, *ch*. 35, p. 10a and *ch*. 1, p. 1b. Cf. also Torii, "Chin shang-ching," pp. 167-68.
  63. *SCPM*, *ch*. 3, p. 5a; *ch*. 165, p. 9a. It was a common practice of both the Ch'i-tan and Jurchen. The Manchus still practiced it during the Ch'ing. See Wang Kuo-wei, "Meng-ku tsa-chi" [Notes on the Mongols], in his *Kuan-t'ang chi-lin*, pp. 811-13. *SCPM*, *ch*. 18, p. 4a. It was also a Ch'i-tan custom. See Torii, "Chin shang-ching," pp. 179-80.

Chapter 2

  1. *LS*, *ch*. 1, p. 1b; *ch*. 3, p. 3b; *ch*. 7, p. 5a. The Ch'i-tan changed the official title of a Jurchen chieftain from *hsiang-wen* to *i-li-chin*, applied from the chief of the civil government to the chief of an army. For these two titles see *HCSL*, p. 129, n. 42, and p. 432.
  2. *LS*, *ch*. 15, p. 2a. For Jurchen raids, see Hsüeh Chü-cheng, *Chin Wu-tai shih*, *ch*. 32, p. 7a; *LS*, *ch*. 8, pp. 3b, 5a. For trade between the Jurchen and the Ch'i-tan, see *LS*, *ch*. 11, p. 1a; *ch*. 60, p. 1a; *SMCW*, *ch*. 1, pp. 6b-7a.
  3. Hsüeh Chü-cheng, *Chiu Wu-tai-shih*, *ch*. 73, p. 8b.

Hu Chiao, the writer of this account, stayed in the Liao kingdom in 947-53.

4. They sent horses to Liao in 1080, 1083, 1087 and 1095. See *LS*, *ch*. 24, pp. 3a, 5b, 7a; *ch*. 25, p. 1a; *ch*. 26, p. 2a; *ch*. 60, pp. 3b-4a.

5. For studies of the tributary system, see John K. Fairbank, ed., *The Chinese World Order: Traditional China's Foreign Relations*. See also Fairbank's earlier study, "Synarch under the Treaties," in *Chinese Thought and Institutions*, ed. Fairbank, pp. 206-9.

6. *CS*, *ch*. 1, p. 5a.

7. *KS*, pp. 62, 78. For early relations between the Jurchen and Koryŏ, see also Michael C. Rogers, "The Regularization of Koryŏ-Chin Relations (1116-1131)," *Central Asiatic Journal* 6, no. 1 (1961): 56, n. 27.

8. According to *KS*, p. 62, the Jurchen paying tribute to Koryŏ in 948 was a Koryŏ official. Examples of their raids on Koryŏ are many; e.g., *KS*, pp. 83, 172. For the genealogy chart see ibid., p. 92.

9. Hsüeh Chü-cheng, *Chiu Wu-tai-shih*, *ch*. 32, p. 14a; *SS*, *ch*. 1, p. 10b; Hsü Sung, *Sung-hui-yao chi-kao*, p. 7711.

10. *SS*, *ch*. 5, p. 15b; Hsü Sung, *Sung-hui-yao chi-kao*, p. 7711, recorded it in 962. Teng-chou is now P'eng-lai.

11. *SS*, *ch*. 5, p. 13b; Hsü Sung, *Sung-hui-yao chi-kao*, p. 7712 recorded it in 992.

12. Ibid., p. 7148; *SCPM*, *ch*. 3, p. 8; *ch*. 1, p. 1a.

13. *HCSL*, p. 115.

14. Horses existed in Manchuria during the Han dynasty. See Ch'en Shou, *Wei-chih*, *ch*. 30, pp. 11b and 17b. For more details about the importance of the horse to the Jurchen, see Jing-shen Tao, "The Horse and the Rise of the Chin Dynasty," *Papers of the Michigan Academy of Science, Arts, and Letters*, 53 (1968): 183-89.

15. *KS*, p. 91.

16. *CS*, *ch*. 1.

17. Torii, "Chin shang-ching," pp. 150-51.

18. According to *CS*, *ch*. 1, the successions are as follows:

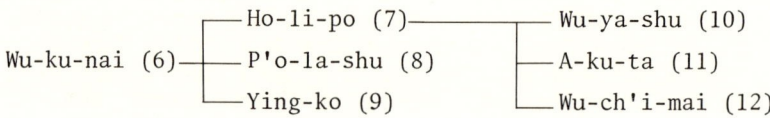

19. All the information here is based on *CS*, *ch*. 1. For a study of the early history of the Jurchen as recorded in *CS*, see Ikeuchi Hiroshi, "Kinshi seiki no kenkyū" [A study of the "Imperial Genealogy" of the Dynastic History of the Chin], *Mansen chiri rekishi kenkyū hōkoku*, no. 11 (1926),

pp. 117-313. The "Five Nations" may have located near the present Ussuriysk, Maritime Province, according to archaeological excavations. See A. P. Okladnikov, *The Soviet Far East in Antiquity*, p. 258.

20. *TCKC*, *ch*. 1, p. 1a.

21. Owen Lattimore first propounded the concept of the "frontier reservoir" organized on the borders of China by different peoples who were able to develop considerable strength in preparation for invading China. See his *Inner Asian Frontiers of China*, pp. 238-51 and 542-49. Also cf. his *Studies in Frontier History: Collected Papers, 1928-1958*, especially pp. 7-118.

22. *CS*, *ch*. 2, p. 4b. According to *SCPM*, *ch*. 3, p. 9a, one of the ill deeds of Liao missions was that they requested Jurchen girls and women to accompany them when they were on business trips.

23. *TCKC*, *ch*. 10; *CS*, *ch*. 2, pp. 4b-5a.

24. *CS*, pp. 5a-7b, 9b-10b.

25. *LS*, *ch*. 28, pp. 2b-3a, for Yeh-lü Chang-nu; *CS*, *ch*. 2, p. 11a, and *LS*, *ch*. 28, pp. 3b-4a for Kao Yung-ch'ang.

26. *KSKK* (1), pp. 96-97.

27. For details see *SCPM*, *ch*. 1, 2, 4, 5-7 and 9-12. Li Hsin-ch'uan provided a summary in *HNYL*, *ch*. 1. Wu Ching-hung, "Sung Chin kung Liao chih wai-chiao" [The Sung diplomacy toward the Chin for an alliance against the Liao], *Tung-fang tsa-chih* 43, no. 18 (1947): 45-52; Hsü Yü-hu, "Sung Chin hai-shang lien-meng ti kai-kuan" [A general observation of the alliance between the Sung and Chin], *Ta-lu tsa-chih* 11, no. 12 (1955): 24-28; Chao T'ieh-han, "Sung Chin hai-shang chih-meng shih-mo chi" [An historical account of the alliance between the Sung and the Chin], *Ta-lu tsa-chih* 25, nos. 5-7 (1962): 9-14, 14-19, 26-34.

28. The question of identifying the so-called Sixteen Prefectures of Yen and Yün (*Yen Yün shih-liu chou*) has been a confusing and complicated one since Sung times. See Chao T'ieh-han, "Yen Yün shih-liu chou ti ti-li fen hsi" [A geographical analysis of the sixteen prefectures of Yen and Yün] in *Sung Liao Chin shih yen-chiu lun-chi* [Collected essays on the history of the Sung, Liao, and Chin dynasties], pp. 53-62. The six prefectures returned to Sung were: Yu (now Peking), Chi (now Chi), Ching (now Tsun-hua), T'an (now Mi-yün), Shun (now Shun-i), Cho (now Cho-chou), and I (now I). Two Ch'i-tan nobles assumed the reins of government, but failed. They were Yeh-lü Nieh-li or Ch'un 淳 (1122-23) and Yeh-lü Ya-li (1123). See *SCPM*, *ch*. 5-12; *LS*, *ch*. 29, pp. 3a-5a; and *CS*, *ch*. 2, pp. 17a-18a and *ch*. 76, pp. 10a-11a for Nieh-li. Also *LS*, *ch*. 29, pp. 6a-b; *CS*, *ch*. 3, p. 1a and *ch*. 74, p. 10a for Ya-li.

29. *CS*, *ch*. 3, pp. 3a, 8a. See also Michael C. Rogers, "The Regularization of Koryŏ-Chin Relations (1116-1131)," p. 62.

30. He was captured by Wan-yen Lou-shih near the present Ying County, Shansi. See *CS*, *ch*. 3, p. 5b; *LS*, *ch*. 30, p. 1b.

31. There is an account of Qarā-Khitay in *HCSL*, pp. 619-74 (Appendix 5).

32. *SCPM*, *ch*. 19, pp. 7a-10a. For Kuo Yao-shih, see *SCPM*, *ch*. 9, pp. 12a-14a and *ch*. 10, pp. 3a-4a. Kuo was a Po-hai whose troops were largely Chinese from Liao-tung and Yen. Cf. also *CS*, *ch*. 82, pp. 1b-2a; *SCPM*, *ch*. 15, p. 12a.

33. *SCPM*, *ch*. 4, pp. 9a-11a; *ch*. 11, pp. 6a-12a; *ch*. 12, pp. 1a-3a and 9a-11a; *ch*. 22, pp. 8a-9a. Cf. Chao Tieh-han, *Sung Liao Chin*, pp. 53-54.

34. A-ku-ta promised only orally. See *SCPM*, *ch*. 4, pp. 3a-7a; *HNYL*, *ch*. 1, p. 7a; *CS*, *ch*. 74, p. 3b, records that Nien-han asked Wu-ch'i-mai not to return northern Shansi to Sung and Wu-ch'i-mai said, "The late emperor (A-ku-ta) promised to return this area; we ought to give it to Sung."

35. *SCPM*, *ch*. 12, pp. 10a-11a; *ch*. 13-15; *ch*. 17, pp. 2a-4a, 11a-12a; *ch*. 18. Also *ch*. 133, pp. 1a-2b.

36. *SPCM*, *ch*. 8, p. 12a; *ch*. 22, p. 6a. A contemporary writer wrote that the Yen Chinese employed by the Jurchen such as Liu Yen-tsung and Shih Li-ai wanted to include their native region in the Chin. See *SCPM*, *ch*. 24, p. 12a. For Liu Yen-tsung, see *CS*, *ch*. 78, p. 2a; for Shih Li-ai, see *CS*, *ch*. 78, p. 7b; for Kao Ch'ing-i see *SCPM*, *ch*. 141, pp. 4a-5a and *ch*. 178, pp. 5a-6a; for Tso Chi-kung, see *CS*, *ch*. 75, p. 9a and *TCKC*, *ch*. 2, p. 5a. Tso wrote a poem to A-ku-ta:

> Oh, my lord,
> People are talking about giving up Yen;
> But please don't listen to such gossip,
> For one inch of land is one inch of gold.

37. *CS*, *ch*. 74, pp. 3b-4a and 12a; *ch*. 71, pp. 4a-b. Sung also promised to lend Wo-li-pu some provisions, but soon refused to do so. See *SCPM*, *ch*. 15, pp. 9a-10a; *ch*. 19, p. 6a.

38. According to Li Kang (1085-1140), who defended Pien-ching, Jurchen troops were less than 60,000 men, including 30,000 Ch'i-tan and Po-hai. See Li Kang, *Ching-k'ang ch'uan-hsin lu* [Authentic records of the Ching-k'ang period], *ch*. 2, p. 1a. Cf. "Sung Government at Mid-Season: Translation of and Commentary on the *Ching-k'ang ch'uan-hsin lu*" (Ph. D. diss. by John W. Haeger, University of California, Berkeley, 1970). *SCPM*, *ch*. 30, p. 1a, records that the Jurchen army contained less than 50,000 men; see also *CS*, *ch*. 74, p. 13a; *SS*, *ch*. 358, pp. 3b-5a; Li Kang, *Ching-*

k'ang ch'uan-hsin lu, *ch.* 1, pp. 8b-9a and *ch.* 2, p. 3a; *SCPM*, *ch.* 29, pp. 11a-12a; *ch.* 30, pp. 1a-2a.

39. *CS*, *ch.* 82, p. 15a; *SCPM*, *ch.* 83-84.
40. *CS*, *ch.* 44, p. 1a.
41. *SCPM*, *ch.* 3, p. 7a; *ch.* 244, p. 8a; Lü I-hao, *Chung-mu chi*, *ch.* 1, pp. 5a-6a; *ch.* 2, p. 13b.
42. *SCPM*, *ch.* 30, p. 5a; *HNYL*, *ch.* 136; *SS*, *ch.* 366, "Biography of Liu Ch'i." The horse team has been traditionally considered as the "*kuai-tzu ma*." But Teng Kuang-ming in his *Yüeh Fei chuan* [A biography of Yüeh Fei], Appendix, pp. 275-78, argues that it did not refer to a team of horses but to the two wings of cavalry columns.
43. *SCPM*, *ch.* 36, pp. 8a-b.
44. See Ch'en Kuei's account in *SCPM*, *ch.* 139, pp. 5b-17b. Also *ch.* 53, pp. 4a-5a; *ch.* 97, p. 2a.
45. L. C. Goodrich and Feng Chia-sheng, "The Early Development of Firearms in China," *Isis* 36 (1945-46): 114-23, 250-51; Wang Ling, "On the Invention and Use of Gunpowder and Firearms in China," *Isis* 37 (1947): 160-78; Chao T'ieh-han, *Huo-yao ti fa-ming* [The invention of gunpowder]; Feng Chia-sheng, "Huo-yao ti fa-hsien chi-ch'i ch'uan-pu" [The discovery and diffusion of gunpowder], *Shih-hsüeh chi-k'an* [Historical journal] 5 (1947): 29-84. A general account is provided by Yoshida Mitsukuni, in *Sō-Gen jidai no kagaku gijutsu shi* [A history of science and technology in the Sung-Yüan periods], ed. Yabuuchi Kiyoshi, pp. 211-34.
46. *KCC*, *ch.* 11; *CS*, *ch.* 113, "Biography of Ch'ih-chan Ho-hsi."
47. T'ao Chin-sheng [Jing-shen Tao], *Chin Hai-ling-ti ti fa Sung yü Ts'ai-shih chan-i ti k'ao-shih* [A study of the Chin Emperor Hai-ling's invasion of the Southern Sung and the battle of Ts'ai-shih: 1161], pp. 96-100, 108-20.

Chapter 3

1. *CS*, *ch.* 55, pp. 1a-b; also cf. chap. 1, note 55, above.
2. *KSKK* (2), pp. 113-62.
3. *CS*, *ch.* 1, p. 6a; *ch.* 70, pp. 2a-b.
4. *CS*, *ch.* 2, pp. 9b, 11b; *ch.* 71, p. 2b. Cf. *KSKK* (2), pp. 113-62.
5. For these local officials, see *KSKK* (1), pp. 237-39, 451-72.
6. For the Manchu Banners, see Franz Michael, *The Origin of Manchu Rule in China*, chap. 6. See also *CS*, *ch.* 44, pp. 11b-12a.
7. For example, A-ku-ta ordered Lu-shih to garrison

Huang-lung Prefecture. See *CS*, *ch*. 2, p. 12b.
    8. See chap. 4, pp. 48-51, below.
    9. *CS*, *ch*. 77, p. 12b; *ch*. 81, pp. 5b-6a; *ch*. 128, pp. 5a and 6a; *ch*. 95, p. 13a. For Wang Fu, see Lo Chi-tsu, "Chin ch'ung-i-chün chieh-tu-shih Wang Fu mu-chih pa" [Note on the tablet inscription of Wang Fu] *Manshu Shigaku* 3, no. 2 (1940): 35. Other examples are: Chang Ch'ung (*CS*, *ch*. 71, p. 6b); Chai Chao-yen, Hsü Hsing (*CS*, *ch*. 2, p. 19); Liu Kung-chou 劉公弗, Wang Yung-fu 王永福 (*CS*, *ch*. 2, pp. 10b-11a; *ch*. 71, p. 7a).
    10. Below is a chart of examples of foreign *meng-an* and *mou-k'e*:

Name		Title	Time Received	Sources (in *CS*)
CHINESE				
Lu K'e-chung	盧克忠	hereditary *mou-k'e*	1116	128/2
Ho Shih	霍石	*meng-an*	1118	2/13
Han Ch'ing-ho	韓慶和	*meng-an*	1118	2/13
Chang Ying-ku	張應古	*meng-an*	1118	2/13
Liu Chung-liang	劉仲良	*meng-an*	1118	2/13
Li Hsiao-kung	李孝功	*meng-an*	1118	2/13
Liu Hung	劉宏	hereditary *meng-an*	1118	2/13
K'ung Ching-tsung	孔敬宗	hereditary *meng-an*	1118	75/5
Wang Po-lung	王伯龍	hereditary *meng-an*	1118	81/5b-6a
Kao Ts'ung-yu	高從祐	*meng-an*	1118	44/2b
Wang Liu-erh	王六兒	*mou-k'e*	1118	44/2b
Yang Hsün-ch'ing	楊詢卿	*mou-k'e*	1119	2/14
Lo Tzu-wei	羅子偉	*mou-k'e*	1119	2/14
Wang Cheng	王政	*mou-k'e*	1115-23	128/4
Chao Wei	趙賦	*meng-an*	1115-23	81/3
Li Ch'u-o-chih	李雛訛只	*meng-an*	1115-23	81/14
Kuo Chi-chung	郭企忠	*meng-an*	1125	82/8b
Li San-hsi	李三錫	*meng-an*	1123-35	75/4b
Li Ching	李靖	*po-chin*	1123-35	3/2b
CH'I-TAN				
Yeh-lü Huai-i	懷義	*mou-k'e*	1115-23	81/11b
I-la Ch'eng	移剌成	*meng-an*	1123-35	90/5
PO-HAI				
Erh-ko	二哥	*meng-an*	1118	2/13

Notes: Chapter 3   137

Name		Title	Time Received	Sources (in *CS*)
Li Shih	李石	hereditary *mou-k'e*, *meng-an*	1115-23	86/1
Ta-kao	大㚒	*meng-an* *wan-hu*	1115-23 1123-35	80/11a-b
Kao Liu-ko	高六哥	*meng-an*	1115-23	81/8
Kao Chen	高楨	*meng-an*	1115-23	84/12b
Kao Piao	高彪	*meng-an*	1123-35	81/8

HSI

| Hsiao Wang-chia-nu | 蕭王家奴 | *meng-an* | 1123 | 81/12b |
| Hsiao I | 蕭翊 | *wan-hu* | 1123-35 | 82/5b-6 |

11. *CS*, *ch*. 82, p. 6a, recorded that Hsiao Kung 蕭恭 was kept as a hostage. A-ku-ta kept the family of Yeh-lü Yü-tu as hostage. See *CS*, *ch*. 133, p. 3b. In the note of a poem concerning Liu Shan-ch'ang 劉善長, Hung Hao wrote, "His father guarded Pei-an, and (he) was a hostage at the age of nine." See Hung Hao, *P'o-yang chi*, *ch*. 2, pp. 8b-9a.

12. *CS*, *ch*. 2, pp. 7a, 11a, 20a, 11b, 13b, 15b, 18b, 19b, 20b, 21b, 22a; *ch*. 3, pp. 3a, 4a-b, 5a-b, 8b, 11b.

13. *HNYL*, *ch*. 4, p. 1b, recorded that they killed numerous Chinese like "cutting the hemp," and the odor of corpses spread over several hundred *li*.

14. *CS*, *ch*. 2, pp. 11a, 19a; *ch*. 3, pp. 2b, 3a, 4a, 15b.

15. Ibid., *ch*. 2, p. 21b; *ch*. 76, pp. 8b-9a; *SCPM*, *ch*. 16, pp. 5a-11a; *ch*. 133, p. 1b, recorded that when A-ku-ta captured a city, he often moved its people to Shang-ching. The so-called *nei-ti* or "interior" of Chin means the Shang-ching area; see ibid., *ch*. 24, p. 1b.

16. *CS*, *ch*. 3, pp. 2a, 5b, 11b; *ch*. 74, p. 5b; *SCPM*, *ch*. 115, p. 8a; *HNYL*, *ch*. 4, p. 6a.

17. The purpose of the transfer of Chinese population to Manchuria is self-evident, although the unequal treatment of Chinese and Jurchen is not clear in early Chin for lack of data. However the deficit is made up later; see chapter 4, pp. 49-50, below. For Ch'i-tan policy of transfer of Chinese, cf. *HCSL*, pp. 48, 52, 143, 194, and 405.

18. *CS*, *ch*. 3, pp. 6b, 9b, 15a-b.

19. For Yang P'u, see *TCKC*, *ch*. 2, pp. 1b-2a; *CS*, *ch*. 71, p. 4a; *ch*. 24, p. 5a; *SS*, *ch*. 22, p. 8b; *HNYL*, *ch*. 1, pp. 3b and 4a. See also *CS*, *ch*. 2, pp. 13a, 20a.

20. *CS*, *ch*. 76, p. 14a; *ch*. 78, p. 8b; *ch*. 73, p. 9b;

ch. 3, p. 17a.
21. Ibid., *ch.* 78, p. 8b.
22. Cf. *KSKK* (2), pp. 165-69.
23. *HNYL*, *ch.* 12, p. 18a.
24. For the Chang family, see *KCS*, pp. 123-52. For the Li family, see *KCS*, pp. 443-70.
25. For Han Fang, see *SCPM*, *ch.* 166, p. 5a; for Chang Yung-chih, see *CS*, *ch.* 105, pp. 7a-b.
26. *CS*, *ch.* 78, pp. 8b-9a.
27. Hung Hao, *P'o-yang chi*, Appendix, p. 9b. For Yü-wen Hsü-chung, see Mao Wen, "Yü-wen Hsü-chung nien-p'u" [Chronological biography of Yü-wen Hsü-chung] in *Liao Chin shih-shih lun-wen chi* [Essays on the history of the Liao and Chin], pp. 1-28.
28. Hung Hao, *P'o-yang chi*, *ch.* 4, p. 10a; *CS*, *ch.* 88, p. 13a, recorded Wu-lu's opinion about Yü-wen.
29. Data taken from *HNYL*, *ch.* 1, pp. 29b-31a; *ch.* 2, pp. 17b-18a; *SCPM*, *ch.* 72, pp. 3a-5a, 8a-9a; *ch.* 77, pp. 10a-13a; *ch.* 78, pp. 1a-4a; *ch.* 79, p. 8a; *ch.* 81, pp. 4a-5a, 8a; *ch.* 97, pp. 7a-12a; *CS*, *ch.* 74, p. 5a.
30. *CS*, *ch.* 2, p. 16b; A-ku-ta ordered to move Ch'i-tan imperial devices, books, etc., to Shang-ching in early 1122 (the twelfth month of 1121). For the development of Buddhism in Shang-ching, cf. Torii Ryuzō, "Chin shang-ching ch'eng fu-ssu k'ao" [Buddhist temples in Shang-ching of the Chin dynasty], *Yen-ching Journal of Chinese Studies*, no. 34 (1948), pp. 107-32.
31. *TCKC*, *ch.* 2, p. 7a; *CS*, *ch.* 28, p. 2a; *ch.* 29, p. 10b; *ch.* 2, p. 11b.
32. Torii, "Chin shang-ching," pp. 142-43. Chung Pang chih, "Hsüan-ho i-ssu feng-shih hsing-ch'eng-lu," *BIHP*, pp. 277-78.
33. *CS*, *ch.* 75, p. 2a; *ch.* 30, p. 1a; *ch.* 3, pp. 6a-b.
34. *HCSL*, pp. 428-504.
35. For A-ku-ta's attack on Yen-ching and its surrender, see *SCPM*, *ch.* 12, p. 4a; *HNYL*, *ch.* 1, p. 6b; *CS*, *ch.* 75, p. 8b and *ch.* 78, p. 1b. In the spring of 1123 the Bureau of Military Affairs already existed. See *CS*, *ch.* 2, p. 21b. Cf. also *KCS*, pp. 154-81. He has a thorough study and evaluation of the career of Nien-han (Tsung-han), the most powerful general in early Chin.
36. Chang Chüeh killed Tso Chi-kung in 1123. Liu was the head of the Bureau of Military Affairs in 1123-1128. According to *CS*, *ch.* 3, p. 3b, in 1124 he already served as *chih shu-mi-yüan shih*. Cf. *KCS*, p. 178, n. 15. The Bureau of Military Affairs was in P'ing Prefecture in 1123-24. See *CS*, *ch.* 78, p. 8b; *SCPM* *ch.* 24, p. 2a, recorded that before Wo-li-pu took Yen-ching in 1124, Liu stayed in P'ing Prefecture.

Notes: Chapter 3   139

37. *CS*, *ch*. 3, p. 6b. At the time the grand marshal was Kao, the heir apparent. *CS*, *ch*. 44, p. 12a, states that the grand marshal was always *an-pan po-chi-lieh* and stayed in the central government. After Kao's death, however, Nien-han became grand marshal in 1135, and Wu-chu was grand marshal in 1139-48.

38. For the power of Nien-han and Wo-li-pu, see below. Wo-li-pu later became *Nan-ching lu tu-t'ung* or general-in-chief in the Nan-ching route. Liu Yen-tsung was *Han-chün tu-t'ung* or general-in-chief of Chinese armies, under the command of Wo-li-pu. See *CS*, *ch*. 78, pp. 2a and 8b; *ch*. 74, p. 12a.

39. *CS*, *ch*. 78, pp. 1b and 8b; *ch*. 3, p. 10b; *ch*. 127, p. 3b.

40. Ibid., *ch*. 78, pp. 8a-b, states that at the court there were Jurchen officials, using Jurchen titles, and the Chinese chamberlains only administered North China. See also ibid., *ch*. 3, p. 13b.

41. Although *SCPM*, *ch*. 45, p. 9a, says that Nien-han had his own Bureau of Military Affairs, it seems that after Wo-li-pu and Liu Yen-tsung's death their bureau was moved to Shansi in 1128. Tan gave Nien-han a position in the central government in 1135, and moved the bureau to Yen-ching again. Toyama Gunji considers that it still existed in Yen-ching during 1128-35, though its power was reduced due to the increase of power of Nien-han's bureau. See *KCS*, pp. 164-65. Mikami Tsugio thinks that in 1128 the two bureaus merged into one. See *KSKK* (2), pp. 462-63. I tend to consider that probably there was no bureau under Nien-han at first, because one cannot find in *CS* any reference to its existence in Shansi. Nien-han, of course, had a local government in Shansi similar to the Bureau of Military Affairs in the Yen area.

42. *CS*, *ch*. 44, pp. 1a-b.

43. Ch'en Kung-fu, a contemporary high-ranking Southern Sung official, said that the intention of the Jurchen to prop up the Liu Yü regime was not only to make the Chinese fight among themselves, but also to set up a buffer state between the Jurchen and the Southern Sung Chinese. See *HNYL*, *ch*. 108, p. 1b. The famous Southern Sung general Yüeh Fei also said that the Jurchen could rest and watch the Chinese fighting among themselves. See *SS*, *ch*. 365, p. 13a. Wan-yen P'u-lu-hu said that Jurchen policy was for self-defense and for having the people and the soldiers take some rest. See *SS*, *ch*. 475, p. 12b. Ch'in K'uei, another Sung high-ranking official, considered that those Jurchen who favored the Liu Yü regime wanted to keep a firm hold on the land north of the Yellow River. See *HNYL*, *ch*. 87, pp. 22a-b.

44. *Tiao-fa lu* [Records of consoling the people and punishing the rebellious] *SPTK* (3rd series ed.), *ch.* 2, p. 6a.

45. *SCPM, ch.* 115, p. 11a; *ch.* 132, p. 5a. Cf. also *KCS,* pp. 170-71.

46. *SCPM, ch.* 141, pp. 4a-5a; *HNYL, ch.* 32, pp. 9b-10b; *ch.* 35, pp. 8b-9b. The Jurchen gave Shansi to Liu in 1131; see *CS, ch.* 3, p. 15b.

47. *CS, ch.* 3, pp. 14a-b. *HNYL, ch.* 53, p. 9b, states that the grand marshal made all the important decisions for Liu Yü, and that Jurchen troops stayed along the Yellow River and the Huai River, and also in Shensi and Shantung.

48. Cf. *KCS,* pp. 232-309. Also T'ao Chin-sheng, *Pien-chiang-shih yen-chiu-chi,* pp. 33-49.

49. Cf. *KSKK* (2), pp. 471-73, and pp. 474-75 for Mikami's evaluation.

50. *CS, ch.* 3, p. 2a, 3b. Hsi-yin (*CS, ch.* 73, p. 14b); Shih-ku-nai, P'o-lu-ho (*CS, ch.* 3, p. 2a) and Ying-chu-k'o (*CS, ch.* 3, p. 10b) also had these privileges.

51. *CS, ch.* 74, pp. 3b-4a, 10b, 12a; *SCPM, ch.* 45, p. 9a; *HNYL, ch.* 8, pp. 14b-15a, says that Nien-han and Hsi-yin decided to bring the two Sung emperors to Manchuria.

52. See Wolfram Eberhard's theory of superstratification in his *Conquerors and Rulers: Social Forces in Medieval China,* pp. 27-28. The feudal forces were not strong enough to achieve a real superstratification. For various theories of the formation of the state, see Lawrence Krader, *Formation of the State,* especially pp. 44-45, for the conquest theory. See also Franz Oppenheimer, *The State* (New York: B. W. Huebsch, 1922), pp. 42-43.

Chapter 4

1. For the debate see *CS, ch.* 77, "Biography of Ta-lan."

2. In the early years the highest military authority rested on the generals such as Nien-han and Wo-li-pu. Later the Bureau of Military Affairs replaced the offices of these generals. Cf. *CS, ch.* 44.

3. One of Tan's teachers was Han Chi-hsien. See *SCPM, ch.* 166, p. 5a; also *TCKC, ch.* 12, p. 5a. *SMCW, ch.* 1, p. 2b, states: "After the death of Sheng-kuo 繩果 (Jurchen name of Tsung-chün 宗峻, Tan's father), *gurun* 固碖 (Wo-pen) took his wife; therefore the present king (Tan) grew up in *gurun*'s home." *SCPM, ch.* 166, p. 3a, also records that Wo-pen was Tan's uncle, who took Tan's mother, and treated Tan as his own son. For Tan's character, see *TCKC, ch.* 12, pp. 3b-4a; *SCPM, ch.* 166, p. 5a; *CS, ch.* 4,

p. 7a; *ch*. 105, pp. 4b-5a.

4. See Hsi-yin's tablet in Hsü Ping-ch'ang, "Chiao Chin Wan-yen Hsi-yin sheng-tao-pei shu-hou," p. 14. Hung Hao's poems written for Hsi-yin's sons whose Chinese names were Yen-ch'ing 彥清 and Yen-shen 彥深 are in *P'o-yang chi*, *ch*. 1, pp. 6a-b, 8a, 10b, 12b, 13b, 14a, and 14b-15a.

5. Hung Hao, *P'o-yang chi*, *ch*. 1, p. 11a; *ch*. 4, p. 10a.

6. *CS*, *ch*. 70, pp. 3a-5a. Two other associates of Wo-pen were also important: Wan-yen Hsü and Mou-liang-hu, both of whom loved Chinese books and helped Wo-pen organize the new government. See *CS*, *ch*. 66, pp. 1a-b, 3a; *ch*. 73, p. 9b.

7. *SCPM*, *ch*. 166, p. 4a. See also *KCS*, pp. 172-74. *CS*, *ch*. 73, p. 15a; *ch*. 76, pp. 1b-2a; *ch*. 69, p. 1b; *ch*. 77, p. 14a. See *SCPM*, *ch*. 166, pp. 8a-9a for the power struggle and the official reasons for the execution of P'u-lu-hu and O-lu-kuan.

8. *CS*, *ch*. 77, pp. 14a-b. See also *SCPM*, *ch*. 197, pp. 6a-9a and *CS*, *ch*. 73, p. 15a. Hsi-yin's death was probably the result of his rivalry with Wu-chu. See Hsi-yin's tomb tablet in Hsü Ping-ch'ang, "Chiao Chin Wan-yen Hsi-yin sheng-tao-pei shu-hou," pp. 14 and 17. See also *SCPM*, *ch*. 197, p. 2a.

9. For government organization, see *KSKK* (2), pp. 163-343, 495-570.

10. Teng Ssu-yü, *Chung-kuo k'ao-shih chih-tu shih* [A history of Chinese examination system], pp. 211-13. See also chap. 5, below. See also *TCKC*, *ch*. 35, pp. 5a-6a; *CS*, *ch*. 51, p. 6a.

11. *CS*, *ch*. 4, pp. 2a, 3a, 4a. In the same year he forbade princes to enter palaces with swords.

12. Ibid., pp. 2b, 4a-b, 7a; *ch*. 39, p. 1b; *ch*. 30, p. 1a; *ch*. 12, p. 1a; *ch*. 28, p. 1a.

13. For political and diplomatic developments under Tan see *KCS*, pp. 310-420.

14. *CS*, *ch*. 4, p. 7a; *ch*. 89, pp. 6b-7a, record the case of T'ien Chüeh.

15. Ibid., *ch*. 63, p. 10b; *TCKC*, *ch*. 13.

16. *SCPM*, *ch*. 231, p. 5b.

17. *KCC*, *ch*. 1, p. 1a.

18. Ibid.; *SCPM*, *ch*. 242, p. 11a, attributes this poem to his Han-lin scholar Ts'ai Kuei. For his other poems see *SCPM*, *ch*. 231, pp. 5a-b; Yüeh K'o, *T'ing-shih* (*SPTK hsü-pien* ed.), *ch*. 8, pp. 10a-12a. There is one *tz'u* cited in *Shui-hu chuan* [All Men are Brothers], *ch*. 11.

19. *CS*, *ch*. 129, pp. 7a, 13a.

20. Ibid., *ch*. 89, p. 17a.

21. Ibid., *ch*. 5, p. 6a.

22. *HNYL*, *ch*. 162, p. 24a; *CS*, *ch*. 83, p. 5a; *ch*. 73, p. 12a.
23. Fan Ch'eng-ta, *Shih-hu chü-shih shih-chi* (*SPTK* ed.), *ch*. 12, p. 11a; Chou Lin-chih, *Hai-ling chi*, appendix, p. 2a; *CS*, *ch*. 24, pp. 2a-b, *ch*. 5, p. 16a.
24. *CS*, *ch*. 28, p. 2b; *ch*. 5, pp. 6a, 15b; *ch*. 125, p. 4a.
25. Ibid., *ch*. 51, p. 2b. *HNYL*, *ch*. 164, p. 5b, records the revision of the examination system and the introduction of the palace examination in 1153. *CS*, *ch*. 5, p. 9a.
26. *CWT*, *ch*. 34, pp. 2-4: "Wei-hsien chien miao-hsüeh pei" [Inscribed tablet of the establishment of local temple school in the Wei county]. See *TCKC*, *ch*. 13, p. 1b; *HNYL*, *ch*. 161, p. 13a.
27. *CS*, *ch*. 5, pp. 14a-b; *ch*. 55, pp. 1b-2a.
28. Cf. *KSKK* (2), pp. 243-47, 344-48.
29. Jing-shen Tao, "The Influence of Jurchen Rule on Chinese Political Institutions," *The Journal of Asian Studies* 30, no. 1 (1970): 127.
30. Ibid., It is generally believed that the *t'ing-chang* was first practiced in the Yüan period. See F.W. Mote, "The Growth of Chinese Despotism," *Oriens Extremus* 8, no. 1 (1961): 27-28. For this practice in the Ming period see Meng Shen, *Ming-tai shih* [History of the Ming dynasty] (Taipei: Chung-hua ts'ung-shu wei-yüan-hui, 1957), pp. 81-82; Charles O. Hucker, *The Traditional Chinese State in Ming Times (1368-1644)* (Tucson: The University of Arizona Press, 1961), p. 48; and his *The Censorial System of Ming China*, p. 318. Also Jing-shen Tao, "Influence of Jurchen Rule," p. 127 and Chuang Lien, "Ming-tai t'ing-chang chih-tu so-yüan" [The origin of the institution of flogging in the Ming dynasty]. In his *Ming Ch'ing shih-shih ts'ung-t'an* [Miscellaneous notes to the history of the Ming-Ch'ing periods] (Taipei: Hsüeh-sheng shu-chu, 1972), pp. 1-16.
31. Tao, "Influence of Jurchen Rule," pp. 127-28.
32. For details see *KSKK* (1), pp. 444-50.
33. *CS*, *ch*. 44, pp. 3a, 12b-13a; *ch*. 132, p. 5a; *ch*. 83, p. 14a. See also *HNYL*, *ch*. 164, p. 5a.
34. Wu-lu later maintained that Liang's purpose was to ward off his clansmen around the old capital and to prevent them from rising against him. See *CS*, *ch*. 8, pp. 6b-7a.
35. *CS*, *ch*. 48, pp. 1a-b.
36. Ibid., *ch*. 74, p. 13a.
37. *HNYL*, *ch*. 69, p. 20a; *TCKC*, *ch*. 8, p. 2a. In 1193 there were 176,000 households under *meng-an* and *mou-k'e* in Manchuria, as compared with the total of 615,624 *meng-an* and *mou-k'e* households in Manchuria and North China recorded

in 1182. See *CS*, *ch*. 50, pp. 8b-9a; *ch*. 46, p. 8a; *ch*. 47, p. 22a.

38. *TCKC*, *ch*. 36, p. 3a. There is no evidence recorded in the *CS* indicating the ban on intermarriage between the Jurchen and the Chinese. But the ban was lifted in 1191. See chap. 8, pp. 95-98, below.

39. *CS*, *ch*. 66, p. 4a; *ch*. 83, p. 14a; *ch*. 47, p. 1b.

40. Ibid., *ch*. 57, pp. 21a-b. See also KSKK (1), pp. 208-15.

41. This is according to *CS*, *ch*. 80, p. 12a. *CS*, *ch*. 44, p. 3a, records it in 1145. See also KSKK (1), pp. 143-46.

42. *CS*, *ch*. 44, p. 3a; *ch*. 5, p. 7b. Hung Hao, *P'o-yang chi*, *ch*. 4, p. 11a. Cf. also KSKK (1), pp. 137-41.

43. KSKK (1), pp. 143-51, 157-61.

44. *CS*, *ch*. 70, p. 12b; *ch*. 86, pp. 5b, 6b, 8b; *ch*. 67, pp. 7a-8b.

45. KSKK (2), pp. 225-35.

46. *CS*, *ch*. 47, pp. 1a, 21a; KSKK (1), pp. 270-74.

47. See chap. 6, pp. 73-75, below.

48. *CS*, *ch*. 46, p. 2a. For modern studies of taxation and population, cf. KSKK (1), pp. 253-90; Ping-ti Ho, "An Estimate of the Total Population of Sung-Chin China," in *Etudes Song in memoriam Etienne Balazs*, ed. Françoise Aubin, series 1, no. 1, pp. 3-53.

49. *CS*, *ch*. 47, pp. 13b-14a. Corn or wheat stalks were collected by the government for the purpose of feeding horses in winter.

50. Ibid., p. 21a; *ch*. 50, p. 4b. Ku Tsu-yü in *Tu-shih fang-yü chi-yao* [Important records of historical geography], *ch*. 12, p. 533, noted that in the Ch'ing-yüan County there was a so-called Chi-liang ch'eng or "food storage town," where in the Chin dynasty the Jurchen stored food.

51. *CS*, *ch*. 70, p. 10a; *ch*. 77, p. 6a. Other examples are *ch*. 72, pp. 9a and 15a; *ch*. 80, pp. 1b, 9b; HNYL, *ch*. 40, p. 2a; *TCKC*, *ch*. 6, pp. 7b-8a. See *CS*, *ch*. 46, p. 12a.

52. *CS*, *ch*. 97, "Land system" (*t'ien-chih*). For slavery in the Chin, cf. **Kuan Yen-hsiang**, "Chin-tai ti nu-li chih-tu" [Slavery in the Chin dynasty], *Hsien-tai shih-hsüeh* 3, no. 2 (1937): 1-11; Chang Po-ch'üan, "Chin-tai nu-li wen-t'i ti yen-chiu" [A study of the problem of slavery in the Chin dynasty], in *Sung-Liao-Chin she-hui ching-chi shih lun-chi* [Collected essays on Sung, Liao, and Chin social and economic history], ed. Chou K'ang-hsieh, 2: 226-32.

53. *CS*, *ch*. 46, p. 9b. Ping-ti Ho has estimated the population at between 40 million and 50 million; see "An Estimate of the Total Population of Sung-Chin China."

54. For the relationship between conquest wars and so-

cial structure, cf. Stanislav Andreski, *Military Organization and Society*, pp. 31-33. For political struggles and social unrest, see T'ao Chin-sheng, "Chin-tai ti cheng-chih ch'ung-t'u" [Political conflicts in the Chin], *BIHP*, 43, no. 1 (1971): 135-61.

Chapter 5

1. For Ch'i-tan local government and the officials of the southern region, see *HCSL*, pp. 445-50.
2. The organization of the Chin political system has been carefully examined by Mikami Tsugio; see *KSKK* (2). The characteristics of the Chin bureaucracy are based upon T'ao Chin-sheng, "Chin-tai ti cheng-chih chieh-kou" [The political structure of the Chin], *BIHP* 41, no. 4 (1969): 578-82.
3. T'ao, "Chin-tai ti cheng-chih chieh-kou," p. 580.
4. For the Yüan, cf. Ch'i-ch'ing Hsiao, "The Military Establishment of the Yüan Dynasty" (Ph.D. diss., Harvard University, 1969), pp. xxxii-xliv.
5. For details see T'ao, "Chin-tai . . . chieh-kou, pp. 583-85.
6. Adapted from ibid., p. 585, table 3.
7. See pp. 61-64.
8. T'ao, "Chin-tai . . . chieh-kou, pp. 580-82.
9. Political recruitment refers to the function of filling the roles in political systems. There are two general methods in the political recruitment: one is based upon universalistic or general criteria, the other is based upon particularistic criteria. The former includes the selection of officials by lot, by election, or by performance, such as an examination. The latter is the recruitment from a particular tribe or ethnic group. Although most traditional and primitive political systems tend to recruit into political roles on the basis of particularistic and ascriptive criteria, it is argued that no political system recruits purely on the basis of such criteria. See Gabriel A. Almond and G. Bingham Powell, Jr., *Comparative Politics: A Developmental Approach*, pp. 47-48. Karl A. Wittfogel has pointed out that the recruitment and maintenance of the Ch'i-tan government were based upon particularistic criteria, and the Ch'i-tan especially emphasized the *yin* privilege (or protection) to ensure the control of offices by Ch'i-tan nobility. See his "Public Office in the Liao Dynasty and the Chinese Examination System," *Harvard Journal of Asiatic Studies* 10 (1947): 13-40. Yet the Ch'i-tan also devised an examination system, which, though limited in its scope, channeled a number of Chinese into the political system. See *HCSL*, pp. 454-56.

Notes: Chapter 5   145

10. T'ao Chin-sheng, "Chin-tai ti cheng-chih ch'ung-t'u," pp. 144-45.
11. E.g., Liu Yen-tsung. See *HNYL, ch.* 14: entry for 1128, *Hsin-hai* of 3rd month, quoting *Yen-yün lu* [Records of the Yen and Yün].
12. *CS, ch.* 51, p. 6a; *HNYL, ch.* 28, p. 7b.
13. *CS, ch.* 51, p. 6a; *SMCW, ch.* 129, p. 12a.
14. *CS, ch.* 51, p. 7b; *ch.* 52, p. 4a. The practice invoked political conflicts between the northerners and the southerners. See T'ao, "Chin-tai . . . ch'ung-t'u," pp. 145-47.
15. *CS, ch.* 51, pp. 10a-b.
16. Ibid.
17. Adapted from Tao, "Chin-tai . . . chieh-kou," p. 586. The category "Miscellaneous" includes sponsorship, transfer from the clerical service, protection, and other methods. Those whose information is unavailable are also included.
18. Ibid., p. 586.
19. For details see Jing-shen Tao, "The Jurchen *Chin-shih* Degree in the Chin Dynasty," *Proceedings of the Third East Asian Altaistic Conference, August 17-24, 1969* (Taipei, 1970), pp. 221-33.
20. See Jing-shen Tao, "The Influence of Jurchen Rule on Chinese Political Institutions," p. 129, n. 44.
21. See T'ao, "Chin-tai . . . ch'ung-t'u," for a discussion of political conflicts.
22. The names Chang A-hai 張阿海 and Wang Nu-shen 王奴申 appeared on the list of Jurchen *chin-shih* who passed the examination in 1224. But Chang might be a Po-hai and Wang Nu-shen might be Wan-yen Nu-shen. However, for a Jurchenized Chinese to have a name such as Nu-shen is very likely. See Wang Tsing-ju, "Yen-t'ai Nüchen-wen chin-shih t'i-ming-pei ch'u-shih" [A preliminary study of the Yen-t'ai stone tablet in Jurchen script], *Shih-hsüeh chi-k'an*, no. 3 (1937), pp. 49-68.
23. E. A. Kracke, Jr., *Civil Service in Early Sung China, 960-1067,* p. 59.
24. The number of *chin-shih* recruited between 1123 and 1136 was unclear. It was recorded, however, that in 1126 the government conferred 73 degrees and 810 persons received the degree in 1128. See *HNYL, ch.* 14, p. 11a, note. Fang Chuang-yu estimated the total of *chin-shih* conferred during the entire Chin period at more than 10,000. See his "Liao-Chin-Yüan k'o-chu nien-piao" [Tables on Liao, Chin, and Yüan examinations], *Shuo-wen Yüeh-k'an* 3, no. 12 (1944): 23.
25. The totals of the Ming and Ch'ing periods are respectively 24,594 and 26,747; and the averages per annum for

the Ming and Ch'ing are 89.1 and 100.2, respectively. See Ping-ti Ho, *The Ladder of Success in Imperial China: Aspects of Social Mobility, 1368-1911*, p. 189, table 22. Using the materials provided in Araki Toshikazu, *Sō-dai kakyo seidō kenkyū* [The civil service examination of the Sung dynasty], pp. 450-61, I have worked out the averages per examination in the Northern and Southern Sung at 457.8 and 446.4, respectively; and the averages per annum at 193.6 and 148.8, respectively. The Southern Sung per annum average is about the same as that of the Chin.

26. *CS*, *ch*. 55: introductory paragraph. The numbers of civil and military officials in the early Sung are given in Kracke, *Civil Service*, p. 55. In 1046 the total of officials was only slightly over 12,700.

27. Sung Lien et al., *Yüan-shih*, *ch*. 163, pp. 10a-b. Cf. also Su T'ien-chüeh, *Kuo-ch'ao wen-lei* [Anthology of Yüan literature], *ch*. 10, "Biography of Chang Te-hui." Qubilai Qan asked Chang Te-hui whether it was true that the collapse of the Liao was caused by the people's indulgence in Buddhism, while the employment of Chinese literati destroyed the Chin. Chang replied that during the Chin period the Chinese did not occupy important positions, so that they should not bear the responsibility for the fall of the dynasty. Cf. Yao Ts'ung-wu, "Chang Te-hui *Ling-pei chi-hsing tsu-pen chiao-chu*" [The complete text of Chang Te-hui's *Record of a journey beyond the northern ranges*, edited with notes], *Bulletin of the College of Arts, National Taiwan University* 11 (1962): 1-38.

28. *CS*, *ch*. 73, p. 17b; *ch*. 8, p. 6b. Discussing the appointment of Jurchen *chin-shih* as officials in the Presidential Council, Shih-tsung praised the Confucianists (*ju*) and criticized the bureaucrats (*li*).

29. *CS*, *ch*. 7, p. 2a: " 諸府尸多闕員 當選進士 "; also *ch*. 86, p. 3b. According to *CS*, *ch*. 86, p. 3b. According to *CS*, *ch*. 8, p. 6b, both Chinese and Jurchen *chin-shih* should be appointed as *ling-shih*.

30. Ibid., *ch*. 73, pp. 17a-b.

31. Note to a poem entitled "T'i T'ai-ho ming-ch'en-pei hou," *Ch'iu-chien hsien-sheng ta-ch'üan wen-chi* (*SPTK*), *ch*. 32, p. 11a.

32. *ISC*, *ch*. 27, p. 12b; also quoted in Karl A. Wittfogel, "Public Office in the Liao Dynasty and the Chinese Examination System," p. 36.

33. "Chang Wen-chen-kung shen-tao-pei" 張文貞公神道碑 [Epitaph of Chang Wen-chen-kung], in *ISC*, *ch*. 16, p. 1b.

34. T'ao Chin-sheng, "Chin-tai . . . chieh-kou," p. 582.

Notes: Chapter 5   147

35. *CS, ch.* 52, pp. 2b-4a. For the importance of the *yin* privilege in the Liao, see Wittfogel, "Public Office."
36. Wittfogel, "Public Office," p. 35.
37. The information about these men's entrance is usually "as a son of the imperial clansman" (*i-tsung-shih tzu*) or "as a close relative of the imperial family" (*i huang-chia chin-ch'in*), without specifying whether it was protection or not. Examples are Kao (膏 , *CS, ch.* 66, p. 11b); I (奕 , ibid., p. 12b); Tsung-heng (宗享 , *CS, ch.* 70, p. 7a); Ch'eng-yü (承裕 , *CS, ch.* 93, p. 9a), etc. See also *CS, ch.* 88, p. 17b.
38. *CS, ch.* 6, p. 24b.
39. E.g., Tsung-hsien 宗賢 , whose biography is in ibid., *ch.* 70.
40. Ibid., *ch.* 56; concerning the role of the *chin-shih chü*, see *KCC, ch.* 7, p. 13a.
41. For the *mang-an* and *mou-k'e*, see chap. 4, pp. 48-49, above.
42. *CS, ch.* 57, pp. 11a-b; *ch.* 52, pp. 9a-b.
43. *KSKK* (1), pp. 225-35.
44. *CS, ch.* 69, pp. 2a-b; *ch.* 74, pp. 17b-18a.
45. For hereditary selection and its relation to profession see Yao Ts'ung-wu, "Shuo Liao-ch'ao Ch'i-tan-jen ti shih-hsüan chih-tu" [On the institution of hereditary selection of the Ch'i-tan of the Liao dynasty], in *Tung-pei-shih lun-ts'ung*, 1: 255-338.
46. Adapted from T'ao, "Chin-tai . . .chieh-kou," p. 588.
47. *CS, ch.* 52: introductory paragraph. It describes the differences between civil service officials (*wen-tzu kuan* 文資官) and military officers (*san kuan* 散官 or *yu-chih* 右職).
48. T'ao, "Chin-tai . . . chieh-kou," pp. 580-81.
49. *CS, ch.* 55, pp. 9a-10a. For **Northern** Sung practices see Kracke, *Civil Service*, pp. 84-99.
50. *CS, ch.* 52, p. 3a. The rules were not fixed throughout the dynasty. In 1175, for example, there was the ruling that no **terms were** counted for the prime ministers and the commissioners of military affairs, and for officials of the third grade, 50 months constituted a term. See *CS, ch.* 54, pp. 4b-5a.
51. *CS, ch.* 52, p. 4a. Before 1162 the *chin-shih* could be appointed as military aide in the local administration.
52. *CS, ch.* 54, pp. 13a-b. This information is taken from the first of the ten points about recruitment that Emperor Chang-tsung ordered the Presidential Council to reconsider in 1189.

53. *CS, ch.* 53, pp. 9b-10a. But the palace chief could only obtain the seventh grade according to the rules of 1162.

54. Even Shih-tsung, who was very much concerned with the benefits of his tribesmen, once complained that it was a ridiculous sequence. The answer from an official was that this was done according to tradition, so that it should not be abolished. See *CS, ch.* 88, p. 17b.

55. In the cases of palace chiefs and imperial guards, the interval was between their first appointments and their appointments as ministers; in the cases of Jurchen and Chinese *chin-shih*, the years between their receiving the degree and their appointments as ministers are counted. The comparison is based upon the careers of 16 imperial guards and palace chiefs, 14 Jurchen *chih-shih* and 23 Chinese *chin-shih*, on whom the data are available. For the Jurchen imperial guards and palace chiefs, the cases are found in the period approximately from the 1140s to the 1220s; for Jurchen *chin-shih*, from the 1170s to the 1230s, and for the Chinese *chin-shih*, from the 1120s to the 1230s.

56. *CS, ch.* 104, "Biography of Ao-t'un Chung-hsiao"; *ch.* 111, p. 16a. There are three *feng-yü* in the survey. See also *ch.* 54, pp. 6a-7b.

57. E.g., six years for P'u-san Shih-kung (biography in *CS, ch.* 132), nine years for Wan-yen Ho-ta (biography in *CS, ch.* 112), and ten years for Tsung-hsien (biography in *CS, ch.* 70).

58. Only Chang Ju-pi (biography in *CS, ch.* 83) advanced to the ranks of ministers within 19 years, but he was actually a sinicized Po-hai.

59. This is obvious from the tables in *KSKK* (2), pp. 319, 324-25, 427, 428-30, 451-52. Cf. Robert M. Marsh's findings on differences in official advancement between the Manchus and Chinese in *The Mandarins: The Circulation of Elites in China, 1600-1900*, chapter 6.

60. Wittfogel, "Public Office," pp. 32-33, 36.

61. Max Weber's ascription of the roots of the examination system to the conflicts between the feudal order and the literati is relevant here. See H. H. Gerth and C. Wright Mills, trans. and eds., *From Max Weber: Essays in Sociology*, pp. 416-26.

62. See Yanai Watari, "Gen-chō keshiku kō" [On the kesig in the Yüan dynasty], in *Mōkoshi kenkyū*, pp. 211-62.

63. The Ch'i-tan *chin-shih* recruited per annum was less than 20. See Wittfogel, "Public Office," p. 21. According to the numbers given in Fang Chuang-yu, "Liao-Chin-Yüan k'o-chü nien-piao," the Yüan average per annum seems to have been a little higher than that of the Liao.

Chapter 6

1. For the nativistic movement or revitalization movement, see Ralph Linton, "Nativistic Movements," *American Anthropologist* 45 (1943): 230-40; Anthony F. C. Wallace, "Revitalization Movements: Some Theoretical Considerations for Their Comparative Study," *American Anthropologist* 58 (1956): 264-81.
2. For the treaties between the Sung and the Chin, see Herbert Franke, "Treaties between Sung and Chin," in *Etudes Song*, ed. Aubin, pp. 55-84.
3. *CS*, *ch*. 129, "Biography of Li T'ung."
4. The exact number of troops is unclear. I have estimated it at 500,000; see T'ao Chin-sheng, *Chin Hai-ling-ti fa Sung yü Ts'ai-shih chan-i ti k'ao-shih*, pp. 142-50. Haraguchi Hitoshi in "Kinkoku seiryū matsu seinan gun no dōin sosu ni tsuite" [On the number of Chin troops mobilized to invade the south in the late Cheng-lung period], *Tōyō Shigaku* 21 (1959): 25, estimates the number at 600,000.
5. *CS*, *ch*. 6, pp. 15a-b; *SS*, *ch*. 33, pp. 16a-18a; *ch*. 361, pp. 13a-16a. Liu Shih-chü, *Hsü Sung pien-nien tzu-chih t'ung-chien* [A Supplement to the comprehensive mirror for aid in government of the Sung dynasty], *ch*. 8.
6. Shih-tsung's Jurchen name and his posthumous title are used, for his two Chinese names, Pao 褎 and Yung 雍, would cause a confusion if used.
7. *CS*, *ch*. 64, pp. 2a-b. Toyama Gunji has proved that she was a native of Po-hai, not a Chinese. See *KCS*, pp. 453-59.
8. *CS*, *ch*. 64, pp. 2a-3a; *ch*. 86, pp. 1a-3a.
9. Ibid., *ch*. 64, pp. 3a-4b. Wu-lu's hatred of Liang is seen in his coronation proclamation. The complete text is in *HNYL*, *ch*. 193, pp. 7a-8a and *SCPM*, *ch*. 233, pp. 2b-6b.
10. *CS*, *ch*. 44, pp. 12b-13a; *ch*. 72, p. 6a. See also *KCS*, pp. 451-53 and *CS*, *ch*. 86, p. 5b.
11. Examples are Shuang, K'o-hsi (*CS*, *ch*. 69, pp. 2a-b); Ching (*ch*. 74, pp. 15b-16a); and Yung-yüan (*ch*. 76, pp. 15b-16a).
12. *CS*, *ch*. 46, p. 12a.
13. Ibid., *ch*. 7, pp. 4a-b; *ch*. 89, p. 17a.
14. Ibid., *ch*. 7, p. 5b.
15. Ibid., *ch*. 88, "Biography of T'ang-kua An-li"; *ch*. 8, p. 5b.
16. Ibid.
17. Ibid., *ch*. 7, pp. 8b-9a.
18. Ibid., *ch*. 6, p. 14b; *ch*. 76, pp. 16a-b.
19. *KCC*, *ch*. 8, p. 3b; *ISC*, *ch*. 20, pp. 5b-6a; *CS*, *ch*. 104, p. 10a; *ch*. 49, pp. 6b, 7a, 7b, 9a, 12b.

20. *CS*, *ch*. 70, p. 5a.
21. Ibid., *ch*. 47, pp. 2a, 3a.
22. Ibid., p. 4a; *ch*. 83, p. 4b.
23. Ibid., *ch*. 47, pp. 4a-b, 6a; *ch*. 7, p. 19b.
24. Ibid., *ch*. 47, p. 2b.
25. *Kuan-min* 官民 ; see *CS*, *ch*. 47, p. 3b.
26. Ibid., pp. 4a, 5a-b, 6a-b; *ch*. 90, pp. 11a-b.
27. Ibid., *ch*. 47, pp. 3b, 4b, 6b, 22a; *ch*. 46, p. 8a.
28. Cf. *KSKK* (3), pp. 196-232.
29. *CS*, *ch*. 88, pp. 13a, 14a; *ch*. 47, p. 3b.
30. Ibid., *ch*. 47, p. 4b; *ch*. 88, pp. 4a, 6a, 16a-b; *ch*. 92, p. 5a; *ch*. 91, pp. 3b-4a; *ch*. 7, pp. 2a, 13b; *ch*. 95, pp. 5b-6a. Such relief works did not concern the Chinese. Cf. also *KSKK* (3), pp. 196-232.
31. *CS*, *ch*. 88, p. 16a; *ch*. 6, p. 14b; *ch*. 8, pp. 16a-b.
32. For Ch'i-tan rebellions, see *KCS*, pp. 90-105.
33. See *CS*, *ch*. 6-8. From 1178 to 1188 Shih-tsung always went to the Spring River in the first month of a year and returned in the second month. He went to Chin-lien ch'-uan in 1172, 1174, 1175, 1176, 1180, 1182 and 1187. Almost every year he went hunting in autumn or winter, or in both seasons, in the suburbs of Yen-ching. The "Spring River" is a general term and does not denote a specific river.
34. Ibid., *ch*. 6, pp. 11a, 20b; *ch*. 131, p. 6b.
35. Ibid., *ch*. 73, p. 13b; *ch*. 4, p. 3b.
36. Ibid., *ch*. 70, p. 3a: Tsung-hsien attended the Jurchen language school before 1125.
37. Ibid., *ch*. 51, pp. 5a, 11b, 12a; *ch*. 99, p. 1a.
38. Ibid., *ch*. 7, pp. 4b-5a.
39. Ibid., pp. 6a-b; *ch*. 73, pp. 4b-5a; *ch*. 9, p. 1b; *ch*. 8, p. 12a.
40. Ibid., p. 6a. A Bureau for Translation of Classics was set up in 1164.
41. Ibid., *ch*. 99, p. 1a; For the importance of these works, see Herbert Franke, "Chinese Historiography under Mongol Rule: The Role of History in Acculturation," *Mongolia Studies* 1 (1974): 21-22. See also *CS*, *ch*. 8, pp.5b, 6a; *ch*. 51, pp. 13a-b.
42. *CS*, *ch*. 7, p. 5b; *ch*. 8, p. 20b.
43. Ibid., *ch*. 70, p. 13b. It was early in 1162 that Shih-tsung ordered the grouping of the Jurchen.
44. *CS*, *ch*. 83, pp. 11a-b; *ch*. 7, p. 19b; *ch*. 47, pp. 5b-6b; *ch*. 88, p. 3a; also *KSKK* (3), pp. 217-28 for Shih-tsung's land reform.
45. *KSKK* (2), pp. 432-33.
46. Chang Wei and others, *Ta-Chin chi-li* [Compendium of ceremonies of the Great Chin], *ch*. 36, "Sacrificial ceremony at the Confucian temple"; *CS*, *ch*. 35, "The Confucian temple"; K'ung Yüan-ts'o,*K'ung-shih tsu-t'ing kuan-chi* [Ex-

Notes: Chapter 6   151

tensive records of the ancestral hall of the K'ung family],
ch. 2, p. 19a.
    47. *CS*, *ch*. 28, *chiao* ("State sacrifices").
    48. Chang Wei et al., *Ta-Chin chi-li*, *ch*. 35, "The
investiture ceremony at Ch'ang-pai Mountain"; *CS*, *ch*. 35,
"Ch'ang-pai Mountain."
    49. *CS*, *ch*. 35, "Worship of the Heaven."
    50. *CS*, *ch*. 8, p. 6a. The Jurchen song composed by
Shih-tsung is in *ch*. 39, pp. 6b-7a. See also ch. 39, p. 1a.
    51. *CS*, *ch*. 8, p. 5b.
    52. *CS*, *ch*. 7, p. 6a; Shih-tsung told the officials
they should pay attention to more practical ways to govern
the people.
    53. For the tax see Ogawa Hiroto, "Kindai no butsur-
yokusen ni tsuite" [On the property tax of Chin], *Tōyōshi
Kenkyū* 5, no. 6 (1940): 420-37; 6, no. 1 (1941): 43-60;
no. 3, 193-217.
    54. Sogabe Shizuo asserts that the tax was an equiv-
alent of the miscellaneous tax (*tsa-yao*) of the T'ang dynasty, the corvée, and the tax paid in lieu of corvée (*mien-
fu ch'ien* or *mien-i ch'ien*) in the Northern Sung, both
antecedents of the poll tax (*ting shui*) of the Yüan dynasty.
See his "Tō no zatsuyō no Kin Gen ni oyoboshita eikyo -- Kin
no butsuryokusen to Gen no teizei no zenshin" [The influence
of the miscellaneous tax of T'ang on Chin and Yüan -- The
antecedent of the property tax of Chin and the ting tax of
Yüan], *Rekishi Kyōiku* 2, no. 6 (1954): 14-19.
    55. Ogawa Hiroto, "Kindai no butsuryokusen ni tsuite,"
Tōyōshi Kenkyū 6 (1941), no. 1: 54; no. 3: 202, 208-9.
    56. *KSKK* (1), pp. 168-69; *CS*, *ch*. 88, pp. 9b-10a.
    57. *ch*. 8, p. 15b; *ch*. 89, p. 17a; *ch*. 47, p. 2a.
    58. The government began to send such agricultural
advisers in 1131. For details see *CS*, *ch*. 47, pp. 1a, 2a,
4b; also *ch*. 6, pp. 10b, 23a; *ch*. 8, p. 10b.
    59. Ibid., *ch*. 8, pp. 5b, 10b, 13a; *ch*. 6, pp. 18a-b,
21a, 23b, 27a; *ch*. 7, pp. 2a, 6a, 12b.
    60. Among the nobility only Chin, who was to become
Shih-tsung's successor, was good at Jurchen. As indicated
above, when Chin was still a young man he once talked in
Jurchen at Shih-tsung's court. That demonstrates, however,
that to speak Jurchen at the court was a rare practice.
    61. *CS*, *ch*. 51, p. 13a. The Jurchen at first may
have used Ch'i-tan as a medium in the translation process.
See *HCSL*, p. 253, note.
    62. See note 59 above; *CS*, *ch*. 88, p. 16a.
    63. Ibid., p. 24b. Chu Hsi, the great Southern Sung
Neo-Confucianist, commented on Shih-tsung's rule of benevolence: "The people of the Central Plain (*chung-yüan*) called
him Small Yao and Shun." See Huang Tsu-hung, ed., *Chu-tzu*

yü-lei ch. 133, p. 11b. For modern studies of Shih-tsung's career, see Yao Ts'ung-wu, "Chin-shih-tsung tui-yü chung-yüan han-hua yü Nü-chen chiu-su ti t'ai-tu, " *Tung-pei-shih lun-ts'ung*, 2: 118-74; *KSKK* (3), pp. 233-67.

64. The term *Chung-hsing* is found in *CWT*, *ch.* 35, p. 16; *ch.* 37, p. 2a; *ch.* 39, p. 15a; and *ch.* 39, p. 8a. Mao Hui's "Lu-chou ju-hsüeh pei" [Tablet on the Confucian school in Lu-chou],in ibid., *ch.* 39, pp. 7b-8b, is representative of contemporaneous opinions about Shih-tsung's rule according to the Chinese way of government.

65. Mao Hui, "Lu-chou ju-hsüeh pei," p. 8a; in *CWT*, *ch.* 40, pp. 15b-16a, there is a tablet on the deeds of Wu-yen Kung-jui.

66. Cf. Mao Wen, "Chin-tai hsüeh-chih chih yen-chiu" [A study of the school system in the Chin dynasty], *Kuo-hsüeh lun-ts'ung*, no. 7 (1936), pp. 26-36. In 1189, the total of students in local schools reached 5,000.

67. Cf. chap. 5 above.

Chapter 7

1. From this point of view, Wittfogel's emphasis in *HCSL* on the Jurchens' ability to maintain their culture seems too generalized. He agrees, however, that complete assimilation took place after the fall of the alien dynasty (p. 15). An excellent study of other aliens in China after their dynasty was destroyed is Henry Serruys, *The Mongols in China during the Hung-wu Period, 1368-1398.*

2. *CS*, *ch.* 9, p. 2b.

3. He executed Prince Cheng (Yün-tao) in 1193 and Prince Hao (Yün-chung) in 1195. See T'ao Chin-sheng, "Chin-tai ti cheng-chih Ch'un-t'u," p. 155.

4. *CS*, *ch.* 45, p. 10b recorded that in 1201 the government ordered the use of bigger sticks. See also *CS*, *ch.* 99, p. 7b; *ch.* 129, p. 2b.

5. Ibid., *ch.* 45, pp. 11a-12a. There is the remark that the code was "actually the T'ang code" (p. 11a). Cf. Niida Noburu, "Kindai keiho kō" [A study of the criminal law of the Chin dynasty], *Tōyōshi Kenkyū* (n.s.), 1, no. 1 (1944): 1-36; 1, no. 2 (1944): 86-125.

6. Yeh Ch'ien-chao, *Chin-lü chih yen-chiu* [A study of the Chin legal code], which is a translation of the Japanese version published earlier by the author, pp. 9-10.

7. Niida Noburu, "Kindai keiho kō," p. 34; Yeh Ch'ien-chao, *Chin-lü chih yen-chiu*, p. 8.

8. Niida, "Kindai keiho kō," p. 111, Yeh, *Chin-lü chih*

yen-chiu, pp. 83-84.

9. Niida, "Kindai keiho kō," Yeh, *Chin-lü chih yen-chiu*, p. 92. Other differences, such as the use of money instead of cloth, and the disappearance of *pu-ch'ü*, were already discernible in the Sung.

10. Yeh, *Chin-lü chih yen-chiu*, pp. 39, 48, 89, 109.

11. Chin made a trophy out of Han's head. See *CS*, *ch*. 12, p. 18a; *ch*. 98, pp. 10b-11a.

12. *CS*, *ch*. 10, p. 14b; *ch*. 12, pp. 5a, 15b; *ch*. 11, p. 7a; *ch*. 12, p. 5a for the war in 1206. For the Jurchen ceremony see *ch*. 35, "the kowtow ceremony of our dynasty."

13. *CS*, *ch*. 10, p. 11a. According to Mikami Tsugio, the extant book *Ta-Chin chi-li* is not the *Ta-Chin i-li*. See *KSKK* (2), pp. 35-40.

14. *CS*, *ch*. 12, p. 5a; *ch*. 44, p. 6b; *ch*.10, p. 5a, 7b.

15. Ibid., *ch*. 100, pp. 4b-5a.

16. For example, he accepted some courtiers' advice in 1189 and hunted in the suburbs of the capital. See *CS*, *ch*. 9, pp. 4a, 5b; also *ch*. 100, pp. 4a-5a.

17. Cf. the opinions of Liang Hsiang (ibid., *ch*. 96, pp. 10a-14b); Tung Shih-chung (*ch*. 95, pp. 15b-16b), and Hsü An-jen (*ch*. 96, pp. 9b-10a). Other Chinese opposed to hunting were Chang Ju-lin (*ch*. 83, p. 9a), Chia Hsüan, (*ch*. 95, p. 15b); Sun T'o (*ch*. 9, p. 4a); Chia I-ch'ien (*ch*. 106, p. 8a), and Liu T'o (*ch*. 100, pp. 4b-5a).

18. They were Wan-yen Wu-che (*CS*, *ch*. 9, p. 4a) and Nien-ko Tsun-ku (*ch*. 95, p. 15b). For a discussion of the problem of hunting, see Yao Ts'ung-wu hsien-sheng i-chu cheng-li wei-yüan hui, *Yao Ts'ung-wu hsien-sheng ch'üan-chi (3) -- Liao-Chin-Yüan-shih chiang-i (I) Chin-ch'ao shih* [Complete works of Professor Yao Ts'ung-wu (3) Lecture notes on the history of the Liao, Chin, and Yüan dynasties (B) History of the Chin dynasty], pp. 207-13.

19. Cf. the unpublished article by Hok-lam Chan, "In Search of Dynastic Legitimacy: The 'Orthodox Succession' Debates during the Later Reigns of the Jurchen Chin Dynasty (1194-1214)."

20. For the translation of the text see Herbert Franke, "Treaties between Sung and Chin," pp. 78-79.

21. Chang Wei and others, *Ta-Chin chi-li* [Compendium of ceremonies of the Great Chin], *ch*. 2, pp. 17-18.

22. *CS*, *ch*. 28, pp. 1a, 3a. *CWT*, *ch*. 29, p. 6a. In the discussion on the posthumous title of Tan, the annotation to the character *wei* 威 reads, "*Wei* means that all the barbarians are submissive."

23. For various opinions on this issue see *Ta-Chin te-yün t'u-shuo* [Discussions on the dynastic virtue and

element of the Great Chin, with illustration]. *SKCS*, 4th ser. ed. The "production" scheme is like this: Fire→Earth→Metal→Water→Wood→Fire.

24. Ibid., pp. 16a-17b.
25. *CS*, *ch*. 107, p. 17b.
26. Chao Ping-wen, *Hsien-hsien lao-jen fu-shui wen-chi* (*SPTK*), *ch*. 10, p. 9a.
27. *CS*, *ch*. 14, pp. 2b, 7a.
28. Cf. T'ao Chin-sheng, "Chin-Yüan chih-chi Nü-chen yü Han-jen t'ung-hun chih yen-chiu" [A study of Sino-Jurchen intermarriage in the twelfth century], in T'ao, *Pien-chiang-shih yen-chiu-chi*, pp. 77-78.
29. Liu Ch'i says that after Chu-hu Kao-ch'i became prime minister in the Chen-yu era (1213-16), the influence of the *li* 吏 or petty bureaucrats increased and even superseded that of the *chin-shih* degree holders. These bureaucrats without degrees were antagonistic to the scholar-officials. See *KCC*, *ch*. 7, pp. 4b, 5b.
30. *CS*, *ch*. 129, pp. 17a-18a.
31. Examples are Jen Te-mao 任德懋 (*ISC*, *ch*. 29, p. 4a), Pi Tzu-lun 畢資倫 (*CS*, *ch*. 124, p. 11b); Lung Yen-ch'ang 龍延常 (*CS*, *ch*. 98, p. 13a), and Hu Hsin 胡信 (*CS*, *ch*. 98, p. 15a). The term *cha* is a disputable one. Here I follow Ch'en Shu's reading. See his "Cha-chun k'ao-shih ch'u-kao" [First draft of a study of *cha-chün*], *BIHP* 20, no. 2 (1949): 251-300.
32. *KCC*, *ch*. 7, p. 12b; also *CS*, *ch*. 44, p. 9a.
33. For discussions on this policy, see *CS*, *ch*. 118, pp. 3b-4b.
34. Examples are Li P'ing 李平 (*CS*, *ch*. 15, p. 4a); Li Hsüan 李宣 (*CS*, *ch*. 17, p. 15a); Kuo Chung-yüan 郭仲元 (*CS*, *ch*. 103, p. 3b); Kao La-ko 高臘哥 (*CS*, *ch*. 17, p. 15a; *ch*. 107, p. 2b); Chang Tzu-cheng 張子政; Ch'en Cheng 陳政 (*CS*, *ch*. 112, p. 4a); Liu Shou 劉壽 (*CS*, *ch*. 113, p. 17b); Li Po-yüan 李伯淵 (*CS*, *ch*. 115, p. 7b); Ching An-min 靖安民 (*CS*, *ch*. 118, p. 3a); and T'an Hsin 譚信 (*MAC*, *ch*. 24, p. 5a) for *meng-an* or *ch'ien-hu*. Examples of hereditary *ch'ien-hu* are a eunuch named Sung Ch'i-nu 宋乞奴 (*CS*, *ch*. 116, p. 13a); Kuo Yung-an 國用安 (*CS*, *ch*. 117, p. 7b); and T'ien Shih-ko 田十哥 (*CS*, *ch*. 17, p. 4a). An example of *mou-k'e* or *pai-hu* (head of a hundred men) is Ching An-min (*CS*, *ch*. 118, p. 13a). Examples of hereditary *pai-hu* are Ch'iang Shen 強伸 (*CS*, *ch*. 111, p. 12b); Wang Pin 王賓 (*CS*, *ch*. 117, p. 5a); and Yang Wo-yen 楊沃衍 (*CS*, *ch*. 123, p. 6a). Examples of *wan-hu* are Sung Tzu-yü 宋子玉 (*CS*, *ch*. 15, p. 2b); Hu-yen Yü 呼延棫 (*CS*, *ch*. 16, p. 12a); Sun Chung-wei 孫仲威 (*CS*, *ch*. 16, p. 14a);

Wang A-lü 王阿虜 (*CS*, *ch.* 17, p. 13b); Fan Ch'iao 璞僑 (*CS*, *ch.* 17, p. 13b); Wang Chang 王章 (*CS*, *ch.* 111, p. 5a); Ch'i Chen 齊鎮 (*CS*, *ch.* 111, p. 5a); Ch'en Cheng 陳政 (*CS*, *ch.* 112, p. 4a); and Ma K'uan 馬寬 (*CS*, *ch.* 115, p. 5a). Ch'i-tan people appointed *meng-an* and *mou-k'e* are I-ta Yüan 瑗 (*CS*, *ch.* 118, p. 10b); and I-la P'u-a 蒲阿 (*CS*, *ch.* 112, p. 8a).
    35. *CS*, *ch.* 16, p. 18a-b.
    36. *CS*, *ch.* 117, p. 9a; *ch.* 118, pp. 3a-4b. There was a Ch'i-tan, I-la Chung-chia-nu among the nine dukes. Cf. also Sun K'e-k'uan, *Yüan-tai Han-wen-hua chih huo-tung* [The activities of Chinese culture in the Yüan dynasty], pp. 54-65.
    37. See chap. 3 above.
    38. *CS*, *ch.* 9, p. 9a; *ch.* 103, p. 19a; *ch.* 104, p. 10a; *ch.* 49, pp. 6b-7b, 9a, p. 12b; *ch.* 109, p. 9b.
    39. Wan-yen K'uan occupied land in Shantung, Hopei, and Shansi. See *CS*, *ch.* 98, p. 12a. See also ibid., *ch.* 47, p. 9a, for Jurchen taking extra land by reporting fictitious members of their households to the government and by monopolizing the distribution of land to the peasants.
    40. *CS*, *ch.* 98, p. 12a.
    41. For such a measure see ibid., *ch.* 14, pp. 10b, 16a, 16b, 19a; *ch.* 15, pp. 9a-b; *ch.* 16, p. 5b; *ch.* 106, pp. 5b-6a; *ch.* 107, pp. 4a-5a; *ch.* 109, p. 10b. Chang Hsing-chien 張行簡, a contemporary high official, said that the so-called official land was actually taken from the common people. See *CS*, *ch.* 106, p. 5b.
    42. Ibid., *ch.* 109, p. 10b.
    43. Ibid., *ch.* 107, p. 17a.
    44. Ibid., *ch.* 108, p. 14a.
    45. Ibid., *ch.* 108, p. 20a; *ch.* 109, pp. 2a, 12a; *ch.* 44, pp. 8a, 13a; *ch.* 102, p. 15a. After 1200 the Chinese names for *meng-an* and *mou-k'e*, *ch'ien-hu* and *pai-hu*, were used very often. This in itself indicates sinicization.
    46. *CS*, *ch.* 44, pp. 9a-10a; *ch.* 103, pp. 1a-5b; *ch.* 104, pp. 11a-b; *ch.* 108, p. 17a; *ch.* 111, p. 1b; *ch.* 123, p. 3b.
    47. Ibid., *ch.* 106, p. 15a; *ch.* 104, pp. 11a-b; *ch.* 108, p. 20b. Government troops were all foot soldiers who were rarely equipped with horses. See *ch.* 113, p. 8a.
    48. The last emperor said this in 1233; see ibid., *ch.* 119, p. 4b.
    49. For the fall of the Chin, see *CS*, *ch.* 18 and Wang O, *Ju-nan i-shih* [Remnant events of Ju-nan] *ch.* 4.
    50. For English translations of important passages in the *KCC*, see Hok-lam Chan, *The Historiography of the Chin Dynasty*, pp. 148-63.

51. Ibid., pp. 160, 161.
52. See chap. 4, above.
53. Su T'ien-chüeh, *Kuo-ch'ao wen-lei* [Anthology of Yüan literature], *SPTK* ed., *ch.* 38, p. 1b; also Yang Huan, *Huan-shan i-kao* [Extant drafts of Huan-shan.], *ch.* 1, p. 5a.
54. Su T'ien-chueh, *Tzu-ch'i wen-kao*, *ch.* 22, "Biography of An Hsi."
55. *CS*, *ch.* 125, "Introduction," *ch.* 46, p. 4b.
56. Wang O, *Ju-nan i-shih*, *ch.* 4, pp. 7a-9b. On Wang O's life and his remarks on the last Chin emperor, see Hok-lam Chan, "Prolegomena to the *Ju-nan i-shih*: A Memoir on the Last Chin Court under the Mongol Siege of 1234," *Sung Studies Newsletter* 10 (1974): 2-19.
57. Wang O, *Ju-nan i-shih*, pp. 8a-b.
58. Yao Ts'ung-wu, "Chang Te-hui *Ling-pei chi-hsing* tsu-pen chiao-chü," *Bulletin of the College of Arts, National Taiwan University* 11 (1962): 21.
59. Hao Ching, "Li-cheng i," [Memorial on establishment of government policies] in Su T'ien-chüeh, *Kuo-ch'ao wen-lei*, chap. 14, p. 5b.
60. Hsü Heng, "Shih-wu wu-shih" [Five Points on Present Affairs] in Su, *Kuo-ch'ao wen-lei*, *ch.* 13, pp. 3a-4a.
61. It is clear that the Chinese were not loyal to the Jurchen at the end of the dynasty. A great number of Chinese defected to the Mongols and the Southern Sung Chinese; others rose against their masters and a number of Jurchen were killed. See Meng Ssu-ming, *Yüan-tai she-hui chieh-chi chih-tu* [Social classes in the Yüan dynasty], pp. 17-18. Cf. also Igor de Rachewiltz, "Personnel and Personalities in North China in the Early Mongol Period," *Journal of the Economic and Social History of the Orient* 9, pt. 1-2 (1966): 105-6, 141-42.
62. For a discussion of the causes for the downfall of the Chin, see Chan, *Historiography of Chin*, pp. 164-65.

Chapter 8

1. *CS*, *ch.* 9, p. 11b.
2. Emperor Hui-tsung's daughters were married to Jurchen imperial clansmen. See *CS*, *ch.* 3, p. 14a; six daughters of Hui-tsung (*Hun-te kung*) were married to the imperial household. Cf. also Wang Ch'eng-ti, *Ch'ing-kung i-yü*; Anon., *Shen-yin yü* and *Sung-fu chi* in *Ching-k'ang pai-shih* [Romances of the Ching-k'ang era] (*Chi-mao ts'ung-pien* ed.), *ts'e* 2.
3. *CS*, *ch.* 13, p. 1a; *ch.* 14, p. 1a; *ch.* 17, p. 1a.
4. See p. 40, above.
5. *ISC*, *ch.* 28, pp. 10a-11a. The marriage took place

Notes: Chapter 8   157

no later than 1161, because it is recorded in his son's epitaph that the son was born in 1162.

6. *MAC*, *ch*. 29, p. 4a.

7. As a slave girl, Miss Li was taken to the imperial palace and taught to read. Her teacher discovered her talent and recommended her to the emperor. See *CS*, *ch*. 64, pp. 10b-15a.

8. See T'ao Chin-sheng, *Pien-chiang-shih yen-chiu chi*, pp. 78-82.

9. Cf. Sun K'e-k'uan, *Yüan-tai Han-wen-hua chih ho-tung* [The activities of Chinese culture in the Yüan dynasty], pp. 250-70; Igor de Rachewiltz, "Personnel and Personalities in North China in the Early Mongol Period," pp. 88-144.

10. Sung, et al., *Yüan-shih*, *ch*. 147, "Biography of Shih T'ien-ni."

11. Wang P'an 王磐, "Chung-shu-yu-ch'eng-hsiang Shih-kung shen-tao pei" 中書右丞相史公神道碑, in Su T'ien-chüeh, *Kuo-ch'ao wen-lei* [Anthology of Yüan literature], *ch*. 58, pp. 1a-9a.

12. Table 7 is based on Liu Ch'i, "Ku Pei-ching-lu hsing-liu-pu shang-shu Shih-kung shen-tao-pei ming" 故北京路行六部尚書史公神道碑銘, in *CWT*, *ch*. 55, pp. 6a-8a; Tuan Shao-hsien 段紹先, "I-chou chieh-tu-shih hsing-pei-ching-lu ping-ma tu-yüan-shuai Shih-kung shen-tao-chih-pei" 義州節度使行北京路兵馬都元帥史公神道之碑, in *Yung-ch'ing hsien-chih*, "Yung-ch'ing wen chen," *ch*. 2, pp. 20a-23a; Wang Yün, "Tsung-kuan Shih-kung shen-tao-pei" 總管東公神道碑, in *Ch'iu-chien-hsien-sheng ta-ch'üan wen-chi*, *ch*. 54, pp. 7a-10a; Yao Sui, "P'ing-chang cheng-shih Shih-kung shen-tao-pei" 平章政事史公神道碑, in *MAC*, *ch*. 16, pp. 1a-19a. Yao Sui also wrote an epitaph for another family member, Shih Yao, in *MAC*, *ch*. 16, pp. 9a-14b. The most important source is Ts'ui Hsüan 崔銑, "Shih-shih ch'ing-yüan chih pei" 史氏慶源之碑 [The Genealogical Tablet of the Shih Family], in *Yung-ch'ing hsien-chih*, "Yung-ch'ing wen chen," *ch*. 2, pp. 14a-16b.

13. T'ao Tsung-i, *Cho-keng lu* [Writings after farming] *SPTK*, 3rd ser; preface date 1366, *ch*. 1. E.g., Wan-yen equals Wang and Ch'ih-chan equals Chang.

14. Ch'en Chun, *Pei-feng yang-sha lu* [Records of the sands spread by the wind from the north], states that there were some Jurchen having the Chinese surname Na 拏 during the T'ang dynasty. See also *SCPM*, *ch*. 3, p. 5b.

15. *CS*, *ch*. 80, p. 8b; *SCPM*, *ch*. 3, p. 5b.

16. Such include men from the Nü-hsi-lieh 女希烈, Ho-shih-lieh, and Po-chu-lu 李术魯 clans. See Yü Chi, "Kao-lu-kung shen-tao-pei" 高魯公神道碑, in *Tao-yüan hsüeh-ku lu*, *ch*. 17, p. 15b. In *KS* there were many cases of Jurchen chieftains bearing the Kao surname; e.g., Kao Tzu-lo 高子羅, Kao Chih-wen 高之問. See *KS*, pp. 41, 101, and 103. Kao was also one of the most common Po-hai surnames.

17. *CS*, *ch*. 7, pp. 4b-5a; *ch*. 9, p. 13a. As to Chinese counterparts to Jurchen surnames, see Ch'en Shu, *Chin-shih-pu wu-chung* [Five supplements to Chin history], pp. 155-78.

18. For details see Ch'en Shu, *Chin-shih shih-pu wu-chung*, pp. 179-85.

19. *CS*, *ch*. 39, pp. 1b-2a.

20. For Tan and Liang, see chap. 4, pp. 41-47. According to Wang Yü-hsien of the Ch'ing dynasty, *Hui-shih pei-k'ao* [A directory to painting], *ch*. 7, p. 4a, two paintings of bamboos were extant at his time.

21. *ISC*, *ch*. 36, "Ch'in-pien yin" [Preface to discussions on the lute]. Chang-tsung's poems are found in Yüan Hao-wen, *Chung-chou chi*, "Preface," p. 1a; *KCC*, *ch*. 1, pp. 1a-2a; *TCKC*, *ch*. 20, pp. 1a-b, and *ch*. 21, p. 4b; *Ch'üan Chin-shih* [Anthology of Chin poetry], *ch*. 1. For his calligraphy and painting, see *TCKC*, *ch*. 20, pp. 1a-b and *ch*. 21, p. 4b. He was even an expert on drama; see T'ao Tsung-i, *Cho-keng lu*, (*Chin-tai mi-shu*), *ch*. 27, p. 8a.

22. *CS*, *ch*. 19, p. 4a.

23. *KCC*, *ch*. 1, p. 1a. See also Chuang Shen, *Chung-kuo hua-shih yen-chiu hsü-chi* [Studies on Chinese art history, supplementary volume], pp. 371-74. Chuang, however, considers that Hsien-tsung and Prince Hsüan-hsiao were two persons and discusses them separately.

24. *CS*, *ch*. 85, pp. 5b, 9b, and 11a. Their mothers were Chinese.

25. Ibid., *ch*. 10, p. 3b; *ch*. 11, p. 10b.

26. Cf. Toyama Gunji, "Shoshu shōsō no shōga ni tsuite" [Notes on calligraphies and paintings collected by Chin emperor Chang-tsung] in his *KCS*, pp. 660-69.

27. Chuang Shen, *Chung-kuo hua-shih yen-chiu hsü-chi*, pp. 361-64.

28. *KCC*, *ch*. 1, pp. 2a-3b; *CS*, *ch*. 85, pp. 8a-9a. His collected poetry, *Ju-an hsiao-kao*, includes 400 poems.

29. Hsia Wen-yen, *T'u-hui pao-chien* [A precious mirror for painting], *ch*. 4, p. 32.

30. Yüan Hao-wen considers that Wang T'ing-yün's ink bamboo painting was the best after Wen T'ung; see *ISC*, *ch*. 16, p. 12b. Cf. also Susan Bush, "Literati Culture under

the Chin (1122-1234)," *Oriental Art* 15, no. 2 (1969): 109.
  31. Chuang Shen, *Chung-kuo hua-shih*, pp. 355-57. Cf. also the lists of paintings of Liao and Chin painters in Wang Yü-hsien, *Hui-shih pei-k'ao*, ch. 7, pp. 1a-11a.
  32. *ISC*, ch. 36, "Ju-an shih-wen hsü" [On the poetry and literary writings of *Ju-an*].
  33. Fang I, "Yeh-hsien Po-chu-lu yüan-t'ing pei" [Mr. Po-chu-lu's estate at the country of Yeh], in *CWT*, ch. 38, pp. 12a-b. In the stone inscriptions related to the estate, the name Po-chu-lu Hsiao-chung is found; see Pi Yüan, *Shan-tso chin-shih chih* [Records of bronzes and stone tablets in Shantung], ch. 20, pp. 2b-3b.
  34. *CS*, ch. 102, p. 13b; ch. 104, p. 4a; ch. 101, p. 5a; *ISC*, ch. 27, p. 3a; *CWT*, ch. 41, p. 4a; *KCC*, ch. 3, pp. 7a-b; ch. 6, p. 8b.
  35. *CS*, ch. 99. pp. 1a-b, 7a. His collected works, *Hung-tao chi*, 6 ch., does not exist today.
  36. *CWT*, ch. 40, p. 16a.
  37. Liu Wei, "Chung-hsiu fu-hsüeh chiao-yang pei," in *CWT*, ch. 41, pp. 13a-b.
  38. Wang Yün, *Ch'iu-chien hsien-sheng ta-ch'üan wen-chi*, ch. 59, pp. 7a-8a; Hsü An-shang, "Jui-ch'eng wei Ho-shih-lieh Chao-hsing te-cheng chih-pei," in Pi Yüan and Juan Yüan, *Shan-tso chin-shih chih*, ch. 23, pp. 12b-14b.
  39. For his biography see *CS*, ch. 95. According to Hsia Wen-yen, *T'u-hui pao-chien*, ch. 4, p. 33b, he was also a painter, specializing in deer, people, horse, and ink bamboos.
  40. *KCC*, ch. 4, p. 9b; ch. 6, pp. 7b, 8a; Hsia Wen-yen, *T'u-hui pao-chien*, ch. 4, p. 34a.
  41. Bush, "Literati Culture."
  42. Cf. Stephen H. West's forthcoming article, "Literature in the Chin." Also Hsü Wen-yü, "Chin-Yüan ti wen-yu," in Cheng Chen-t'o, ed., *Chung-kuo wen-hsüeh yen-chiu*, pp. 677-714.
  43. For compilation of official history of the Chin, see Chan, *The Historiography of the Chin Dynasty*, pp. 1-5.
  44. Cf. the part on the Chin in Yang Chia-lo, ed., *Liao-Chin-Yüan i-wen chih* [Bibliographies of Liao, Chin, and Yüan], vol. 1.
  45. Ch'ien Ta-hsin, *Pu Liao-Chin-Yüan i-wen chih*, in Yang Chia-lo, *Liao-chin-Yüan*, p. 35.
  46. K.T. Wu, "Chinese Printing under Four Alien Dynasties (916-1368 A.D.)," *Harvard Journal of Asiatic Studies* 13, nos. 3 and 4 (1950): 454, quoting Chang Hsiu-min, "Chin-yüan chien-pen k'ao" [Publications of the *Kuo-tzu-chien* of the Chin dynasty], *T'u-shu chi-k'an* 2, no. 2 (1935): 19-25.
  47. Yeh Te-hui, *Shu-lin ch'ing-hua*, ch. 4, pp. 1a-b.

48. Wu, "Chinese Printing," pp. 456-57, 458.
49. Chang Hsiu-min, "Liao, Chin, Hsi Hsia k'e-shu chien-shih" [A brief history of printing in the Liao, Chin and Hsi Hsia], *Wen-wu*, no. 3 (1959), pp. 12-15.
50. T'ai Ching-nung, "Nu-chen-tsu t'ung-chih-hsia ti Han-yü wen-hsüeh---chu-kung-tiao" [Chinese literature under the rule of the Jurchen---chu-kung-tiao], *Chung-wai Literary Monthly* 1, no. 1 (1972): 9-10. Hu Chi, *Sung Chin tsa-chü k'ao* [A Study of the *tsa-chü* in the Sung and Chin dynasties], p. 7. Yoshikawa Kōjiro, *Gen zatsugeki kenkyū* [Studies of Yüan plays], p. 183.
51. For the *chu-kung-tiao*, see Cheng Chen-t'o, *Chung-kuo su-wen-hsüeh shih* [History of Chinese vernacular literature], chap. 8; T'ai, "Nu-chen-tsu," West, "Literature in the Chin." Cheng Chen-t'o, *Chung-kuo su-wen-hsueh shih*, pp. 109-10; T'ai, "Nu-chen-tsu," pp. 9-10, 11-14, 16-17; T'ao Tsung-i, *Cho-keng lu*, ch. 25,27.
52. See Yoshikawa's discussion in *Gen zatsugeki kenkyū*, pp. 178-84; cf. also Hu Chi, *Sung Chin tsa-chü k'ao*, pp. 67-75; Cheng Chen-t'o, *Chung-kuo su-wen-hsüeh-shih*, pp. 147-54.
53. Wang Kuo-wei, *Sung-Yüan hsi-ch'ü k'ao* [A study of Sung and Yüan drama], pp. 48a-49a.
54. Ibid., p. 49b.
55. Chu Ching's "Preface" (written in 1364) to Huang Hsüeh-so, *Ch'ing-lou chi*; Aoki Masaru, "Nanboku kyoku genryū kō" [Examination of the origin of the southern and northern drama], in *Kano kyōju kanreki kinen shinagaku ronsō*, pp. 849-904.
56. Aoki, "Nanboku," p. 904
57. Yoshikawa, *Gen zatsugeki kenkyū*, pp. 198-206.
58. According to Chao Ching-shen, *Hsi-ch'ü pi-t'an* [Notes on drama], pp. 10-11, Kuan Han-ch'ing died between 1320-24. For a discussion of Kuan Han-ch'ing's date of death see also Yoshikawa, *Gen zatsugeki kenkyū*, pp. 206-11. Pai P'u was only a child when the Chin was destroyed by the Mongols. See ibid., pp. 131-34.
59. Yoshikawa, *Gen zatsugeki kenkyū*, pp. 118-98. For Chin sculpture, see Osvald Siren, "Chinese Sculpture of the Sung, Liao and Chin Dynasties," *Bulletin of the Museum of Far Eastern Antiquities* 14 (1942): 45-64.
60. Sherman E. Lee and Wai-kam Ho, *Chinese Art under the Mongols, The Yüan Dynasty (1279-1368)*, pp. 3-6.
61. Kuan Sung-fang, "Chin-tai tz'u-ch'i ho Chün-yao ti wen-t'i" [The china in the Chin dynasty and the problem of Chün kiln], *Wen-wu ts'ang-k'ao tzu-liao*, no. 2 (1958), pp. 25-26.
62. Chu Hsieh, "Pa-pai-nien-ch'ien ti Pei-ching wei-ta

chien-chu Chin Chung-tu kung-tien t'u k'ao" [A study of the great palace architecture of the Central Capital of the Chin of 800 years ago, with maps], *Wen-wu ts'ang-k'ao tzu-liao* no. 7 (1955), pp. 67-75.

63. *HNC*, *ch*. 6, p. 4b; *ch*. 12, p. 5a. Wang's criticisms of the *Historical Records* are in *chs*. 9-16. See also ibid., *ch*. 30, p. 3a.

64. Ibid., *ch*. 26, pp. 10a-b.

65. *Hsien-hsien-lao-jen fu-shui wen-chi* (*SPTK*), *ch*. 14, pp. 1a-3b; *ch*. 10, p. 7a; *ch*. 18, pp. 4b-5a.

66. For Li Ch'un-fu, see Nogami Shunjō, *Ryōkin no bukkyō* [Buddhism in the Liao and Chin Dynasties], pp. 209-20. Also Tokiwa Daijō, "Kin no Ri Heisan sen meidō shusetsu ni tsuite" [On the *Ming-tao chi-shuo* written by Li P'ing-shan of the Chin], *Hattori sensei koki shukuga kinen rombunshū*, pp. 673-98.

67. "Ch'ung-hsiu mien-pi-an pei," in Chang Chin-wu, ed., *Chin-wen tsui*, *ch*. 41, pp. 7a-8b; see also *KCC*, *ch*. 1, pp. 6b-7b.

68. *KCC*, *ch*. 9, p. 15a.

69. Li Ch'un-fu, *P'ing-shan hsien-sheng Ming-tao-chi shuo* [Commentaries of the *Ming-tao-chi* by Mr. P'ing-shan], 5 *chs*. Li's standpoint is clearly stated in ibid., *ch*. 5, pp. 4b-5b, and conclusion (*ch*. 5, pp. 12b-13b). Cf. also Jao Tsung-i, "San-chiao-lun yü Sung-Chin hsüeh-shu" [The theory of combination of the three religions and the intellectual world of the Sung and the Chin], *Tung-hsi wen-hua*, no. 11 (1968), pp. 24-32.

70. *KCC*, *ch*. 9, p. 16a.

71. Jao, "San-chiao-lun...."

72. Tamura Jitsuzō, "Kittan bukkyō no shakaishi no kōsatsu" [A sociohistorical survey of Ch'i-tan Buddhism], *Otagi Gakuhō* 18, no. 1 (1937): 32-47; Nogami, *Ryōkin no bukkyō*, pp. 221-43.

73. Nogami, *Ryōkin no bukkyō*, pp. 221-43.

74. Historians generally agree on this point. See Takao Yoshikata, "Kindai ni okeru dō futsu nikyō no tokuchō" [Characteristics of Taoism and Buddhism during the Chin dynasty], *Shina Gaku* 5, no. 1 (1929): 150-51; Ch'en Yüan, *Nan-Sung-ch'u Ho-pei hsin-Tao-chiao k'ao* [New Taoist societies in the northern provinces at the beginning of the Southern Sung dynasty], pp. 11-14, 34-38; Yao Ts'ung-wu, "Chin-Yüan ch'üan-chen-chiao ti min-tsu ssu-hsiang yü chiu-shih ssu-hsiang" [Ideas in nationalism and salvation of the world of the Ch'üan-chen sect in the Chin and Yüan dynasties], in *Tung-pei-shih lun-ts'ung*, 2: 175-204; Sun K'e-k'uan, "Ch'üan-chen-chiao k'ao-lüeh" [A brief study of the Ch'üan-chen sect], *Ta-lu tsa-chih* 8, no. 10 (1954); 309-13: Nogami,

Ryōkin no bukkyō, pp. 261-74.

75. Yao, "Chin-Yüan ch'üan-chen-chiao," p. 176; Sun K'e-k'uan, *Yüan-tai tao-chiao chih fa-chan* [The development of Taoism in the Yüan dynasty], p. 244.

76. Cf. works cited in n. 63.

77. Ch'en Yüan, *Nan-Sung-ch'u*, chaps. 3 and 4.

78. Takao, "Kindai ni okeru dō futsu," p. 137; *CS*, *ch*. 91, p. 17a; *ch*. 92, p. 18a; *TCKC*, *ch*. 36, p. 2b. Cf. also Nogami, *Ryōkin no bukkyō*, pp. 179-208.

79. Kuo Ch'eng, "Ning-hai-chou Yü-hsü-kuan pei," in Chang Chin-wu, *CWT*, *ch*. 41, pp. 1a-3a; Liu Tsu-ch'ien, "Chung-nan-shan ch'ung-yang tsu-shih hsien-chi chi," in ibid., *ch*. 14, p. 19b. Wang Ch'u-i was summoned by Shih-tsung in 1187, according to Kuo Ch'eng. "Ning-hai-chou," pp. 1a-b. But Wan-yen Shou wrote that Wang and Ch'iu were summoned; see Wan-yen Shou, "Ch'üan-chen-chiao-tsu pei," in *CWT*, *ch*. 41, pp. 19b-20a; and Ch'iu's own note in *P'an-ch'i chi* (in *Tao-tsang*, printed in 1925, *ts'e* 797), *ch*. 3, pp. 6a-b.

80. Ch'en Yüan, *Nan-sung-ch'u*, pp. 43-46; Liu Tsu-ch'ien, "Chung-han-shan," p. 19b.

81. In Ch'iu, *P'an-ch'i chi*, *ch*. 2, p. 7a, there is a poem dedicated to Shih-tsung. Ch'iu also wrote a poem mourning the death of the emperor (*ch*. 3, pp. 6a-7a). For his poems for the wife of Prince Ts'ao, see *ch*. 2, p. 5b; for Chia-ku Ch'ing-shen, prefect of the Western Capital, see *ch*. 1, pp. 8a-b; for General Chia-ku Lung-hu, see *ch*. 2, p. 6a, and *ch*. 5, p. 12b; for the *meng-an* whose last name was Wen-ti-han, see *ch*. 1, p. 13a; for P'ei-man Cheng-kuo, the defense prefect of Lung-chou, see *ch*. 5, p. 12b; and for the scholar with the surname Wan-yen, see *ch*. 1, pp. 11b-12a.

82. Ch'en Yüan, *Nan-Sung-ch'u*, pp. 20-25. Wan-yen Shou wrote "Ch'üan-chen-chiao-tsu pei," the biography of Wang Che, at the request of Taoist priests Li Chih-yüan and Yü Shan-ch'ing. In the essay Shou called himself a friend of Wang Ch'u-i.

83. For Ch'iu's journal to the West, see Arthur Waley's basic account of the matter and the translation of the *Hsi-yu chi* in *Ch'ang-ch'un: The Travels of an Alchemist*, trans. Arthur Waley.

84. Li Pang-hsien, "Lung-chou Ch'ien-yang-hsien hsin-hsiu Yü-ch'ing-kuan pei," in *CWT*, *ch*. 41, pp. 14a-15b. Note especially Li Pang-hsien and Nien-ko Tzu-yang's discussion on whether the Yü-ch'ing-kuan should be repaired, which reflects the Jurchen belief in Taoism.

85. *HNC*, *ch*. 42, pp. 6a-7b; Takao, "Kindai ni okeru dō futsu," p. 138; *HNC*, pp. 4a-b; Ch'en Yüan, *Nan-Sung-ch'u*, pp. 8, 58.

Notes: Chapter 8

86. *SCPM*, ch. 242, p. 10b; *HNYL*, ch. 183, Ping-tsu of the 12th month, 1159; ch. 150, Ping-wu of the 12th month, 1143. Cf. also ch. 198, Ting-wei of the 3rd month, 1162.

87. Ibid., ch. 180, Wu-wu of the 11th month, 1158. Cf. Ch'üan Han-sheng, "Sung Chin chien ti tsou-ssu mao-i" [The smuggling trade between the Sung and Chin kingdoms], *BIHP* 11 (1947): 427; *HNYL*, ch. 199, Kuei-yu of the 4th month, 1162. Cf. also Hsieh Shen-fu and others, *Ch'ing-yüan t'iao-fa shih-lei* [A compilation of the edicts and the laws of the Ch'ing-yüan era: 1195-1200], ch. 5.

88. For the trade between the two states, see mainly Katō Shigeshi, "Sō to Kinkoku tono bōeki ni tsuite" [On the trade between the Sung and Chin kingdoms], in *Shina keizai-shi kōshō* [Studies in Chinese economic history], 2:247-83; Ch'üan Han-sheng, "Sung Chin chien ti tsou-ssu mao-i," p. 427. Cf. also Ōsaki Fujio, "Sō Kin bōeki no keitai" [Types of trade between the Sung and the Chin], *Hiroshima daigaku bungakubu kiyō*, no. 5 (1954), pp. 159-82. Ōsaki, however, made a number of mistakes in the article. An example is that the Huai Ho was read "Chun Ho."

89. E.g., Liu Yen; see *HNYL*, ch. 180, I-wei of the 12th month, 1158.

90. Examples are: Li Ch'eng (*CS*, ch. 79, p. 3a), K'ung Yen-chou (*CS*, ch. 79, p. 3b), Hsü Wen (*CS*, ch. 79, pp. 4b-5a), and Li Ch'iung (*CS*, ch. 79, pp. 1a-b).

91. Examples are: Hsiao Che-pa, P'u-ch'a T'u-mu, Ta Chou-jen, and Hsiao Ch'i (*Sung-hui-yao chi-kao*, ed. Hsü Sung, p. 7051).

92. *HNYL*, ch. 196, pp. 4a-b.

93. Cheng Yüan-yu, *Sui-ch'ang-shan-ch'iao tsa-lu* [Miscellaneous notes of the Sui-ch'ang Wood-cutter], *Hsüeh-hai lei-pien*, 7: 4191.

94. In 1206 when Chu-hu Yün-shou took Lo-shan (in Honan), he invited Ts'ao Ting to the north as his teacher; see *ISC*, ch. 27, p. 3a.

95. Chao Fu was taken to the north to teach the philosophy of the Ch'en-Chu school after the fall of the Southern Sung; see *MAC*, ch. 15, pp. 3b-4a. Cf. also Huang Tsung-hsi, *Sung-Yüan hsüeh-an* [Schools of thought during the Sung and Yüan dynasties], ch. 83; Sun K'e-k'uan, *Yüan-tai Han-wen-hua chih huo-tung*, pp. 139-63.

96. E.g., a certain Wang Tsun-ku was a scholar of the Ch'eng school; see *ISC*, ch. 16, p. 9b.

97. Cf. Liu Ming-shu, "Sung-tai ch'u-pang-fa chi tui Liao Chin chih shu-chin" [Laws concerning publications during the Sung dynasty and concerning the prohibition of books going to and coming from Liao and Chin], *Bulletin of Chinese Studies* 5, part 1 (1945): 95-114.

98. Chang Hsiu-min, "Liao, Chin, Hsi Hsia k'e-shu chien-shih" pp. 13-15. A check of Chu Hsi's collected works, *Hui-an hsien-sheng Chu-wen-kung wen-chi* (*SPTK*), *ch.* 81, pp. 10b-11b, however, indicates that Chang mistook Ssu-ma Kuang's commentaries for his *Ch'ien-hsü t'u*.

99. The gifts presented to the Chin court by Chang I, a Sung envoy, included a set of Ssu-ma Kuang's *Tzu-chih t'ung-chien*. See *TCKC*, *ch.* 8, p. 2a.

100. *HNC*, *ch.* 34, pp. 3b, 5b, 8a. Hung Mai was disappointed with Wang's criticisms of Ssu-ma Ch'ien; see Sun Te-ch'ien, *Chin-shih i-wen lüeh* [A brief account of Chin works], in *Liao-Chin-Yüan i-wen-chih*, ed. Yang Chia-lo, 1: 91, 171.

101. *TCKC*, *ch.* 13; *CS*, *ch.* 129, p. 7a; *CS*, *ch.* 8, p. 20b and n.12 of chap. 8.

102. Wang Kuo-wei, *Sung-Yüan hsi-ch'ü k'ao*, chap. 6; cf. also T'ai, "Nü-chen-tsu"; Ch'ien Nan-yang, "Sung Chin Yüan hsi-chü pan-yen k'ao" [The performance of drama in the Sung, Chin, and Yüan dynasties], *Yen-ching Journal of Chinese Studies*, no. 20 (1936), p. 192.

103. Cf. Liu Ming-shu, "Sung-tai Liao-Chin wen-hua chih nan-chien" [The culture of Liao and Chin in its southward movement during the Sung], *Bulletin of Chinese Studies* 6 (1946): 91-105.

104. See Yeh Yü's biography written by Yang Wan-li in *Ch'eng-chai chi*, *ch.* 119, p. 5a; cf. Liu Ming-shu, "Sung-tai Liao-Chin wen-hua chih nan-chien," p. 96.

105. Liu Ming-shu, "Sung-tai Liao-Chin," p. 95. Cf. another order issued in the same year in *Sung-shih ch'uan-wen hsü tzu-chih t'ung-chien* [The complete text of Sung history: A continuation to the *Comprehensive Mirror for Aid in Government*], *ch.* 24, Kuei-wei of the 8th month, 1163.

106. Hsieh Shen-fu et al., *Ch'ing-yüan t'iao-fu shih-lei* [A compilation of the edicts and the laws of the Ch'ing-yüan era: 1195-1200], *ch.* 3, [Miscellaneous orders] (*tsa-ch'ih*);Liu Ming-shu, "Sung-tai Liao-Chin," pp. 96, 99.

Chapter 9

1. For discussions of the sinicization of the Manchus, see *HCSL*, pp. 10-15; Mary Wright, *The Last Stand of Chinese Conservatism: The Tung-chih Restoration, 1862-1874*, pp. 51-56; John K. Fairbank, *The United States and China*, rev. ed. (New York: Viking Press, 1958), pp. 77-82; and Ping-ti Ho, "The Significance of the Ch'ing Period in Chinese History," *Journal of Asian Studies* 26, no. 2 (1967): 191-93.

2. Wittfogel in *HCSL* stresses the basic differences implicit in Jurchen and Chinese societies. He says, "These

differences are as striking as the trends towards assimilation which were much more marked than under the preceding Liao dynasty" (p. 8).

3. For North American Indians see Oscar Lewis, *The Effects of White Contact upon Blackfoot Culture*, American Ethnological Society, Monograph no. 6 (New York: J.J. Austin, 1942), pp. 38-40. For South American Indians see Julian H. Steward, *Native Peoples of South America* (New York and London: McGraw Hill, 1959), chap. 14. A new appraisal of the problem is Ronald E. Gregson, "The Influence of the Horse on Indian Cultures of Lowland South America," *Ethnohistory* 16, no. 1 (1969): 33-50.

4. These are Max Weber's usages. See *The Theory of Social and Economic Organization*, pp. 346-51, 368.

5. According to Milton Gordon's criteria for measuring assimilation, the sinicization of the Jurchen would be almost complete, although we do not have much data concerning the behavioral aspects of the Jurchen. Gordon's assimilation variables are: change of cultural patterns to those of host society; large-scale entrance into cliques, clubs, and institutions of host society, on primary group level; large-scale intermarriage; development of sense of peoplehood based exclusively on host society; absence of prejudice, absence of discrimination, and absence of value and power conflict. See Milton Gordon, *Assimilation in American Life*, p. 71, table 5.

6. Meng Ssu-ming, *Yüan-tai she-hui chieh-chi chih-tu* [The social classes in the Yüan period], pp. 32-34.

7. See note 63 of chap. 1.

8. For example, see Lo Fu-ch'eng, *Nü-chen i-yü* [Translations of Jurchen documents]. n.d., n.p., in the rare book section, Harvard-Yenching Library; also the texts in Grube, *Die Sprache und Schrift der Jucen*, pp. 106-44.

9. Cf. Ch'en Wen-shih, "Ch'ing-t'ai-tsung shih-tai ti chung-yao cheng-chih ts'u-shih" [Important political measures of Ch'ing-t'ai-tsung], *BIHP* 40, part 1 (1968): 295-371.

10. Henry Serruys, C.I.C.M., "Remains of Mongol Customs in China During the Early Ming Period," *Monumenta Serica* 16 (1957): 171-90, 148-67.

11. For the Yüan classification of the households (*hu-chi*), see Huang Ch'ing-lien, "Yüan-tai *hu-chi* chih-tu yen-chiu," unpublished M.A. thesis, National Taiwan University, 1974; Liu Ming-shu, "Yüan Se-mu-jen ming-ch'eng chi ch'i chieh-chi chih-tu yüan-yüan yü Chin-yüan shou" [A theory that the name Se-mu-jen and the class system of the Yüan originated from the Chin], *Chin-ling hsüeh-pao* 10 (1940): 31-42.

12. For the reservoir theory see my *Pien-chiang-shih*

yen-chiu chi, p. 17 and notes 6 and 7.

13. Robert Hartwell suggests that industrial production, such as iron and coal output, dropped by half during the three centuries after 1078, and that one of the factors for such a trend seems to have been the Jurchen and later Mongol invasions and conquests. See Hartwell, "A Revolution in the Chinese Iron and Coal Industries during the Northern Sung, 960-1126 A.D.," *Journal of Asian Studies* 21, no. 2 (1962): 153-62.

Glossary

Abahai. *See* T'ai-tsung
A-ch'eng 阿城
A-li. *See* Wan-yen
A-li-ho-man. *See* Wan Yen
a-li-hsi 阿里喜
a-she po-chi-lieh 阿捨勃極烈
A-shih 阿什
A-su ch'eng 阿陳城
An-ch'u-hu 按出虎
An-ch'un 按春
an-pan po-chi-lieh 諳班勃極烈
cha-chün 乣軍
ch'a-shih 茶食
chai-shih 寨使
Chang Chiu-ch'eng 張九成
Chang Chüeh 張覺
Chang Chün 張鈞
Chang-nu. *See* Yeh-lü
Chang Pang-ch'ang 張邦昌
Chang Shih 張栻
Chang Te-hui 張德輝
Chang Tsai 張載
Chang-tsung. *See* Wan-yen Chin
Chang T'ung-ku 張通古
Chang Yung-chih 張用直
Ch'ang. *See* Wan-yen Ta-lan
Ch'ang-ch'un 長春
ch'ang-sheng chün 長勝軍
Chao Kou 趙構 (Emperor Kao-tsung of the Sung)
Chao Ping-wen 趙秉文
ch'ao-ch'ien ko 超遷格

Chen-ting 真定
Ch'en Kung-fu 陳公輔
Ch'eng Hao 程顥
Ch'eng-hui. See Wan-yen
Ch'eng I 程頤
Ch'i 齊
ch'i 奇
Ch'i-tan 契丹
Chia I 賈誼
Chia-ku Te-ku 夾谷德固

Chiang Min-piao 江民表
Chiang-ning 江寧
chiao-fang ch'iang-tzu 教坊腔子
chieh 秸 or 稭
chieh-tu shih 節度使
ch'ien-hu 千戶
Ch'ien-yüan 乾元
chih-hou 祗候
Chih-ning. See Wan-yen
Ch'ih-chan Hui 赤盞暉
Chin 金
Chin or Ma-ta-ko (Emperor Chang-tsung). See Wan-yen
Chin i ju wang 金以儒亡

chin-shih 進士
chin-shih chü 近侍局
ching-t'ung 經童
Ch'ing-lo she 清樂社

Ch'ing-yüan 慶元
chou-hsien 州縣
Chou Tun-i 周敦頤
Chu-erh-ch'e 主兒扯
Chu Hsi 朱熹
Chu-hu Yün-shou 术虎筠壽
chu-kung-tiao 諸宮調
Chu-li-chen 朱理真
Chu-shen 珠申、諸申
Ch'u 楚
Ch'u-ts'ai. See Yeh-lü
Ch'üan-chen 全真
ch'üan-nung shih 勸農使

ch'üeh-hsüeh 怯薛
ch'un-shui 春水
chün-hu 軍戶
chün-shuai 軍帥
chung-hsiao chün 忠孝軍

Chung-hsing shih-chi 中興事迹

Chung-hua min-tsu 中華民族
erh-shui 二稅
feng-yü 奉御
fu-yin 府尹
Fu-yü 夫餘
Hai-ku 海古
Hai-ku-le 海古勒

Glossary

Hai-ling. *See* Wan-yen Liang
hai-tung-ch'ing 海東青

Han Chi-hsien 韓企先
Han Fang 韓昉
Han-jen 漢人
han-lin yüan 翰林院
Han-p'u. *See* Wan-yen
Hao Ching 郝經
Hao-jan. *See* Yeh-lü
Hei-shui 黑水
Hei-shui Mo-ho 黑水靺鞨

Ho-che. *See* Wan-yen
Ho-li-po. *See* Wan-yen
Ho-pao 劾保
Ho-shih-lieh Chao-hsing 紇石烈昭信
Hsi-hsiang 西廂
Hsi Liao 西遼
Hsi-nei. *See* Wan-yen
Hsi-tsung. *See* Wan-yen Tan
Hsi-t'uan-shan 西團山
Hsi-yin. *See* Wan-yen
Hsieh Liang-tso 謝良佐
Hsieh-lieh. *See* Wan-yen
Hsieh-yeh. *See* Wan-yen
Hsien-chou 咸州
Hsin Ch'i-chi 辛棄疾
Hsing-hsiu 行秀 (Wan-sung lao-jen) 萬松老人

hsing-hsüeh 心學
Hsing-kuo ling-ying chu 興國靈應主
hsing-t'ai shang-shu sheng 行臺尚書省
Hsing-yüan 興元
Hsü An-shan 許安上
hsüan-hui yüan 宣徽院
Hsüan-tsung. *See* Wan-yen Hsün
Hsün (Emperor Hsüan-tsung) *See* Wan-yen
hu 胡
Hu Chiao 胡嶠
Hu-chou 湖州
Hu-li-kai 胡里改
hu-wei 護衛
hua 華
Hua-feng pu-ching 華風不競

Huai-i 淮夷
Huang-hsi 潢霫
Huang T'ing-chien 黃庭堅

Hui 濊
Hung Hao 洪皓
Hung Mai 洪邁

i-cheng yüan 益政院
I-chien chih 夷堅志
I-la Fu-seng 移剌福僧

I-la Nien-ho 移剌粘合

jen 任
Jurchen. See Nü-chen
k'ang 炕
Kao. See Wan-yen Hsieh-yeh
Kao Ch'ing-i 高慶裔
Kao-tsung. See Chao Kou
Kao Yung-ch'ang 高永昌
k'e-tzu 刻字
ken-pen 根本
Koguryŏ 高句麗
Koryŏ 高麗
ku 古
kuai-tzu ma 拐子馬
Kuan Han-ch'ing 關漢卿
Kuang-ning 廣寧
kuo-hsiang 國相
kuo-lun hu-lu po-chi-lieh 國論忽魯勃極烈
kuo-lun po-chi-lieh 國論勃極烈
kuo-tzu chien 國子監
Kuo Yao-shih 郭藥師
Li Ch'un-fu 李純甫
Li K'an 李侃
Li Kang 李綱
Li Shih 李石
Liang (King Hai-ling). See Wan-yen

Liao 遼
Liao-yang 遼陽
Lin Chih-ch'i 林之奇
ling-shih 令史
Liu An-shih 劉安世
Liu Ch'i 劉祁
Liu Chih-yüan 劉知遠
liu-k'o ch'eng 留可城
liu-shou 留守
Liu Ts'ung-i 劉從益
Liu Yen-tsung 劉彥宗
Liu Yü 劉豫
Liu Yüan-kuei 劉元規
Lo-shan chü-shih 樂善居士
Lou-shih. See Wan-yen
Lou Yüeh 樓鑰
lu 路
Lu I 盧益
Lu Yen-lun 盧彥倫
Lü. See Yeh-lü
Lü Tsu-ch'ien 呂祖謙
Luan-chou 灤州
Ma-chi 馬紀
Ma K'uo 馬擴
Man-yin-i 滿尸伊
Ma-ta-ko. See Wan-yen Chin
Mi-li-mi-shih-han ch'eng 米里米石罕城
meng-an 猛安

Glossary

Meng Hao 孟浩
Meng-yang. See Wan-yen
Ming-ch'ang 明昌
Ming-chou 明州
Mo 貊
Mo-ho 靺鞨
mou-k'e 謀克
Mou-liang-hu (Tsung-hsiung).
    See Wan-yen
Mou-yen. See Wan-yen
Na-ho Ch'un-nien
    納合椿年
Na-ho Liu-ko
    納合六哥
Na-lan 納蘭
na-po 捺鉢
nan-tu 南渡
nei-ch'ao 內朝
Nieh-li. See Yeh-lü
Nien-han (Tsung-han). See
    Wan-yen
Nien-han fa-so
    粘罕髮索
Ning-chiang chou
    寧江州
niu-chü 牛具
niu-t'ou 牛頭
Nü-chen 女真 (Jurchen)
Nü-chen hsiao-tzu
    女真小字

Nü-chen kuo-tzu-hsüeh
    女真國子學
Nü-chen pu-tsu chieh-tu shih
    女真部族節度使
Nü-chih 女直
O-lu-kuan (Tsung-chün). See
    Wan-yen
pai-hu 百戶
Pa-hai. See Wan-yen
Pa-hu-lu. See Wan-yen
Pai P'u 白樸
Pen-ch'ao p'u-tieh
    本朝譜牒
Pi. See Wan-yen
pien-chiang min-tsu
    邊疆民族
P'ing-chou 平州
po-chi-lieh 勃極烈
po-chin 孛堇
Po-chu-lu Hsiao-chung
    孛朮魯孝忠
Po-hai 渤海
Po-ti. See Wan-yen
P'o-la-shu. See Wan-yen
P'o-lu huo. See Wan-yen
P'u-ch'a 蒲察
P'u-kan 僕幹
P'u-li po-chin chai
    蒲里孛堇寨
P'u-lu-hu (Tsung-p'an). See

Wan-yen
P'u-san 僕散
san-kung 三公
san-shih 三師
Sa-kai. See Wan-yen
Sha-men 沙門
shan-hu 山呼
Shang-ching 上京
shang-shu ling 尚書令
shang-shu sheng 尚書省

shao-fan 燒飯
shao-fu chien 少府監
she-liu 射柳
shih 實
Shih I-sheng 施宜生
Shih-ku-nai. See Wan-yen
Shih Li-ai 時立愛
Shih-lu. See Wan-yen
Shih Lun 史倫
Shih-mo Shih-chi
　石抹世勣
Shih T'ien-tse 史天澤
Shih-tsung. See Wan-yen
　Wu-lu
Shou. See Wan-yen
shu-mi yüan 樞密院
Shou-chou 朔州
Ssu-ma Ch'ien 司馬遷
Ssu-ma Kuang 司馬光
Sui-k'o. See Wan-yen

Su-shen 肅慎
Su T'ien-chüeh 蘇天爵

Sung Ch'in-tsung 宋欽宗

Sung Hsiao-tsung 宋孝宗

sung-hsüeh-lei 送血淚
Sung Hui-tsung 宋徽宗

Ta-shih. See Yeh-lü
Ta-lan (Ch'ang). See Wan-yen
Tan (Emperor Hsi-tung). See
　Wan-yen
Ta-tao 大道
Ta-ting 大定
ta-wei 打圍
T'ai-ho 泰和
t'ai-hsüeh 太學
T'ai-i 太乙
T'ai-tsu. See Wan-yen A-ku-
　ta
T'ai-tsung 太宗 (Abahai,
　the Ch'ing emperor).
　See also Wan-yen Wu-ch'i-
　mai
T'ang-kua An-li 唐括安禮

tao-hsüeh 道學
tao-i 島夷
T'ao Tsung-i 陶宗儀
Te-ming. See Wan-yen

Glossary

te-yün 德運
Teng-chou 登州
t'i-fa ling 薙髮令
tiao-min fa-tsui 弔民伐罪
tieh po-chi-lieh 迭勃極烈
tien-ch'ien ma-pu-chün tu-chih-hui shih 殿前馬步軍都指揮使
tien-ch'ien tu-tien-chien ssu 殿前都點檢司
T'ien Chüeh 田殼
T'ien hui 天會
T'ien-tsu ti 天祚帝
t'ing-chang 廷杖
T'o-sa po-chin chai 托撒孛菫寨
Ts'ai-shih 采石
ts'an-shih cheng-shih 參知政事
Ts'ao Ts'ao 曹操
Tso Chi-kung 左企弓
Tsung-chen 宗真
Tsung-chün. See Wan-yen O-lu-kuan
Tsung-fu. See Wan-yen
Tsung-han. See Wan-yen Nien-han
Tsung-hsien. See Wan-yen
Tsung-hsiung. See Wan-yen Mou-liang-hu
Tsung-kan. See Wan-yen Wo-pen
tsung-kuan 總管
Tsung-p'an. See Wan-yen P'u-lu-hu
Tsung-pi. See Wan-yen Wu-chu
tsung ssu-p'in 從四品
Tsung Tse 宗澤
Tsung-wang. See Wan-yen Wo-li-pu
tsung wu-p'in 從五品
tu po-chi-lieh 都勃極烈
Tu Shan-fu 杜善夫
tu yüan-shuai fu 都元帥府
T'u-tan Ch'üan 徒單全
T'u-tan I 徒單鎰
Tun-en ch'eng 鈍恩城
t'un-t'ien chün 屯田軍
Tung Chieh-yüan 董解元
tz'u 詞
tz'u-chang 詞章
tz'u-shih 刺史
wai-ch'ao 外朝
wan-hu 萬戶
Wan-yen A-ku-ta 完顏阿骨打 (Emperor T'ai-tsu 太祖)

Glossary

A-li 阿里
A-li-ho-man 阿里合懣
Ch'eng-hui 承暉
Chih-ning 志寧
Chin 璟 or Ma-ta-ko 麻達葛 (Emperor Chang-tsung 章宗)
Han-p'u 函普
Ho-che 劾者
Ho-li-po 劾里鉢
Hsi-nei 習揑
Hsi-yin 希尹
Hsieh-lieh 科烈
Hsieh-yeh 斜也 (Kao 杲)
Hsün 珣 (Emperor Hsüan-tsung 宣宗)
Liang 亮 (King Hai-ling 海陵)
Lou-shih 婁室
Meng-yang 孟陽
Mou-liang-hu 謀良虎 (Tsung-hsiung 宗雄)
Wan-yen Mou-yen 謀衍
Nien-han 粘罕 (Tsung-han 宗翰)
O-lu-kuan 訛魯觀 (Tsung-chün 宗雋)

Pa-hai 跋海
Pa-hu-lu 把胡魯
Pi 弼
Po-ti 孛迭
P'o-la-shu 頗拉淑
P'o-lu-huo 婆盧火
P'u-lu-hu 蒲盧虎 (Tsung-p'an 宗磐)
Sa-kai 撒改
Shih-ku-nai 實古迺
Shih-lu 石魯
Shou 璹
Shou-chen 守貞
Shuang 爽
Sui-k'o 綏可
Ta-lan 撻懶 (Ch'ang 昌)
Tan 亶 (Emperor Hsi-tsung 熙宗)
Te-ming 德明
Tsung-fu 宗輔
Tsung-hsien 宗憲
Wan-yen Wo-li-pu 斡離不 (Tsung-wang 宗望)
Wo-lu 斡魯
Wo-pen 斡本 (Tsung-kan 宗幹)
Wu-ch'i-mai 吳乞買 (Emperor T'ai-tsung 太宗)

Glossary

Wu-chu 兀朮 (Tsung-pi 宗弼)
Wu-ku-nai 烏古迺
Wu-lu 烏魯
Wu-lu 烏祿 (Emperor Shih-tsung 世宗)
Wu-ya-shu 烏雅束
Ying-chu-k'o 銀朮可
Ying-ko 盈歌
Yung-chi 永濟 (King Wei-shao 衛紹)
Yün-ch'eng 允成
Yün-kung 允功
Wang An-shih 王安石
Wang Kuai 王澮
Wang Jo-hsü 王若虛
Wang O 王鶚
Wang Yün 王惲
wei-ch'i 圍棋
Wei-shao. See Wan-yen yung-chi
wen 文
Wen-tu 溫都
wo-chi 窩集
Wo-li-pu (Tsung-wang). See Wan-yen
Wo-lu. See Wan-yen
Wo-pen. See Wan-yen
Wo-tsu 沃沮
Wu-che 烏者

Wu-chi 勿吉
Wu-ch'i-mai (Emperor T'ai-tsung). See Wan-yen
Wu-chu (Tsung-pi). See Wan-yen
Wu-ku-lun Chen 烏古倫貞
Wu-ku-nai. See Wan-yen
Wu-kuo pu 五國部
wu-li ch'ien 物力錢
Wu-lin-ta Shuang 烏林答爽
Wu-lin-ta Su 烏林答肅
Wu-lu (Emperor Shih-tsung). See Wan-yen
wu po-chi-lieh 吳勃極烈
Wu-t'a ch'eng 塢塔城
Wu-ya-shu. See Wan-yen
Wu-yen Kung-jui 烏延公稅
Ya-li. See Yeh-lü
Yang Huan 楊奐
Yang P'u 楊璞
Yang Shih 楊時
Yang Yün-i 楊雲翼
Yeh-lan 耶懶
Yeh-lü Chang-nu 耶律章奴

Ch'u-ts'ai 楚材
Hao-jan 浩然
Lü 履
Nieh-li 捏里
Ta-shih 大石
Ya-li 雅里
Yü-tu 余睹
Yen Ting-chi 閻鼎吉
Yen-Yün 燕雲
Ying-chu-k'o. *See* Wan-yen
Ying-ko. *See* Wan-yen
yu fu-yüan-shuai 右副元帥
yü-shih t'ai 御史台
Yü-tu. *See* Yeh-lü
Yü-wen Hsü-chung 宇文虛中
Yü Yün-wen 虞允文
Yüan Hao-wen 元好問
yüan-pen 院本
Yüeh-chou 越州
Yung-chi (King Wei-shao). *See* Wan-yen
Yün-ch'eng. *See* Wan-yen
Yün-kung. *See* Wan-yen

Bibliography

Primary Sources

Anon. *Ta-Chin te-yün t'u-shuo* 大金德運圖說 [Discussions on the dynastic virtue and element of the Great Chin, with illustration]. 1 *ch*. *SKCS*, 4th ser. ed.

Anon. *Chin-yüan pei-lu* 金源碑錄 [Collected stone tablets of the Chin]. Rare book in the Fu ssu-nien Library, Institute of History and Philology, Academia Sinica.

Anon. *Sung-shih ch'üan-wen hsü tzu-chih t'ung-chien* 宋史全文續資治通鑑 [The complete text of Sung history: continuation to the comprehensive mirror for aid in government]. 36 *ch*. Taipei: Wen-hai 文海, 1969.

Anon. *Tiao-fa lu* 弔伐錄 [Records of consoling the people and punishing the rebellious]. 2 *ch*. *SPTK* 3rd ser. ed.

Chang Chin-wu 張金吾. *Chin-wen tsui* 金文最 [Anthology of Chin literature]. 60 *ch*. Soochow shu-chü 蘇州書局 ed., 1895.

Chang Wei 張暐. *Ta-Chin chi-li* 大金集禮 [Compendium of ceremonies of the Great Chin]. 40 *ch*. *Ts'ung-shu chi-ch'eng* ed.

Chao Ping-wen 趙秉文. *Hsien-hsien lao-jen fu-shui wen-chi* 閑閑老人滏水文集 [Collected works of the old man Hsien-hsien]. 20 *ch.* SPTK ed.

Chao Meng-fu 趙孟頫. *Sung-hsüeh-chai wen-chi* 松雪齋文集 [Collected works of Sung-hsüeh-chai]. 10 *ch.* and appendix. SPTK ed.

Ch'en Chun 陳準. *Pei-feng yang-sha lu* 北風揚沙錄 [Records of the sands spread by the wind from the north]. 1 *ch.* *Shuo-fu* 說郛 ed.

Cheng Yüan-yu 鄭元祐. *Sui-ch'ang-shan-ch'iao tsa-lu* 遂昌山樵雜錄 [Miscellaneous notes of the Sui-ch'ang woodcutter]. In *Hsüeh-hai lei-pien* 學海類編. 7: 4186-91. Wen-hai 文海 ed.

Ch'eng Cho 程卓. *Shih-Chin lu* 使金錄 [Report on the mission to the Chin]. 1 *ch.* *Yü-yüan ts'ung-shu* 芋園叢書 ed.

Ch'iu Ch'u-chi 丘處機. *P'an-ch'i chi* 磻溪集 [Collected works of P'an-ch'i]. In *Tao-tsang* 道藏. 6 *ch.* Shanghai: Han-fen lou 涵芬樓 1925, *ts'e* 797.

Chou Lin-chih 周麟之. *Hai-ling chi* 海陵集 [Collected works of Hai-ling]. 23 *ch.* and appendix. *Hai-ling ts'ung-k'e* 海陵叢刻 ed.

Chou Te-ch'ing 周德清. *Chung-yüan yin-yün* 中原音韻 [The rhyme of the Central Plain]. In *San-ch'ü ts'ung-k'an* 散曲叢刊. Chung-hua shu-chü 中華書局 ed., n.d.

Chuang Chung-fang 莊仲方, ed. *Chin-wen ya* 金文雅 [Anthology of Chin prose]. 19 *ch.* Kiangsu shu-chü 江蘇書局, 1891.

Chung Pang-chih 鍾邦直. "Hsuan-ho i-ssu feng-shih hsing-ch'eng-lu" 宣和乙巳奉使行程錄 [Report of the mission of the year I-ssu (1125) of the Hsüan-ho period]. In *BIHP* 6, no. 2 (1936): 266-79.

Fan Ch'eng-ta 范成大. *Lan-p'ei lu* 攬轡錄 [Records of holding the reins]. 7 pp. *Chih-pu-tsu-chai ts'ung-shu* 知不足齋叢書 ed.

Hsia Wen-yen 夏文彥. *T'u-hui pao-chien* 圖繪

Bibliography

寶鑑 [A precious mirror for painting]. 8 *ch*. Chieh-lü ts'ao-t'ang 借綠草堂 ed., 1365.

Hsieh Shen-fu 謝深甫 et al. *Ch'ing-yüan t'iao-fa shih-lei* 慶元條法事類 [A compilation of the edicts and the laws of the Ch'ing-yüan era: 1195-1200]. 36 *ch*. Rare book in the National Central Library, Republic of China.

Hsü Meng-hsin 徐夢莘 . *San-ch'ao pei-meng hui-pien* 三朝北盟會編 [Compendium on the northern alliance under the three reigns: 1101-1161]. 250 *ch*. Taipei: Wen-hai ed., 1962.

Hsü Sung 徐松 , ed. *Sung-hui-yao chi-kao* 宋會要輯稿 [Collected drafts on government institutions of the Sung dynasty]. 8 vols. Shanghai: Chung-hua shu-chü ed., 1957.

Hu P'ing-chih 胡聘之 . *Shan-yu shih-k'e ts'ung-pien* 山右石刻叢編 [Collected stone tablets of Shansi]. 40 *ch*. 1901 ed.

Huang Hsüeh-so 黃雪簑 . *Ch'ing-lou chi* 青樓集 [Collected works of Ch'ing-lou]. 1 *ch*. *Ku-chin shuo-hai* 古今說海 ed.

Huang Tzu-hung 黃子洪 , ed. *Chu-tzu yü-lei* 朱子語類 [Collected sayings of Chu Hsi]. 140 *ch*. 1872 ed.

Hung Hao 洪皓 . *P'o-yang chi* 鄱陽集 [Collected works of P'o-yang]. 4 *ch*. and appendix. *San-jui-t'ang* 三瑞堂 ed., 1870.

_____. *Sung-mo chi-wen* 松漠紀聞 [Travel records of the pine and desert area]. 2 *ch*. and appendix. *Liao-hai ts'ung-shu* 遼海叢書 ed.

Hung Mai 洪邁 . *Yung-chai sui-pi* 容齋隨筆 [Random notes of Yung-chai]. 74 *ch*. *SPTK* ed.

K'ung Yüan-ts'o 孔元措 . *Kung-shih tsu-t'ing kuang-chi* 孔氏祖庭廣記 [Extensive records of the Ancestral Hall of the K'ung family]. 12 *ch*. *Hsü ku-i ts'ung-shu* 續古逸叢書 .

Li Ch'un-fu 李純甫 [Chih-ch'un 之純]. *P'ing-shan hsien-sheng Ming-tao chi shuo* 屏山先生鳴道集說 [Commentaries of the *Ming-tao chi*]. 5 *ch*. Ming ed. In the Pei-p'ing t'u-shu-kuan 北平圖書館 .

Li Hsin-ch'uan 李心傳. *Chien-yen i-lai ch'ao-yeh tsa-chi* 建炎以來朝野雜記 [Miscellaneous notes since the chien-yen era: 1127-1162]. 40 ch. *Wu-ying-tien chü-chen-pan ch'üan-shu* 武英殿聚珍版全書 ed.

———. *Chien-yen i-lai hsi-nien yao-lu* 建炎以來繫年要錄 [Annual records of important events since the Chien-yen era: 1127-1162]. 200 ch. *Kuang-ya ts'ung-shu* 廣雅叢書 ed.

Li Kang 李綱. *Ching-k'ang ch'uan-hsin lu* 靖康傳信錄 [Authentic records of the Ching-k'ang period]. 3 ch. *Ssu-pu pei-yao* 四部備要 ed.

Liu Ch'i 劉祁. *Kuei-ch'ien chih* 歸潛志 [Records of the Kuei-ch'ien-t'ang]. 14 ch. *Chih-pu-tsu-chai ts'ung-shu* ed.

Lou Yüeh 樓鑰. *Kung-k'uei chi* 攻媿集 [Collected works of Kung-k'uei]. 112 ch. SPTK, 2d ser.

Lü I-hao 呂頤浩. *Chung-mu chi* 忠穆集 [Collected works of Chung-mu]. 8 ch. SKCS ed.

Lu Yu 陸游. *Lao-hsüeh-an pi-chi* 老學庵筆記 [The Lao-hsüeh-an notes]. 10 ch. *Pai-hai* 稗海 ed.

Pi Yüan 畢沅, and Juan Yüan 阮元. *Shan-tso chin-shih chih* 山左金石志. [Records of bronzes and stone tablets in Shantung]. 24 ch. I-wen 藝文 ed., 1966.

Su T'ien-chüeh 蘇天爵. *Kuo-ch'ao wen-lei* 國朝文類 [Anthology of Yüan literature]. 70 ch. SPTK ed.

Sung Lien 宋濂 et al. *Yüan-shih* 元史 [Dynastic history of the Yüan]. 210 ch. Po-na ed.

Tai Piao-yüan 戴表元. *Yen-yüan Tai-hsien-sheng wen-chi* 剡源戴先生文集 [Collected works of Mr. Tai of Yen-yüan]. 30 ch. SPTK ed.

T'ao Tsung-i 陶宗儀. *Cho-keng lu* 輟耕錄 [Writings after farming]. 30 ch. *Chin-tai mi-shu* 津逮秘書 ed.

T'o-t'o 脫脫 et al. *Chin-shih* 金史 [Dynastic history of the Chin]. 135 ch. Po-na ed.

———. *Liao-shih* 遼史 [Dynastic history of the

Bibliography

———. *Sung-shih* 宋史 [Dynastic history of the S'ung]. 496 *ch*. Po-na ed.

Ts'ai Sung-nien 蔡松年. *Ming-hsiu chi* 明秀集 [Collected works of Ming-hsiu]. 6 *ch*. *Chiu-Chin-jen chi* 九金人集 ed.

Wang Jo-hsü 王若虛. *Hu-nan i-lao chi* 滹南遺老集 [Collected works of the remnant old man of Hu-nan]. 45 *ch*. SPTK ed.

Wang Kuo-wei 王國維. *Meng-ta pei-lu chien-chu* 蒙韃備錄箋注 [Annotated *Meng-ta pei-lu*]. 15 pp. In *Wang-chung-k'o-kung i-shu* 王忠慤公遺書. Ser. 3, 1927.

———. *Hei-ta shih-lüeh chien-chu* 黑韃事略箋注 [Annotated *Hei-ta shih-lüeh*]. 24 pp. In *Wang-chung-k'o-kung i-shu*. Ser. 3.

Wang O 王鶚. *Ju-nan i-shih* 汝南遺事 [Remnant events of Ju-nan]. 4 *ch*. *Chi-fu ts'ung-shu* 畿輔叢書 ed.

Wang Yün 王惲. *Ch'iu-chien hsien-sheng ta-ch'üan wen-chi* 秋澗先生大全文集 [Complete works of Mr. Ch'iu-chien]. 100 *ch*. SPTK ed.

Wen Wei-chien 文惟簡. *Lu-t'ing shih-shih* 虜廷事實 [Facts about the barbarian court]. 3 pp. *Shuo-fu* ed.

Yang Huan 楊奐. *Huan-shan i-kao* 還山遺稿 [Extant drafts of Huan-shan]. *Shih-yüan ts'ung-shu* 適園叢書.

Yang Wan-li 楊萬里. *Ch'eng-chai chi* 誠齋集 [Collected works of Ch'eng-chai]. 133 *ch*. SPTK ed.

Yao Sui 姚燧. *Mu-an chi* 牧庵集 [Collected works of Mu-an]. 36 *ch*. SPTK ed.

Yeh Lung-li 葉隆禮. *Ch'i-tan kuo-chih* 契丹國志 [History of the Ch'i-tan kingdom]. 27 *ch*. *Ssu-ch'ao pieh-shih* 四朝別史, Sao-yeh shan-fang 掃葉山房 ed.

Yü Chi 虞集. *Tao-yüan hsüeh-ku lu* 道園學古錄 [Tao-Yüan's records of learning from the past]. 50 ch. SPTK ed.

Yüan Hao-wen 元好問. Chung-chou chi 中州集 [Works of the central region]. 10 ch. SPTK ed.

———. I-shan hsien-sheng wen-chi 遺山先生文集 [Collected works of Mr. I-shan]. 40 ch. SPTK ed.

———. Yüan-i-shan shih chien-chu 元遺山詩箋注 [Annotated poems of Yüan I-shan]. 14 ch. Ssu-pu pei-yao ed.

Yüeh K'o 岳珂. T'ing-shih 桯史. 15 ch. SPTK ed., 2d ser.

Yü-wen Mao-chao 宇文懋昭. Ta-chin-kuo chih 大金國志 [History of the Great Chin kingdom]. 40 ch. In Ssu-ch'ao pieh-shih.

Secondary Sources

Books and Articles in Chinese, Japanese, and Korean

Aoki Masaru 青木正兒. "Nanboku kyoku genryu kō" 南北曲源流考 [The origin of southern and northern drama]. In *Kano kyōju kanreki kinen shinagaku ronsō* 狩野教授還曆紀念支那學論叢, pp. 849-944. (Kyoto: kōbundō 弘文堂 1928).

Aoki Tomitarō 青木富太郎. "Genshō gyoja kō" 元初行省考 [Examination of the province in early Yüan]. *Shigaku Zasshi* 51, nos. 4-5 (1940): 480-501, 614-45.

Aoyama Kosuke 青山公亮. "Kinchō kotai shōshoshō kō" 金朝行臺尚書省考 [Examination of the mobile presidential council in the Chin dynasty]. *Taihaku teikoku daigaku bunsei gakubu shigaku ka kenkyū nembo* 台北帝國大學文政學部史學科研究年報 no. 1 (1934), pp. 151-62.

Araki Yoshikazu 荒木敏一. *Sō-dai kakyo seido kenkyū* 宋代科舉制度研究 [The civil service examination of the Sung dynasty]. Kyoto: Kyoto University, 1969.

Chang Hsiu-min 張秀民. "Chin-yüan chien-pen k'ao" 金源槧本考 [Publications of the

Kuo-tzu-chien of the Chin dynasty]. *T'u-shu chi-k'an* 2, no. 1 (1935): 19-25.

―――. "Liao, Chin, Hsi Hsia k'e-shu chien-shih" 遼金西夏刻書簡史 [A brief history of printing in the Liao, Chin, and Hsi Hsia]. *Wen-wu*, no. 3 (1959), pp. 11-16.

Chang Po-ch'uan 張博泉. "Chin-tai nu-pei wen-t'i ti yen-chiu" 金代奴婢問題的研究 [A study of the problem of slavery in the Chin dynasty]. *Sung-Liao-Chin she-hui ching-chi-shih lun-chi* 2: 226-32.

Chao Ching-shen 趙景深. *Hsi-ch'ü pi-t'an* 戲曲筆談 [Notes on drama]. Shanghai: Chung-hua shu-chü, 1963.

Chao I 趙翼. *Nien-erh-shih cha-chi* 廿二史劄記 [Notes on the twenty-two histories]. 36 *ch*. Kuang-ya shu-chü 廣雅書局.

Chao T'ieh-han 趙鐵寒. *Huo-yao ti fa-ming* 火藥的發明 [The invention of gunpowder]. Taipei: Chung-hua ts'ung-shu wei-yüan-hui 中華叢書委員會, 1960.

―――. "Sung-Chin hai-shang chih-meng shih-mo chi" 宋金海上之盟始末記 [An historical account of the alliance between the Sung and the Chin]. *Ta-lu tsa-chih* 25, nos. 5-7 (1962): 9-14, 14-19, 26-34.

―――. "Yen-Yün shih-lui-chou ti ti-li fen-hsi" 燕雲十六州的地理分析 [A geographical analysis of the sixteen prefectures of Yen and Yün]. In *Sung-Liao-Chin shih yen-chiu lun-chi*, pp. 53-62.

Ch'en Hsiang-wei 陳相偉. "Chi-lin huai-te ch'in-chia-t'un ku-ch'eng tiao-ch'a chi" 吉林懷德秦家屯古城調查記 [Archaeological investigation of an old town in Kirin]. *Kaogu*, no. 2 (1964), pp. 79-82.

Ch'en Lo-su 陳樂素. "San-ch'ao pei-meng hui-pien k'ao" 三朝北盟會編考 [A study of the *San-ch'ao pei-meng hui-pien*]. *BIHP* 6, nos. 2-3 (1936): 193-279.

Ch'en Shu 陳述. "Cha-chün k'ao-shih ch'u-kao" 紮

軍考釋初稿 [First draft of a study of the *cha-chün*]. *BIHP* 20, no. 2 (1949): 251-300.

———. *Chin-shih shih-pu wu-chung* 金史拾補五種 [Five supplements to Chin history]. Peking: K'o-hsüeh ch'u-pan-she 科學出版社, 1960.

Ch'en Wen-shih 陳文石. "Ch'ing-t'ai-tsung shih-tai ti chung-yao cheng-chih she-shih" 清太宗時代的重要政治設施 [Important political measures of Ch'ing-t'ai-tsung]. *BIHP* 40, pt. 1 (1968): 295-371.

Ch'en Yüan 陳垣. *Nan-Sung ch'u Ho-pei hsin Tao-chiao k'ao* 南宋初河北新道教考 [New Taoist societies in the northern provinces at the beginning of the Southern Sung dynasty]. Peking: The Catholic University of Peking, 1941.

———. *Yüan hsi-yü-jen hua-hua k'ao* 元西域人華化考 [The sinicization of the westerners in the Yüan]. *Li-yün shu-wu ts'ung-k'an* 勵耘書屋叢刊, ts'e 1-2, 1934. 8 ch. English translation and annotation: Ch'ien Hsing-hai and L. Carrington Goodrich, *Western and Central Asians in China under the Mongols*. Los Angeles: *Monumenta Serica* at the University of California, 1966.

Cheng Cheng-t'o 鄭振鐸. *Chung-kuo su-wen-hsüeh shih* 中國俗文學史 [History of Chinese vernacular literature]. 2 vols. Peking: Tso-chia ch'u-pan-she 作家出版社, 1957. Reprint. Hong Kong, 1963.

Cheng Ch'ien 鄭騫. "Tung-hsi-hsiang yü tz'u chi nan-pei-ch'ü ti kuan-hsi" 董西廂與詞及南北曲的關係 [The relationship between the *Tung-hsi-hsiang* and the *tz'u* and southern and northern drama]. *Bulletin of the College of Arts, National Taiwan University*, no. 2 (1951), pp. 113-37.

Ch'eng Shuo-lo 程溯洛. "Nü-chen pien-fa k'ao" 女真辮髮考 [A study of the queue of the Jurchen]. *Shih-hsüeh chi-k'an*, no. 5 (1947), pp. 241-65.

Chi-fu t'ung-chih 畿輔通志 [General history of the Chih-li Province]. 300 *ch*. 1934 ed.

Chia Lan-p'o 賈蘭坡, and Yen Yen 顏誾. "Hsi-t'uan-shan jen-ku ti yen-chiu pao-kao" 西團

山人骨的研究報告 [A report on the human bones of Hsi-t'uan-shan]. *K'ao-ku hsüeh-pao*, no. 2 (1963), pp. 101-9.

Chien Po-tsan 翦伯贊, *Chung-kuo-shih lun-chi* 中國史論集 [Collected essays on Chinese history]. Chungking: Wen-feng shu-chü 文風書局, 1943.

Ch'ien Mu 錢穆. "Sung i-hsia Chung-kuo wen-hua chih ch'ü-shih" 宋以下中國文化之趨勢 [Trends of Chinese cultural development since the Sung]. *Ssu-hsiang yü shih-tai*, no. 31 (1944), pp. 18-28.

Ch'ien Nan-yang 錢南揚. "Sung-Chin-Yüan hsi-chü pan-yen k'ao" 宋金元戲劇搬演考 [The performance of drama in the Sung, Chin, and Yüan dynasties]. *Yen-ching Journal of Chinese Studies*, no. 20 (1936), pp. 177-94.

Chin Yü-fu 金毓黻. *Sung-Liao-Chin shih* 宋遼金史 [History of the Sung, the Liao, and the Chin]. Shanghai: Commercial Press, 1946. Reprint. Taipei: Lo-t'ien ch'u-pan-she 樂天出版社, 1964.

──── . *Tung-pei t'ung-shih* 東北通史 [History of the Northeast]. Chungking: Wu-shih-nien-tai ch'u-pan-she 五十年代出版社, 1941. Reprint. Taipei: Lo-t'ien ch'u-pan-she, 1971.

Chong In-Ji 鄭麟趾. *Koryŏ sa* 高麗史 [History of Koryŏ]. 137 *ch.* Seoul: Yonhi Taehakkyo 延禧大學 ed., 1955.

Chou Chieh 州杰. "Nei-meng-ku chao-meng Liao-t'ai-tsu ling tiao-ch'a san-chi" 內蒙古昭盟遼太祖陵調查散記 [Notes on the investigation of the mausoleum of Liao-t'ai-tsu]. *Kaogu*, no. 5 (1966), pp. 263-66.

Chu Hsi-tsu 朱希祖. "Chin k'ai-kuo-ch'ien san-shih yü Kao-li ho-chan nien-piao" 金開國前三世與高麗和戰年表 [A chronological table of peace and war between the Chin and Koryŏ, 1094-1115]. *Yen-chin Journal of Chinese Studies*, no. 15 (1934), pp. 101-61.

──── . "Chin-yüan hsing-shih k'ao" 金源姓氏考 [A study of the surnames of the Chin]. *Chung-*

Shan ta-hsüeh wen-shih-hsüeh yen-chiu-so yüeh-k'an 2, nos. 3 and 4 (1934): 1-8.

_____. *Wei-ch'i lu chiao-pu* 偽齊錄校補 [Criticisms and supplements to the records of the puppet Ch'i]. Chungking: Tu-li ch'u-pan-she 獨立出版社, 1944.

_____. *Wei-ch'u lu chi-pu* 偽楚錄輯補 [Supplements to the records of the puppet Ch'u]. Taipei: Cheng-chung shu-chü 正中書局 ed., 1955.

Chu Hsieh 朱偰. "Pa-pai-nien-ch'ien ti Pei-ching wei-ta chien-chu Chin Chung-tu kung-tien t'u k'ao" 八百年前的北京偉大建築金中都宮殿圖考 [A study of the great palace architecture of the Central Capital of the Chin of 800 years ago, with maps]. *Wen-wu ts'ang-k'ao tzu-liao*, no. 7 (1955), pp. 67-75.

Chuang Shen 莊申. *Chung-kuo hua-shih yen-chiu hsü-chi* 中國畫史研究續集 [Studies in the history of Chinese painting, supplementary volume]. Taipei: Cheng-chung shu-chü, 1972.

Ch'üan Han-sheng 全漢昇. "Sung-Chin chien ti tsou-ssu mou-i" 宋金間的走私貿易 [The smuggling trade between the Sung and Chin kingdoms]. *BIHP* 11 (1947): 425-47.

Chung-kuo shang-ku-shih pien-chi wei-yüan-hui 中國上古史編輯委員會 *Chung-kuo shang-ku-shih (tai-ting-kao)*. Vol. 1: *Shih-ch'ien pu-fen* 中國上古史（待定稿）第一本史前部分 [Draft of ancient history of China. Vol. 1, Prehistory]. Taipei: Institute of History and Philology, Academia Sinica, 1972.

Fang Chuang-yu 方狀猷. "Liao-Chin-Yüan k'o-chü nien-piao" 遼金元科舉年表 [Tables on Liao, Chin, and Yüan examinations]. *Shuo-wen yüeh-k'an* 3, no. 12 (1944): 23-34.

Feng Chia-sheng 馮家昇. "Ch'i-tan ming-hao k'ao-shih" 契丹名號考釋 [The origin of the name Ch'i-tan]. *Yen-ching Journal of Chinese Studies*, no. 13 (1933), pp. 1-48.

_____. "Ho-yao ti fa-hsien chi-ch'i ch'uan-pu" 火藥的發現及其傳佈 [The discovery and diffusion of gunpowder]. *Shih-hsüeh chi-k'an*, no. 5

Bibliography

(1947), pp. 29-84.

Feng-t'ien t'ung-chih 奉天通志 [General history of Feng-t'ien]. 260 *ch*. 1934 ed.

Fu Lo-huan 傅樂煥. "Liao-tai ssu-shih na-po k'ao wu-p'ien" 遼代四時捺鉢考五篇 [Nat-pat: the seasonal life of the Khitan grand khans]. *BIHP* 10 (1942): 223-347.

Fu Ssu-nien 傅斯年. *Tung-pei shih-kang* 東北史綱 [Outline history of the Northeast]. Nanking: Institute of History and Philology, Academia Sinica, 1932.

Fu Ta-li 傅達禮 et al. *Wu-t'i ch'ing-wen chien* 五體清文鑑 [A glossary of five languages in the Ch'ing dynasty]. 3 vols. Peking: Min-tsu ch'u-pan-she, 民族出版社 1957.

Fujida Akira 藤枝晃. *Seifuku ōchō* 征服王朝 [Conquest dynasties]. Osaka: Akita ya, 1948.

Han Ju-lin 韓儒林. "Nü-chen i-ming k'ao" 女真譯名考 [A study of the transcription of the name Nü-chen]. *Studia Serica* 3, nos. 1-4 (1943): 1-11.

Haraguchi Hitoshi 原口仁. "Kingaku seiryū matsu seinangun no dōin sōsū ni tsuite" 金國正隆末征南軍の動員總數について [On the number of Chin troops mobilized to invade the south in the late Cheng-lung period]. *Tōyō Shigaku*, no. 21 (1959), pp. 17-26.

Hei-lung-chiang po-wu-kuan 黑龍江博物館. "Hei-lung-chiang La-lin-ho yu-an k'ao-ku tiao-ch'a" 黑龍江拉林河右岸考古調查 [Archaeological investigation of the Lalin River banks]. *Kaogu*, no. 12 (1964), pp. 603-6.

Ho Chien-min 何建民, trans. and ed. *Sui-T'ang shih-tai hsi-yü-jen hua-hua k'ao* 隋唐時代西域人華化考 [The sinicization of foreigners during the Sui and T'ang dynasties]. Shanghai: Chung-hua shu-chü, 1939.

Hsü Ping-ch'ang 徐炳昶. "Chiao Chin Wan-yen Hsi-yin shen-tao-pei shu-hou" 校金完顏希

尹神逵碑書後 [Remarks after examining the epitaph of Wan-yen Hsi-yin]. *Shih-hsüeh chi-k'an*, no. 1 (1936), pp. 3-18.

Hsü Yü-hu 徐玉虎. "Sung-Chin hai-shang lien-meng ti kai-kuan" 宋金海上聯盟的概觀 [A general observation of the alliance between the Sung and the Chin]. *Ta-lu tsa-chih* 11, no. 12 (1955): 24-28.

Hu Chi 胡忌. *Sung-Chin tsa-chü k'ao* 宋金雜劇考 [A study of the plays of the Sung and the Chin]. Shanghai: Chung-hua shu-chü, 1959.

Huang Ta-hua 黃大華. *Chin tsai-fu nien-piao* 金宰輔年表 [Chronological table of Chin high officials]. In *Erh-shih-wu shih pu-pien* 二十五史補編, pp. 8185-8197. K'ai-ming shu-tien 開明書店.

Huang Tsung-hsi 黃宗羲. *Sung-Yüan hsüeh-an* 宋元學案 [Schools of thought during the Sung and Yüan dynasties]. Taipei: Cheng-Chung shu-chü ed., 1959.

Ikeuchi Hiroshi 池內宏. "Kin no kenkoku izen ni okeru kanganshi no kunsho no shogo ni tsuite" 金の建國以前に於ける完顏氏の君長の稱號について [On the titles of the Wan-yen chieftains before the Chin]. *Tōyō Gakuhō* 20, no. 1 (1932): 99-138.

―――. "Kinshi seiki no kenkyū 金史世紀の研究 [A study of the "Imperial Genealogy" of the dynastic history of the Chin]. *Mansen chiri rekishi kenkyū hōkoku* 滿鮮地理歷史研究報告, no. 11 (1926), pp. 177-313.

Jao Tsung-i 饒宗頤. "San-chiao lun yü Sung-Chin hsüeh-shu 三教論與宋金學術 [The theory of combination of the three religions and the intellectual world of the Sung and the Chin]. *Tung-hsi wen-hua*, no. 11 (1968), pp. 24-32.

Katō Shigeshi 加藤繁. *Shina keizaishi kōshō* 支那經濟史考證 [Studies in Chinese economic history]. 2 vols. Tokyo: Tōyō bunko 東洋文庫, 1953.

Ku Tsu-yü 顧祖禹. *Tu-shih fang-yü chi-yao* 讀

Bibliography

史方輿紀要 [Important records of historical geography]. 130 *ch*. Taipei: Hsin-hsing shu-chü 新興書局 ed., 1956.

Ku Yen-wu 顧炎武. *Jih-chih lu* 日知錄 [Notes of knowledge accumulated daily]. 32 *ch*. Taipei: World Book Co., 1962.

Kuan Sung-fang 關松房. "Chin-tai tz'u-ch'i ho Chün-yao ti wen-t'i" 金代磁器和鈞窯的問題 [The China in the Chin dynasty and the problem of Chün kiln]. *Wen-wu ts'ang-k'ao tzu-liao*, no. 2 (1958), pp. 25-26.

Kuan Tung-kuei 管東貴. "Man-tsu ju-kuan-ch'ien ti wen-hua fa-chan tui t'a-men hou-lai han-hua ti ying-hsiang" 滿族入關前的文化發展對他們後來漢化的影響 [The Manchus' cultural borrowing before the conquest of China and its influence on their sinicization]. *BIHP* 40, pt. 1 (1968): 255-79.

_____. "Man-tsu ti ju-kuan yü han-hua" 滿族的入關與漢化 [The Manchu conquest of China aand their sinicization]. *BIHP* 43, pt. 3 (1971): 445-88.

Kuan Yen-hsiang 關燕詳. "Chin-tai ti nu-li chih-tu" 金代的奴隸制度 [Slavery in the Chin dynasty]. *Hsien-tai shih-hsüeh* 3, no. 2 (1937): 1-11.

Kubo Noritada 窪德忠. "Kindai no shindōkyō to bukkyō -- sankyō chōwa shisō kara mita" 金代の新道教と佛教――三教調和思想からみた [The new Taoism and Buddhism in the Chin dynasty--from the viewpoint of the theory of the mixture of the three religions]. *Tōhōgaku*, no. 25 (1963), pp. 68-82.

Lan Wen-cheng 藍文徵. "Hai-shang ti Nü-chen" 海上的女真 [The Jurchen on the sea]. *Min-chu p'ing-lun* 民主評論 4, no. 24 (1953): 676-79.

Li Chien-nung 李劍農. *Sung-Yüan-Ming ching-chi shih kao* 宋元明經濟史稿 [Draft economic history of the Sung, Yüan, and Ming dynasties]. Peking: San-lien shu-tien 三聯書店, 1957.

Li Yu-t'ang 李有棠. *Liao-Chin chi-shih pen-mo* 遼金紀事本末 [Topic accounts from beginning to end of the Liao and Chin histories]. 92 ch. In *Li-ch'ao chi-shih pen-mo* 歷朝紀事本末, 1893.

Liao-Chin-Yüan san-shih yü-chieh 遼金元三史語解 [Dictionary of Liao, Chin, and Yüan histories]. Kiangsu shu-chü, 1878.

Liao-ning-sheng po-wu-kuan 遼寧省博物館. "Liao-ning Ch'ao-yang Chin-tai pi-hua mu" 遼寧朝陽金代壁畫墓 [A Chin tomb with mural paintings at Ch'ao-yang, Liaoning]. *Kaogu*, no. 4 (1962), pp. 182-85.

Ling Ch'un-sheng 凌純聲. *Sung-hua-chiang hsia-yu ti ho-che tsu* 松花江下游的赫哲族 [The Goldi tribe]. Nanking: Institute of History and Philology, Academia Sinica, 1934.

Liu Chieh 劉節. "Hao-t'ai-wang pei k'ao-shih" 好太王碑考釋 [A study of the Hao-t'ai-wang tablet]. *Kuo-hsüeh lun-ts'ung*, no. 1 (1929), pp. 11-54.

Liu Ming-shu 劉銘恕. "Sung-tai ch'u-pan-fa chi tui Liao Chin chih shu-chin" 宋代出版法及對遼金之書禁 [Laws concerning publications during the Sung dynasty and concerning the prohibition of books going to and coming from Liao and Chin]. *Bulletin of Chinese Studies* 5, pt. 1 (1945): 95-114.

———. "Sung-tai Liao-Chin wen-hua chih nan-chien" 宋代遼金文化之南漸 [The culture of Liao and Chin in its southward movement during the Sung]. *Bulletin of Chinese Studies* 6 (1946): 91-105.

Liu Shih-chü 劉時舉. *Hsü Sung pien-nien tzu-chih t'ung-chien* 續宋編年資治通鑑 [A supplement to the comprehensive mirror for aid in government of the Sung dynasty]. 15 ch. Hsüeh-chin t'ao-yüan 學津討原.

Lo Ch'i-tsu 羅繼祖. "Chin ch'ung-i-chün chieh-tu-shih Wang Fu mu-chih pa" 金崇義軍節度使王甫墓誌跋 [Note on the tablet inscription of Wang Fu]. *Manshu Shigaku* 3, no. 2 (1941): 35-36.

Lo Fu-i 羅福頤. *Man-chou chin-shih chih* 滿洲金石志 [Records of bronzes and stone tablets in Manchuria]. 6 *ch.* and *pu-i* 補遺, *wai-pien* 外編. Hsinking: Man-jih wen-hua hsieh-hui 滿日文化協會, 1937.

Mao Ch'i-ling 毛奇齡. *Hsi-ho shih-hua* 西河詩話 [Hsi-ho's talks about poems]. 1 *ch.* Chao-tai ts'ung-shu 昭代叢書.

Mao Wen 毛汶. "Chin-tai hsüeh-chih chih yen chiu" 金代學制之研究 [A study of the school system in the Chin dynasty]. *Kuo-hsüeh lun-ts'ung*, no. 7 (1936), pp. 26-36.

_____. *Liao-Chin shih-shih lun-wen chi* 遼金史事論文集 [Collected essays on the Liao and Chin histories]. Kaifeng: Commercial Press, 1935.

Meng Ssu-ming 蒙思明. *Yüan-tai she-hui chieh-chi chih-tu* 元代社會階級制度 [Social classes in the Yüan dynasty]. Peiping: Harvard-Yenching Institute, 1938.

Mikami Tsugio 三上次男. "Joshin jin no hatten to Kinshō no kansei" 女真人の發展と金初の官制 [The progress of the Jurchen and the government organization in early Chin]. *Rekishigaku Kenkyū* (Old), 4, no. 3 (1935): 277-85.

_____. "Kindai ni okeru chihō tochi seido ni tsuite" 金代に於ける地方統治制度について [The local government system of the Chin dynasty]. *Tōhō Gakuhō* [Tokyo], 14, no. 2 (1943): 145.

_____. *Kinshi kenkyū* 金史研究 [Studies in Chin history]. Tokyo: Chūō-kōran bijutsu shuppan 中央公論美術出版, 1970-73.
Vol. 1, *Kindai Joshin shakai no kenkyū* 金代女真社會の研究 [Studies in the Jurchen society]. 1972.
Vol. 2, *Kindai seiji seido no kenkyū* 金代政治制度の研究 [Studies in the political institutions of the Chin dynasty]. 1970.
Vol. 3, *Kindai seiji shakai no kenkyū* 金代政治社會の研究 [Studies in politics and society of the Chin dynasty]. 1973.

Nichiman bunka kyokai 日滿文化協會.

Manmoshi ronsō 滿蒙史論叢 [Essays on Manchurian and Mongolian history]. Vols. 1-3. Tokyo and Hsinking, 1938-40.

Niida Noboru 仁井田陞. "Kindai keihō kō" 金代刑法考 [A study of the criminal law in the Chin dynasty]. *Tōyōshi Kenkyū* (n.s.) 1, no. 1 (1944): 1-36; no. 2: 86-125.

Nogami Shunjō 野上俊靜. *Ryōkin no bukkyō* 遼金の佛教 [Buddhism in the Liao and Chi Chin dynasties]. Kyoto: Heirakuji shoten, 1953.

Ogawa Hiroto 小川裕人. "Kindai no butsuryokusen ni tsuite" 金代の物力錢に就りて [On the property tax of Chin]. *Tōyōshi Kenkyū* 5, no. 6 (1940): 420-37; 6, no. 1 (1941): 43-60; 6, no. 3 (1941): 193-217.

_____. "Sanjubu Joshin ni tsuite" 三十部女真に就って [On the thirty Jurchen clans]. *Tōyō Gakuhō* 24, no. 4 (1937): 561-601.

Onogawa Hidemi 小野川秀美, comp. *Kinshi goi shusei* 金史語彙集成 [Index to the dynastic history of the Chin]. 3 vols. Kyoto: Kyoto University, 1960-62.

Ōsaki Fujio 大崎富士夫. "Sō Kin bōeki no keitai" 宋金貿易の型態 [Types of trade between the Sung and the Chin]. *Hiroshima daigaku bungakubu kiyo*, no. 5 (1954), pp. 159-82.

Otagi Matsuo 愛宕松男. *Ajia no seifuku ōchō* アジアの征服王朝 [The conquest dynasties in Asia]. Tokyo: Kawabe shobo, 1969.

Shang Chung-lien 尚重濂. "Liang-Sung chih-chi min-chung k'ang-ti-shih yen-chiu" 兩宋之際民眾抗敵史研究 [A study of the history of the resistance movement during the late Northern Sung and the early Southern Sung]. *Hsin-ya hsüeh-pao* 5, no. 2 (1963): 147-238.

Shen K'ai 申鍇. "Wang Jo-hsü" 王若虛. *Kuo-hsüeh chi-k'an* 6, no. 2 (1936): 153-90.

Shih Kuo-ch'i 施國祁. *Chi-pei-chü tsa-chi* 吉貝居雜記 [Random notes of Chi-pei-chü]. 1 ch. *Hsüeh-t'ang ts'ung-k'e* 雪堂叢刻.

Bibliography

____. *Chin-shih hsiang-chiao* 金史詳校 [Careful criticism to the dynastic history of the Chin. 10 *ch*. *Kuang-ya ts'ung-shu*.

____. *Chin-yüan cha-chi* 金源劄記 [Notes on the Chin kingdom]. 2 *ch*. *Yang-shih ch'ien-ch'i-pai-erh-shih-chiu ho-chai ts'ung-shu* 仰視千七百二十九鶴齋叢書

Shimada Masao 島田正郎. "Joshin no konzoku to Kindai kon'inhō" 女真の婚俗と金代婚姻法 [Jurchen marriage customs and Chin marriage laws]. *Meiji daigaku hōritsu ronsō* 39, nos. 4-6 (1966): 639-66.

____. *Pei-ya-chou shih* 北亞洲史 [History of North Asia]. Taipei: College of Chinese Culture, 1964.

Shiratori Kurakichi 白鳥庫吉. "Kittan Joshin Seika monji kō" 契丹女真西夏文字考 [An investigation of the languages of the Ch'i-tan, Jurchen, and Hsi Hsia]. *Shigaku Zasshi* 9, nos. 11 and 12 (1898): 922-36, 1054-68.

____. "Tōko minzolu kō" 東胡民族考 [On the Tung-hu peoples]. *Shigaku Zasshi* 21 (1910): 369-93, 741-62, 1003-26; 22 (1911): 62-88, 589-607, 1265-88, 1381-1407.

Sogabe Shizuo 曾我部靜雄. "Tō no zatsuyo no Kin Gen ni oyobeshita eikyo--Kin no butsunyokusen to Gen no teizei no zenshin" 唐の雜徭の金元に及し太影響──金の物力錢と元の丁税の前身 [The influence of the miscellaneous tax of T'ang on Chin and Yüan--the antecedent of the property tax of Chin and the poll tax of the Yüan]. *Rekishi Kyoiku* 2, no. 6 (1954): 14-19.

Su T'ien-chüeh 蘇天爵. *Tzu-ch'i wen-kao* 滋溪文稿 [Drafts of Tzu-ch'i]. 30 *ch*. *Shih-yüan ts'ung-shu*.

Sun K'e-k'uan 孫克寬. "Ch'üan-chen-chiao k'ao-lüeh" 全真教考畧 [A brief study of the Ch'üan-chen sect]. *Ta-lu tsa-chih* 8, no. 10 (1954): 309-13.

____. *Yüan-tai tao-chiao chih fa-chan* 元代道教之發展 [The development of Taoism in the Yüan].

Taichang: Tung-hai University, 1968.

―――. *Yüan-tai Han-wen-hua chih huo-tung* 元代漢文化之活動 [The activities of Chinese culture in the Yüan dynasty]. Taipei: Chang-hua shu-chü, 1968.

Sung Wen-ping 宋文炳. "Nü-chen han-hua k'ao-lüeh" 女真漢化考略 [A brief study of the sinicization of the Jurchen]. In *Sui-T'ang shih-tai hsi-yü-jen hua-hua k'ao*, pp. 172-94. Edited by Ho Chien-min. Shanghai: Chung-hua shu-chü, 1939.

Ta-lu tsa-chih she 大陸雜誌社, ed. *Sung-Liao-Chin shih yen-chiu lun-chi* 宋遼金史研究論集 [Collected essays on the history of the Sung, Liao, and Chin dynasties]. Taipei: Ta-lu tsa-chih she, 1960.

T'ai Ching-nung 臺靜農. "Nü-chen-tsu t'ung-chih-hsia ti Han-yü wen-hsüeh--*chu-kung-tiao*" 女真族統治下的漢語文學――諸宮調 [Chinese literature under the rule of the Jurchen--*chu-kung-tiao*]. *Chung-wai Literary Monthly* 1, no. 1 (1972): 6-20.

Takao Yoshikata 高雄義堅. "Kindai ni okeru dō futsu nikyō no tokuchō" 金代に於ける道佛二教の特徵 [Characteristics of Taoism and Buddhism during the Chin dynasty]. *Shina Gaku* 5, no. 1 (1929): 137-51.

Tamura Jitsuzō 田村實造. *Chūgoku seifu ōchō ne kenkyū* 中國征服王朝の研究 [Studies on the conquest dynasties in China]. 2 vols. Kyoto: Kyoto University, 1964-71.

―――. "Daikin tokushōda shohi no kenkyū" 大金得勝陀碑頌の研究 [A study of the Te-sheng-t'o tablet]. *Tōyōshi Kenkyū* 2, nos. 5 and 6 (1937): 405-37, 542-60.

―――. "Kittan bukkyō no shakaishi no kōsatsu" 契丹佛教の社會史的考察. [A sociohistorical survey of Ch'i-tan Buddhism]. *Otagi Gakuhō* 18, no 1 (1937): 32-47.

T'ao Chin-sheng (Jing-shen Tao) 陶晉生. *Chin Hai-ling-ti ti fa Sung-yü Ts'ai-shih chan-i ti k'ao-shih* 金海陵帝的伐宋與采石

Bibliography

戰役的考實 [The invasion of the Southern Sung by Emperor Hai-ling of Chin and the battle of Ts'ai-shih: 1161]. Taipei: National Taiwan University, 1963.

_____. "Chin-tai ti cheng-chih chieh-kou" 金代的政治結構 [Political structure of the Chin]. *BIHP* 41, no. 4 (1969): 567-93.

_____. "Chin-tai ti cheng-chih ch'ung-t'u 金代的政治衝突 [Political conflicts in the Chin]. *BIHP* 43, no. 1 (1971): 135-61.

_____. *Pien-chiang-shih yen-chiu chi: Sung Chin shih-ch'i* 邊疆史研究集——宋金時期 [Studies in Chinese frontier history: the Sung and Chin periods]. Taipei: Commercial Press, 1971.

T'ao Hsi-sheng 陶希聖. "Chin-tai meng-an mou-k'e ti t'u-ti wen-t'i" 金代猛安謀克的土地問題 [The land problem in the Chin dynasty]. *Shih-huo pan-yüeh-k'an* 1, no. 8 (1935): 345-52.

_____. "Shih-i chih shih-ssu shih-chi ti ko-chung hun-yin chih-tu" 十一至十四世紀的各種婚姻制度 [Marital institutions during the eleventh to fourteenth centuries]. *Shih-huo pan-yüeh-k'an* 1, no. 12 (1935): 540-44; 2, no. 3 (1935): 139-42.

Teng Kuang-ming 鄧廣銘. "Nau-Sung tui Chin tou-cheng chung ti chi-ko wen-t'i" 南宋對金鬥爭中的幾個問題 [Problems in the Southern Sung's struggles against the Chin]. *Lishi Yanjiu*, no. 2 (1963), pp. 21-32.

_____. *Yüeh Fei chuan* 岳飛傳 [A biography of Yüeh Fei]. Chungking: Sheng-li Ch'u-pan-she 勝利出版社, 1945.

Teng Ssu-yü 鄧嗣禹. *Chung-kuo k'ao-shih chih-tu shih* 中國考試制度史 [A history of the Chinese examination system]. Nanking: 1936. Reprint. Taipei: Hsüeh-sheng shu-chü 學生書局, 1966.

Tōa kenkyūjo 東亞研究所. *Iminzoku no Shina tōchi shi* 異民族の支那統治史 [The rule of China by alien peoples]. Tokyo:

Dai Nippon yubenkai kodansha, 1944.

Tokiwa Daijō 常盤大定. "Kin no Ri Heisan sen meidō shūsetsu ni tsuite" 金の李屏山撰鳴道集説 について [On the *Ming-tao chi-shuo* written by Li P'ing-shan of the Chin]. *Hattori sensei koki shukuga kinen rombunshū* 服部先生古稀祝賀記念論文集, pp. 673-97. Tokyo: Fuzambō 富山房, 1936.

Torii Ryuzō 鳥居龍藏. "Chin Shang-ching-ch'eng chi-ch'i wen-hua" 金上京城及其文化 [Shang-ching of Chin dynasty]. *Yenching Journal of Chinese Studies*, no. 35 (1948), pp. 129-204.

────. "Chin Shang-chin-ch'eng fu-ssu k'ao" 金上京城佛寺考 [Buddhist temples in Shang-ching of the Chin dynasty]. *Yenching Journal of Chinese Studies*, no. 34 (1948), pp. 107-32.

Toyama Gunji 外山軍治. *Kinchōshi kenkyū* 金朝史研究 [Studies on the history of the Chin dynasty]. Kyoto: Kyoto University, 1964.

────. "Kin no Shōsō to Rihi" 金の章宗と李妃 [Chin Chang-tsung and Lady Li]. *Osaka gaikokugo daigaku gakuhō*, no. 29 (1973), pp. 379-88.

────. "Kinjin to sho" 金人と書 [The Chin people and calligraphy]. In *Chūgoku no sho to hito* 中國の書と人 [Calligraphy and calligraphers in China], pp. 149-78. Osaka: Sogen-she 創元社, 1971.

Ts'ao T'ing-chieh 曹廷杰. *Tung-san-sheng yü-ti-t'u-shuo* 東三省輿地圖説 [Maps and explanations of the geography of the Three Eastern Provinces]. 43 pp. *Liao-hai ts'ung-shu*. ed.

Tsuda Sōkichi 津田左右吉. "Kindai hokuhen kō" 金代北邊考 An investigation of the northern borders of the Chin]. *Mansen chiri rekishi kenkyū hōkoku*, no. 4 (1918), pp. 131-226.

────. "Ryō no seido no nijū taikei" 遼の制度の二重體系 [Dualistic structure in Liao insitutions]. *Mansen chiri rekishi kenkyū hōkoku* no. 5 (1918), pp. 181-298.

Bibliography 197

Ts'un-ts'ui hsüeh-she 存萃學社. *Sung-Liao-Chin she-hui ching-chi shih lun-chi* 宋遼金社會經濟史論集 [Collected essays on Sung, Liao, and Chin social and economic history]. Vol. 2. Hong Kong: Ch'ung-wen shu-tien 崇文書店, 1973.

Tung Chu-ch'en 佟柱臣. "Chi-lin hsin-shih-ch'i wen-hua ti san-chung lei-hsing" 吉林新石器文化的三種類型 [Three types of Neolithic cultures in Kirin]. *K'ao-ku hsüeh-pao*, no. 3 (1957), pp. 31-39.

Wan Kuo-ting 萬國鼎. "Chin-Yüan chih t'ien-chih" 金元之田制 [The agrarian changes of the Chin and Yüan dynasties]. *Nanking Journal* 2, no. 1 (1932): 80-104.

Wan Ssu-t'ung 萬斯同. *Chin chiang-hsiang ta-ch'eng nien-piao* 金將相大臣年表 [Chronological table of Chin generals, prime ministers, and high officials]. In *Erh-shih-wu shih pu-pien*, pp. 8167-84.

Wang Chih-jui 王志瑞. *Sung-Yüan ching-chi shih* 宋元經濟史 [Economic history of Sung and Yüan dynasties]. Shanghai: Commercial Press, 1935.

Wang Ching-ju [Tsing-ju] 王靜如. "Yen-t'ai Nü-chen-wen chin-shih t'i-ming-pei ch'u-shih" 宴台女真文進士題名碑初釋 [A preliminary study of the Yen-t'ai stone tablet in Jurchen script]. *Shih-hsüeh yüeh-k'an* 3 (1937): 49-68.

Wang Fu-chih 王夫之. *Sung lun* 宋論 [On the Sung dynasty]. 15 ch. In *Ch'uan-shan i-shu* 船山遺書.

Wang Kuo-wei 王國維. "Chin chieh-hao k'ao" 金界壕考 [The boundary trenches of the Chin dynasty]. *Yenching Journal of Chinese Studies*, no. 1 (1927), pp. 1-14.

_____. *Kuan-t'ang chi-lin* 觀堂集林. 24 ch. In *Wang-ching-an hsien-sheng i-shu* 王靜安先生遺書.

_____. *Sung-Yüan hsi-chü k'ao* 宋元戲曲考 [A Study of Sung and Yüan drama]. Taipei: I-wen ed., n.d.

Wang Yü-hsien 王毓賢. *Hui-shih pei-k'ao* 繪事備考 [A directory to painting]. 8 ch. *SKCS*, 2d ser.

Wen Ch'ung-i 文崇一. "Hui-mo min-tzu wen-hua chi ch'i shih-liao" 濊貊民族文化及其史料 [A study of the culture and source material of the Hui-Mo tribe]. *Bulletin of the Institute of Ethnology, Academia Sinica*, no. 5 (1956), pp. 115-214.

Wu Ching-hung 吳景宏. "Sung-Chin kung Liao chih wai-chiao" 宋金攻遼之外交 [The Sung diplomacy toward the Chin for an alliance against the Liao]. *Tung-fang tsa-chih* 43, no. 18 (1947): 45-52.

Wu Mei 吳梅. *Liao-Chin-Yüan wen-hsüeh shih* 遼金元文學史 [A history of Liao, Chin, and Yüan literature]. Shanghai: Commercial Press, 1934.

Wu T'ing-hsieh 吳廷燮. *Chin fang-chen nien-piao* 金方鎮年表 [Chronological table of important local officials of Chin]. In *Erh-shih-wu shih pu-pien* pp. 8199-8238.

Yabuuchi Kiyoshi 藪內清, ed. *Sō-Gen jidai no kagaku gijutsu shih* 宋元時代の科學技術史 [A history of science and technology in the Sung-Yüan periods]. Kyoto: Kyoto University, 1967.

Yamaji Hiroaki 山路廣明. *Joshingo kai* 女真語解 [A Jurchen-Japanese-English glossary]. Tokyo: Research Room for the Asian and African Languages, 1956.

Yanai Watari 箭內亙. *Mōkoshi kenkyū* 蒙古史研究 [Studies in Mongolian history]. Tokyo: Tōkō Shoin, 1930.

Yang Chia-lo 楊家駱. *Liao-Chin-Yüan i-wen-chih* 遼金元藝文志 [Bibliographies of Liao, Chin, and Yüan]. 2 vols. Taipei: World Co., 1963.

Yang Hsün-chi 楊循吉. *Chin hsiao-shih* 金小史 [A short history of the Chin]. 8 ch. *Liao-hai ts'ung-shu*.

Yao Ts'ung-wu 姚從吾. "Chang Te-hui *Ling-pei chi-hsing* tsu-pen chiao-chu 張德輝嶺北紀行足本校注 [Annotations of the complete text of Chang Te-hui's *Record of a journey beyond the northern ranges*, edited with notes]. *Bulletin of the College of Arts, National Taiwan University* 11 (1962): 1-38.

_____. "Nü-chen han-hua ti fen-hsi" 女真漢化的分析 [An analysis of the sinicization of the Jurchen]. *Ta-lu tsa-chih* 6, no. 3 (1953): 91-103.

_____. *Tung-pei-shih lun-ts'ung* 東北史論叢 [Collected essays on the history of the Northeast]. 2 vols. Taipei: Cheng-chung shu-chü, 1959.

Yao Ts'ung-wu hsien-sheng i-chu cheng-li wei-yuan-hui 姚從吾先生遺著整理委員會. *Yao Ts'ung-wu hsien-sheng ch'üan-chi, III Liao-Chin-Yüan shih chiang-i (2) Chin-ch'ao shih* 遼金元史講義 (2) 金朝史 [Complete works of Professor Yao Ts'ung-wu, Part III, History of the Liao, the Chin, and the Yüan (2) History of the Chin]. Taipei: Cheng-chung shu-chü, 1973.

Yeh Ch'ien-chao 葉潛昭. *Chin-lü chih yen-chiu* 金律之研究 [A study of the Chin legal code]. Taipei: Commercial Press, 1972.

Yeh Te-hui 葉德輝. *Shu-lin ch'ing-hua* 書林清話 [Discussions in the forest of books]. 10 *ch*. Kuang-ku-t'ang 觀古堂, 1920.

Yen Wen-ju 閻文儒. "Chin Chung-tu" 金中都 [The central capital of the Chin]. *Wen-wu*, no. 9 (1959), pp. 8-12.

Yoshikawa Kōjiro 吉川幸次郎. *Gen zatsugeki kenkyū* 元雜劇研究 [Studies of Yüan plays]. Tokyo: Iwanami shoten, 1948. 2d printing, 1954.

Yung-ch'ing hsien-chih 永清縣志 [Records of the Yung-ch'ing country]. 30 *ch*. 1779 ed.

Books and Articles in Western Languages

Allen, Francis R. *Socio-cultural Dynamics: An Introduction to Social Change*. New York: Macmillan, 1971.

Almond, Gabriel A., and Powell, G. Bingham, Jr. *Comparative Politics: A Developmental Approach*. Boston: Little Brown & Co., 1966.

Andreski, Stanislav. *Military Organization and Society*. Berkeley and Los Angeles: University of California Press, 1968.

Aubin, Françoise. "Travaux et tendances de la Sinologie Soviétique récente." *T'oung Pao* 58, nos. 1-5 (1972): 161-71.

_____, ed. *Etudes Song in memoriam Etienne Balazs*. Series 1, no. 1. Paris: Mouton & Co., 1970.

Barth, Frederick, ed. *Ethnic Groups and Boundaries: The Social Organization of Cultural Difference*. Bergen-Oslo: Universtats Foraget, 1969.

Bretschneider, Emilii V. *Medieval Researches from Eastern Asistic Sources*. 2 vols. London: K. Paul, Trench, Trübner & Co., 1887.

Bush, Susan. *The Chinese Literati on Painting: Su Shih (1037-1101) to Tung Ch'i-ch'ang (1555-1636)*. Cambridge, Mass.: Harvard University Press, 1971.

_____. "Literati Culture under the Chin (1122-1234)." *Oriental Art*, n.s., 15 (1969): 103-12.

Chan, Hok-lam. *The Historiography of the Chin Dynasty: Three Studies*. Wiesbaden: Franz Steiner, 1970.

_____. "Prolegomena to the *Ju-nan i-shih*: A Memoir on the Last Chin Court under the Mongol Siege of 1234." *Sung Studies Newsletter* 10 (1974): 2-19.

Chang, Kwang-chih. *The Archaeology of Ancient China*. Rev. and enl. ed. New Haven and London: Yale University Press, 1968.

_____. "Neolithic Cultures of the Sungari Valley, Manchuria." *Southwestern Journal of Anthropology* 17, no. 1 (1961): 56-74.

Cheng Te-k'un. *Archaeology in China*, vol. 1, *Prehistory of China*. Cambridge: Heffer & Sons, 1959.

Chavannes, Edouard. "Voyageurs chinois chez les Khitan et les Joutchen." *Journal Asiatique*, ser. 9, no. 9 (1897), pp. 377-422; ser. 9, no. 11 (1898), pp. 316-439.

Bibliography

De Harlez, Charles J. *Histoire de L'Empire de hin ou Empire d'Or*. Louvan: Charles Peeters, 1887.

De Rachewiltz, Igor. "Personnel and Personalities in North China in the Early Mongol Period." *Journal of the Economic and Social History of the Orient* 9, pt. 1-2 (1966): 88-144.

Eberhard, Wolfram. *Conquerors and Rulers, Social Forces in Mediaeval China*. 2d rev. ed. Leiden: E. J. Brill, 1965.

Eisenstadt, S.N. *The Political Systems of Empires: The Rise and Fall of the Historical Bureaucratic Societies*. New York: The Free Press, 1963.

Fairbank, John K., ed. *The Chinese World Order: Traditional China's Foreign Relations*. Cambridge, Mass.: Harvard University Press, 1968.

Feuerwerker, Albert, ed. *History in Communist China*. Cambridge, Mass.: The M.I.T. Press, 1968.

Franke, Herbert. "Chinese Historiography under Mongol Rule: The Role of History in Acculturation." *Mongolian Studies* 1 (1974): 15-26.

_____. "Treaties between Sung and Chin." In *Etudes Song in memoriam Etienne Balazs*, edited by Françoise Aubin, pp. 55-84.

Gernet, Jacques. *Daily Life in China on the Eve of the Mongol Invasion, 1250-1276*. Translated by H.M. Wright. New York: Macmillan, 1962.

Gerth, H. H., and Mills, C. Wright, trans. and eds. *From Max Weber: Essays in Sociology*. New York: Oxford University Press, 1946.

Gilbert, Lucien. *Dictionnaire historique et géographique de la Mandchourie*. Hong Kong: Imprimerie de la Société des Missions-Etrangères, 1934.

Gordon, Milton M. *Assimilation in American Life: The Role of Race, Religion, and National Origins*. New York: Oxford University Press, 1964.

Grousset, René. *The Empire of the Steppes: A History of Central Asia*. Translated by Naomi Walford. New Brunswick, N.J.: Rutgers University Press, 1970.

Grube, Wilhelm. *Die Sprache and Schrift der Jucen*.

Leipzig: O. Harrassowitz, 1898.

Haenisch, Erich. *Die Ehreninschrift für den Rebellengeneral Ts'ui Lih der Konfucianischen moral, ein Episode aus dem 13, Jahundert.* Berlin: In Kommission bei W. de Gruyter, 1944.

Hambly, Gavin, ed. *Central Asia.* New York: Delacorte Press, 1966.

Herskovits, Melville J. *Acculturation: The Study of Culture Contact.* Gloucester, Mass.: Peter Smith, 1958.

Ho, Ping-ti. "An Estimate of the Total Population of Sung-Chin China." In *Etudes Song in memoriam Etienne Balazs*, edited by Françoise Aubin, pp. 3-53.

_____. *The Ladder of Success in Imperial China: Aspects of Social Mobility, 1368-1911.* New York: Columbia University Press, 1963.

Hsiao Ch'i-ch'ing. "The Military Establishment of the Yüan Dynasty." Ph.D. dissertation, Harvard University, 1969.

Hucker, Charles O. *The Censorial System of Ming China.* Stanford: Stanford University Press, 1966.

Jochelson, V. I. *Peoples of Asiatic Russia.* New York: The American Museum of Natural History, 1928.

Kracke, Edward A., Jr. *Civil Service in Early Sung China, 960-1067.* Cambridge, Mass.: Harvard University Press, 1953.

_____. "Sung Society: Change within Tradition." *Far Eastern Quarterly* 14 (1954-55): 479-88.

Krader, Lawrence. *Formation of the State.* Englewood Cliffs, N. J.: Prentice-Hall, 1968.

Kroeber, A. L., and Parsons, Talcott. "The Concepts of Culture and Social System." *American Sociological Review* 23, no. 5 (1958): 582-83.

LaPiere, Robert T. *Social Change.* New York: MacGraw-Hill, 1965.

Lattimore, Owen. *Inner Asian Frontiers of China.* Boston: Beacon Press ed., 1962.

_____. *Studies in Frontier History: Collected Papers, 1928-58.* London: Oxford University Press, 1962.

Lee, Sherman E., and Ho, Wai-kam. *Chinese Art under the Mongols, the Yüan Dynasty (1279-1368)*. Cleveland: The Museum of Art, 1968.

Levin, M. G. *Ethnic Origins of the Peoples of Northeast Asia*. Toronto: University of Toronto Press, 1963.

Levin, M. G., and Potapov, E. P. *The Peoples of Siberia*. Translated by Scripta Technica, Inc. Chicago: University of Chicago Press, 1964.

Li, Chi. *Manchuria in History*. Peiping: Peking Union Bookstore, 1932.

Ligeti, L. "Notes préliminaire sur le dichiffrement des 'petits caracteres' Joutchen." *Acta Orientalia Academiae Scientiarum Hungaricae* 3, no. 2 (1953): 211-28.

Linton, Ralph. "Nativistic Movements." *American Anthropologist* 45 (1943): 230-40.

Liu, James T. C. "An Administrative Cycle in Chinese History: The Case of Northern Sung Emperors." *Journal of Asian Studies* 21, no. 2 (1962): 137-52.

_____. "Sung Roots of Chinese Political Conservatism: The Administrative Problems." *Journal of Asian Studies* 26, no. 3 (1967): 457-63.

Marsh, Robert M. *The Mandarins: The Circulation of Elites in China, 1600-1900*. New York: The Free Press, 1961.

Menges, Karl H. "Problemata Etymologica." *Studia Sino-Altaica* 10 (1961): 130-40.

Michael, Franz. *The Origin of Manchu Rule in China*. Baltimore: The Johns Hopkins Press, 1942.

Michael, Henry N., ed. *Studies in Siberian Ethnogenesis*. Toronto: University of Toronto Press, 1962.

Moore, Wilbert E. *Social Change*. Englewood Cliffs, N. J.: Prentice-Hall, 1963.

Mote, Frederick W. "The Growth of Chinese Despotism." *Oriens Extremus* 8, no. 1 (1961): 1-41.

Moule, A. C., and Pelliot, Paul I., eds. *Marco Polo, The Description of the World*. 2 vols. London, 1938.

Okladnidov, A. P. *Ancient Population of Siberia and Its Cultures*. Cambridge, Mass.: The Peabody Museum, 1959.

_____. *The Soviet Far East in Antiquity*. Toronto: University of Toronto Press, 1965.

Parker, Edward H. *A Thousand Years of the Tartars*. London: K. Paul, Trench, Trubner & Co. and New York: Alfred A. Knopf, 1924.

Poppe, Nicholas. *Introduction to Altaic Linguistics*. Wiesbaden: O. Harrassowitz, 1965.

Redfield, Robert; Linton, Ralph; and Herskovits, Melville J. "Memorandum on the Study of Acculturation." *American Anthropologist* 38 (1936): 149-52.

Reischauer, Edwin O., and Fairbank, John K. *East Asia: The Great Tradition*. Boston: Houghton Mifflin, 1960.

Rogers, Michael E. "The Regularization of Koryŏ-Chin Relations (1116-1131)." *Central Asiatic Journal* 6, no. 1 (1961): 51-84.

Serruys, Henry. *The Mongols in China during the Yung-lo Period, 1403-24*. Brussels: Institut Belge des Hautes Etudes Chinoises, 1959.

_____. "Remains of Mongol Customs during the Early Ming." *Monumenta Serica* 16 (1957): 137-90.

_____. *Sino-Jürced Relations during the Yung-lo Period, 1403-24*. Wiesbaden: O. Harrassowitz, 1955.

Sickman, Laurence, and Soper, Alexander C. *The Art and Architecture of China*. Rev. ed. Baltimore: Penguin Books, 1960.

Siren, Osvald. "Chinese Sculpture of the Sung, Liao, and Chin Dynasties." *Bulletin of the Museum of Far Eastern Antiquities* 14 (1942): 45-64.

Tao, Jing-shen. "The Horse and the Rise of the Chin Dynasty." *Papers of the Michigan Academy of Science, Arts, and Letters* 53 (1968): 183-89.

_____. "The Influence of Jurchen Rule on Chinese Political Institutions." *Journal of Asian Studies* 30, no. 1 (1970): 121-30.

_____. "Political Recruitment in the Chin Dynasty." *Journal of the American Oriental Society* 94, no. 1 (1974): 24-34.

Tax, Sol, ed. *Anthropology Today: Selections*. Chicago: The University of Chicago Press, 1962.

Thiele, Dagmar. *Der Abschluss eines Vertrages: Diplomatie zwischen Sung-und Chin-Dynastie 1117-1123*. Wiesbaden: Münchener ostasiatische studien vol. 6, 1970.

Vander Zanden, James W. *American Minority Relations: The Sociology of Race and Ethnic Groups*. New York: Ronald Press, 1963. 2d ed., 1966.

Waley, Arthur. *Ch'ang-ch'un: The Travels of an Alchemist*. London: George Routledge & Sons, 1931.

Wallace, Anthony C. *Culture and Personality*. 2d ed. New York: Random House, 1962.

──────. "Revitalization Movements: Some Theoretical Consideration for Their Comparative Study." *American Anthropologist* 58 (1956): 264-81.

Wang, Ling. "On the Invention and Use of Gunpowder and Firearms in China." *Isis* 37, no. 1 (1947): 160-78.

Weber, Max. *The Theory of Social and Economic Organization*. Edited by Talcott Parsons. New York: The Free Press, 1964.

West, Stephen H. "Literature in the Chin." To be published by the Chin Project at the University of Munich.

Wittfogel, Karl A. "Chinese Society and the Dynasties of Conquest." In *China*, edited by H. F. MacNair, pp. 112-26. Berkeley & Los Angeles: University of Califoria Press, 1946.

──────. "Public Office in the Liao and the Chinese Examination System." *Harvard Journal of Asiatic Studies* 10 (1947): 13-40.

──────. *Oriental Despotism: A Comparative Study of Total Power*. New Haven: Yale University Press, 1957.

──────, and Feng Chia-sheng. *History of Chinese Society: Liao (907-1125)*. Philadelphia: The American Philosophical Society, 1949.

Wu, K. T. "Chinese Printing under Four Alien Dynasties," *Harvard Journal of Asiatic Studies* 13 (1950): 447-523.

Wright, Mary C. *The Last Stand of Chinese Conservatism: The Tung-chih Restoration, 1862-74*. Stanford: Stanford University Press, 1957.

Yang, Lien-sheng. "Review of Karl A. Wittfogel and Feng Chia-sheng, *History of Chinese Society, Liao (907-1125)*." *Harvard Journal of Asiatic Studies* 13 (1950): 216-237.

Yü, Ying-shih. *Trade and Expansion in Han China: A Study in the Structure of Sino-Barbarian Economic Relations*. Berkeley and Los Angeles: University of California Press, 1967.

Index

A-li-ho-man, 10
A-li-hsi, 9
A-su, 19
Absorption theory, viii-ix, 121n1
Acculturation, viii, 112; definition of, xi, 122n12, 123n14
Agriculture, 4, 6, 7-8, 28, 29, 47; collective farming, 49, 78; encouragement of, 85; prohibition to abandon farming, 75, 80; prohibition to hinder, 28
Ai-tsung (emperor, r. 1223-34), 92; and the decline of the Chin, 92-94.
Alcoholic liquors, 10, 73, 90
Amalgamation, viii
An-ch'u-hu [An-ch'un], 8, 127n30
An-ch'un. See An-ch'u-hu
An-pan po-chi-lieh, 26, 28. See also Po-chi-lieh
Ancestral temples, 32, 42
Archery, 9, 75, 80, 85
Architecture, 103
Army: Cha, 90; Ch'i-tan, 90; Chinese, 23, 90, 91, 116; decline of morale in, 91; Jurchen, 19, 20, 21, 22, 28, 53
Assimilation, vii, ix, xi, 78, 81, 82, 98, 112, 164n2; definition of, xi; traditional theory, vii-viii; Western theory, viii-ix, 123n14, 165n5

Bandits, 91, 96
Barbarians, vii, 19, 40, 104, 105, 110; invasions by, vii, 111, 117
Battle of Ts'ai-Shih (1161), 23, 68, 70, 108; influence of, 69
Books, 31; Jurchen collection of, 40, 99, 100, 101; publication of, 101
Buddhism, 10, 13, 31, 48, 100, 103, 105-7, 114, 115
Bureaucracy, 30, 39, 41, 89, 92, 113, 154n29; characteristics, 53-54; ethnic composition, 54. See also Government; Officials
Byzantine Empire, 111

Canon of Filial Piety, 56, 77, 81
Cattle, 11
Censors, 41, 46, 53, 58, 60, 61
Ceremonies: Chinese, 42, 44, 78, 86; Jurchen, 78, 85; kowtow, 12, 38
Ch'a-shih (tea and confections), 10
Chai (or *ch'eng*), 7
Chai-shih (fort chiefs), 11
Chang Chüeh, 20, 138n36

Chang Chün, 42
Chang Hsing-chien, 102
Chang Pang-ch'ang (puppet emperor under Chin), 21, 34. See also Ch'u
Chang Shih, 105
Chang Te-hui, 93, 146n27
Chang Tsai, 105
Chang-tsung (emperor, r. 1189-1208), 60, 61, 84, 85, 86, 87, 88, 89, 91, 95, 98, 99, 147n52, 158n21
Chang Yung-chih, 30
Ch'ang-ch'un prefecture, 19
Ch'ang-sheng Chün (Ever Victorious Army), 20, 23
Chao Kou (emperor of Southern Sung, r. 1127-62), 34. See also Sung Kao-tsung
Chao Ping-wen, 88, 99, 101, 105
Chen-kuan cheng-yao, 93
Ch'eng. See Chai
Ch'eng brothers (Ch'eng I and Ch'eng Hao), 105, 109
Ch'i (puppet regime under Chin), 35, 41
Ch'i (unusual), 101
Ch'i-tan, vii, viii, ix, x, 13, 18, 19, 40, 43, 45, 50, 71, 72, 101, 109, 112, 115, 116, 128n33; and Jurchen, 6, 9-10, 11, 13, 14-15, 18, 19, 31-32; language, 12; officials, 27, 28, 57, 78; scholars, 101. See also Liao dynasty
Chia I, 104
Chiang Min-piao, 105
Chiang-ning, 34
Chiao-fang ch'iang-tzu, 102
Chieh-tu shih, 11, 12, 48
Ch'ien-hu (Chinese term for meng-an), 90, 115
Ch'ien-yüan palace, 32
Chih-hou (warders), 62
Chin dynasty, ix-x, 18, 31, 33, 44, 53, 54, 60, 62, 87, 93, 95, 102, 107, 108, 109, 113, 115; decline of, 92-94; dynastic history, 101; and five elements, 86-89, 153-54n23; legitimation of, 43, 44, 69, 87-89. See also Jurchen
Chin i ju wang (the employment of the Chinese literati brought about the destruction of the Chin), 60
Chin-shih chü (bureau of palace attendants), 53, 55, 62
Chin-shih degree, 29, 56-58, 65, 66, 85, 148n55, 154n29; appointment of, 60, 65-66; Jurchen, 57, 58, 61, 66, 76, 77, 80, 83; number enlisted, 56-60, 145nn24-25, 146n28, 147n51, 148n63; and promotion, 66, 67, 148n58. See also Civil service examinations; Officials
Ch'in K'uei 139n43
Ch'in-tsung (Sung emperor), 21
Chinese: artisans, 31; calligraphy, 99; classics, 40, 41, 42, 56, 70, 72, 77, 80, 81, 98, 101, 114, 115; commoners, 74; customs, 39, 42, 43, 71, 81, 86, 105; education, 40, 69, 84, 96, 99, 114; emperors, 81, 82; history, 70, 101, 103-4, 125n5; influence on Jurchen, 10, 12, 13, 29, 38, 80, 81, 82, 98-99, 102; institutions, 25, 30, 37, 38, 39, 40, 42, 43, 44, 93; literati, 60, 61, 92, 98, 100, 115; literature, 98, 99; music, 99, 100; officials, 57, 78, 93, 94; scholar-gentry, 30, 31, 32, 50; scholar-officials, 30, 40,

Index

42, 46, 88, 89, 92, 93; scholars, 31, 93, 101, 104, 109; teachers, 30, 31, 40, 109; values and symbols, 38, 39, 42; virtues, 72, 77, 81, 100; warlords, 90; of the Yen-yün region, 20, 30, 31, 41, 55, 56, 72
Ch'ing dynasty, ix, x, 58, 60, 116; Eight Banners System, 27, 48, 116
Ch'ing-lo she (purity and happiness society), 96
Ch'ing-yüan temple, 31
Ch'iu Ch'u-chi, 107
Chou-hsien, 28, 52
Chou Tun-i, 105
Chu Hsi, 105, 109, 151n63
Chu-ko Liang, 104
Chu-kung-tiao, 102
Ch'u (puppet regime under Chin), 21, 34
Ch'u-ho-tien, 19
Ch'üan-chen. *See* Taoism
Ch'üan-nung Shih (agricultural advisers), 80
Ch'üeh-hsüeh (kesig), 67
Ch'un-shui (Spring River), 76
Chün-hu, 91
Chün-shuai, 27. *See also* Meng-an and *mou-k'e*
Chung-hsiao chün, 91
Chung-hsing (restoration), 82
Chung-hsing Shih-chi (History of the restoration), 101
Činggis Qan, 107
Cities, 32, 44
Civil service: Chin, 61, 64, 65, 67; Northern Sung, 59. *See also* Civil service examinations
Civil service examinations, 33, 41-42, 44, 82, 85, 89, 92, 102, 103, 113, 114; Jurchen *chin-shih*, 57, 58, 61, 66, 76, 77, 80; recruitment of *chin-shih*, 56-60. *See also* Chin-shih degree
Clan, 8, 10, 11, 16, 17
Clothing, 10, 34, 41, 44, 75, 77-78, 85, 110, 114, 116; fastened on left side, 34. *See also* Jurchen, fashions
Coins, 7, 127n122
Commoners, 50, 103, 113. *See also* Chinese; Jurchen
Confucian temples, 42, 44, 82, 86
Confucianism, 60, 105-6, 115; Neo-Confucianists, 105; *tao-hsüeh*, 106.
Conquest dynasties, ix, 55
Cultural diffusion, 107, 110

Deer, 14
Dogs, 14
Drama, 101-3, 110, 115
Dualism, ix, 32, 33, 36, 40, 52, 61, 67, 112, 113

Eastern Jurchen, 6
Economy, 44, 47, 83, 86, 106, 114; decline of, 90-91; fiscal policy, 79, 85, 114; monetary system, 114. *See also* Agriculture; Land; Taxes
Envoys: of Chin to Sung, 108; of Sung to Ch'i-tan, 6; of Sung to Chin, 8, 31, 75
Erh-shui (double-taxed) households, 106

Feng-yü (chiefs of palace service), 62, 65, 66
Feudal forces, 32, 37, 39, 112
Fishing, x, 4, 6, 9, 10
Food, 10, 50
Fu (prose), 41
Fu-yin (mayor), 48
Fu-yü, 4, 5

Funeral practices, 13

Games, 31, 100
Garrison(s), 27, 35, 47
Gold, 8, 10, 14
Government, 11-12, 31, 32, 38, 41, 44, 89, 90, 114, 115; centralization of, 25, 30, 36, 39-40, 42, 43-44, 45, 70-71, 79; relief, 28, 29, 49, 50, 75; tribal political organization, 11-12. *See also* Dualism; Officials
Great Wall, vii, 32

Hai-ling Wang. *See* Wan-yen Liang
Hai-tung-ch'ing, 18-19
Haiku River, 127n29
Han Chi-hsien, 30, 31, 33, 36, 140n3
Han dynasty, 93, 104
Han Fang, 30
Han-jen (the people of Han), 115
Han-lin yüan (*han-lin* academy), 41
Han T'o-chou, 85
Hangchow, 34, 108
Hao Ching, 93
Hei-shui Mo-ho, 5, 6
Hereditary selection, 61, 62, 63, 64, 67, 147n37, n45
Ho-shih-lieh (clan), 10
Ho-shih-lieh Chao-hsing, 100
Horse(s), 11, 17, 112, 127 n22; cavalry, 9, 10, 22, 75, riding of, 9, 10, 22, 75, 80; trade of, 14-16, 108; tribute of, 14-16, 17
Hsi-Hsia 20, 31, 36
Hsi-hsiang (The West Chamber), 102
Hsi-tsung (emperor r. 1123-49), 99. *See also* Wan-yen Tan
Hsieh Liang-tso, 105

Hsien, 28
Hsin Ch'i-chi, 85, 109
Hsing, 73
Hsing-hsiu, 107
Hsing-kuo ling-ying chu (the efficacious state-contructing god), 78
Hsing-t'ai, 90
Hsing-t'ai shang-shu-sheng (mobile presidential council), 35-36, 44
Hsing-Yüan temple, 31
Hsü An-shang, 100
Hsü tzu-chih t'ung-chien (a continuation of the *Tzu-chih t'ung-chien*), 101
Hsüan-hui-yüan (department of court etiquette), 62
Hsüan-tsung (emperor, r. 1213-23), 88, 89, 95. *See also* Wan-yen Hsün
Hu (barbarian), 110
Hu-chou, 34
Hu-li-kai (clan), 10
Hu-wei (imperial guard), 65
Hua (ornate), 92
Hua-feng pu-ching (decline of Chinese customs), 105
Huai-i (barbarians of the Huai), 105
Huai River, 35, 68
Huang-lung prefecture, 19
Huang T'ing-chien, 99, 101
Hui-tsung (Sung emperor), 21, 156n2
Hung Hao, 31, 40, 108, 141n4
Hung Mai, 100, 110
Hung-wen Yüan (academy of letters), 101
Hunting, 4, 6, 8-9, 10, 19, 22, 76, 80, 86, 114, 128n33, 150n33

I-cheng Yüan (bureau for improving state affairs), 93
I-chien chih, 110
I-la Fu-seng, 91
I-la Mai-nu, 101
I-la Nien-ho, 101

Index

I-lou, 3, 4, 5, 126n11
Imperial academy, 44, 82, 101
Indians, 112
Inner court, 30, 54-55, 65, 67
Iron, 7, 10, 17, 114, 166n13

Japan, 116
Jen, 65
Ju-nan i-shih, 93
Jung-chai sui-pi, 110
Jurchen: adoption of Chinese surnames, 77, 114, 157n14; aristocrats, 39, 43, 45, 49, 70, 78, 83, 113, 114; and Ch'i-tan, 6, 14-15, 18, 130n50; *chin-shih* degree, 57-59, 76, 77; and Chinese, vii, 15-16, 18, 156n61; clans, 8, 10-11; commoners, 61, 62, 73, 83; culture, 71, 78, 79, 82, 83, 129n37, 130n44, 152n1; customs, 22, 32, 41, 71, 72, 77, 79, 81, 82, 84, 85 128n33, 130n53, 143n50; dance, 18, 78, 79, 110; demoralization, 72, 75, 78, 155n39, n41; examination system, 57-59, 61, 76, 77, 80, 83, 85, 114; fashions, 42, 71, 110; first appearance, 3; generals, 34, 35, 36, 37, 39, 40, 41, 42; hair style, 34, 41; impoverishment, 75; Jurchenizing movement, 34, 41, 44, and Koryŏ, 15, 18; language, 12, 29, 76-77, 80-81, 85, 115; laws, 11, 152n5; lineages, 110; martial spirit, 60, 75, 76, 114; nobles, 50, 52, 58, 70, 79; origin of, 5-6; pig raising, 5, 8, 127n26; powerful families, 73, 74, 79; renditions of name, 3, 123-24n1; research on, x-xi, 121n3; rise of; 14-16; savage (*sheng*), 6-7; scholars, 99-100; sedentary life of, 6-8; slaves, 11, 16, 18, 28, 29; and stockbreeding, 4, 6, 8, 9; and Southern Sung, 108-10, 163n88; and Sung and Liao, 19-20; tribute to Sung, Liao, and Koryŏ, 14-16; walled towns, 7, 10; warlords, 36-37, 39, 40, 41, 90

K'ang, 8
Kao Ch'ing-i, 35, 36, 41
Kao Yung-ch'ang, 19
K'e-tzu, 12
Ken-pen (foundations), 92
Kirin, 5
Koguryŏ, 5, 16
Koryŏ, relations with the Jurchen, 7, 10, 11, 14, 15-16, 17, 18. See also Jurchen
Ku (archaic), 101
Kuai-tzu ma (horse team), 22
Kuan Han-ch'ing, 102, 103, 160n58
Kuang-ning, 32, 33
Kuang-wu (Han emperor), 81
Kuo-hsiang, 11-12, 27
Kuo-lun hu-lu po-chi-lieh, 27. See also *Tu-po-chi-lieh*
Kuo-tzu chien (Imperial academy), 44, 101
Kuo Yao-shih, 20, 21, 23

Land: government confiscation of, 73, 74; illegal seizure by Jurchen, 48, 73-75, 90-91; and Jurchen landlords, 49, 50, 73-74; ownership of, 73-74, 78, 90-91; redistribution of, 48, 73, 74, 78; tenantry, 74
Later T'ang, 15
Laws, 11, 42, 85; legal dis-

putes between Jurchen and Chinese, 72-73
Lei Yüan, 99
Li Ch'un-fu [Li P'ing-shan], 101, 105, 109
Li K'an, 22
Li P'ing-shan. *See* Li Ch'un fu
Li Shih, 70
Liao dynasty, viii, ix, 9, 11, 14, 15, 17, 18, 19, 20, 28, 43, 52, 56, 62, 67, 69, 87, 88, 92, 103; destruction of, 20; society, viii, ix. *See also* Ch'i-tan
Liao-yang, 6, 70
Ling-shih (assistant secretaries), 60, 89
Literature, 99, 101-3, 114, 115; vernacular, 114, 115. *See also* Drama
Liu An-shih, 105
Liu Ch'i, 92
Liu Chih-yüan, 102
Liu-k'o ch'eng, 11
Liu Pei, 104
Liu Ts'ung-i, 90
Liu Yen-tsung, 30, 36
Liu Yü (puppet emperor under Chin), 35, 37, 41, 139n43
Liu Yüan-kuei, 90
Lo-shan chü-shih (scholar fond of good deeds), 99
Lou Yüeh, 45
Lu I, 31
Lu Yen-lun, 32
Lü Tsu-ch'ien, 105
Lung prefecture, 107

Ma K'uo, 8, 22
Man-yin-i, 16
Manchuria, 3, 4, 5, 16, 18, 21, 28, 40, 47, 51, 112, 115, 116, 117; Chinese captives in, 28-29
Manchus, vii, viii, 27, 58, 111. *See also* Ch'ing dynasty

"Marginal Society", viii
Marriage, 10, 12, 32, 116; with Chinese, 47, 89, 95-98, 114; levirate, 12, 116; polygamy, 12; sororate, 116
Meng-an and *mou-k'e*, 9, 142n37; adjustment, 46-47; Chinese, 48; function, 9, 27, 48-51, 70, 73, 79, 85, 90, 113, 115; hereditary, 43, 48-49, 63, 73, 79, 90, 91; inheritance, 49, 62; organization, 9, 11-12, 25, 27-28, 48-50; Po-hai, 48
Merchants, 56
Military: central control of, 39, 53; decline of military power, 91, 115; organization, 23, 53; power, 21-24; service, 44, 53, 61, 63, 64, 65, 67
Ming dynasty, 46, 60, 103, 115, 116
Mo-ho, 3, 4, 5-6, 124n3
Monetary system, 47
Mongolia, 117
Mongols, vii, viii, ix, x, 23, 58, 67, 69, 90, 91, 93, 111, 112, 116; invasions of Chin, 90, 96, 105, 109, 115
Mou-k'e. *See Meng-an* and *mou-k'e*
Music, 31, 32, 42, 79, 110

Na-ho Liu-ko, 90
Na-lan (clan), 10
Na-po, 9
Nan tu (Southern Crossing), 101
Nativistic movement, 76, 83. *See also* Revitalization movement
Navy: Chinese, 23-24; Jurchen, 23-24, 69, 109
Nei-ch'ao (inner court). *See* Inner court

Index

Nien-han fa-so (Nien-han's pigtail), 110
Ning-chiang prefecture, 14, 19
Niu-chü (oxen unit), 49
Nomads, vii, 8, 9, 111, 112
Northern Sung, 9, 15, 18, 20, 31, 32, 37, 40, 42, 44, 50, 52, 53, 59, 60, 87, 88, 91, 92, 93, 96, 102, 103, 104, 115, 116; and Ch'i-tan, 19-20; and Chin, 19-20
Nü-chen hsiao-tzu (small characters), 76
Nü-chen kuo-tzu-chien (Jurchen imperial academy), 82
Nü-chen pu-tsu chieh-tu shih (Commanding prefect of the Jurchen tribe), 17

Officials, 28, 52, 65, 82; Ch'i-tan, 27, 28, 57, 78; Chinese, 28, 30, 33, 42, 50, 67, 78, 89, 93, 94; Jurchen, 30, 57-58, 62, 63, 67; Northern Sung, 31; Po-hai, 28, 29, 31; promotion of, 65-66; suppression of Chinese, 42, 45, 46, 53
Ox(en), 7, 10, 14, 49

Pai P'u, 102, 115, 160n58
Painting, 99
Pen-ch'ao p'u-tieh (Imperial genealogy of the Chin), 101
Period of disunity (222-589 A.D.), vii
Pien-ching, 9, 21, 22, 23, 31, 32, 34, 35, 44, 89, 90, 91
Po-chi-lieh, 12, 52; abolition of, 41; organization, 25-27
Po-chin, 9, 10, 11. See also *Po-chi-lieh*
Po-chu-lu Hsiao-chung, 100

Po-hai, 3, 4, 28, 29, 48, 57, 69, 78. See also Officials
Poetry, 40, 41, 42, 43, 55
Population, 51; Jurchen, 51, 74-75
Prince Yüan-kung, 84
P'u-ch'a (clan), 10
P'u-kan River, 127n29
P'u-san (clan), 10
Puppet regimes, 33, 34, 35, 37, 38, 41, 116. See also Ch'i; Ch'u

Qārā-Khitay kingdom (Hsi Liao), 20
Qubilai Qan, 54, 93, 107, 146n27

Rebellions: Ch'i-tan, 76; against Ch'i-tan, 18-19; Chinese, 28, 109; against King Hai-ling, 70
Recruitment, political, 144n9, 147n52
Religion, 12-13, 106-7. See also Buddhism; Confucianism; Taoism
"Reservoir" theory, viii
Revival movement, 68, 79, 81, 82, 86, 113-14. See also Revitalization movement; Nativistic movement
Revitalization movement, 68. See also Nativistic movement; Revival movement

Salt, 13, 73, 90, 114
San-ch'ao pei-meng hui-pien, 22
San-shih and San-kung (Three teachers and three dukes), 41
Schools, 82, 100
Sculpture, 103
Shamanism, 4, 12-13, 106. See also Religion
Shan-hu, 44
Shang-ching, 8, 28, 29, 31,

32, 44, 46, 47, 79, 80;
Chinese influence on, 29-32
Shang-shu (Books of History), 76, 93
Shang-shu ling, 30
Shang-shu Sheng (Presidential Council), 45, 116
Shantung, 35
Shao-fan (burning the cooked rice), 13, 115
Shao-fu chien (Imperial Workshops), 56
She-liu (shooting willow wands), 9-10, 76
Shih (realistic), 92
Shih family, 95-96, 97
Shih Li-ai, 30, 36
Shih Lun, 96
Shih-mo Shih-chi, 101
Shih T'ien-ni, 96
Shih T'ien-tse, 97
Shih-tsung (emperor, r. 1161-89), 58, 65, 69, 71, 72, 73, 74, 75, 84, 86, 87, 98, 99, 146n28, 148n54, 149n6, 150n33, 151n52, 63, 162n81; and sinicization, 79-83. See also Wan-yen Wu-lu
Shu Han, 104
Shu-mi yüan (Bureau of Military Affairs), 32, 33, 35, 36, 41
Shuo prefecture, 73
Silver, 10, 108
Sinicization, viii, xi, 30, 39, 40, 41, 68, 70, 71, 84, 86, 92, 93, 94, 95, 98, 113, 114, 116; definition, xi, legal, 85; study of, x. See also Assimilation
Sino-Jurchen synthesis, 78
Sino-Manchu synthesis, 111
Sixteen Prefectures of Yen and Yün, 20. See also Yen-Yün region
Slaves, 11, 18, 28, 29, 50-51, 56, 74-75, 77, 96; market, 50. See also Jurchen
Society: ethnic integration, 71; social classes, 11; social mobility, 58; social structure, 50-51; tribal organization, 27. See also Jurchen
Sociocultural change, xi, 84, 112, 114
Southern Sung, 7, 23, 33, 34, 35, 41, 42, 43, 44, 68, 69, 70, 71, 75, 82, 94, 102, 104, 105, 108, 109, 110, 115; cultural influence on Chin, 109-10; navy, 69; relations with Chin, 82, 85, 108-10, 115; as tributary state of Chin, 68, 87, 88
Ssu-ma Kuang, 99, 104, 105, 109
Su-shen, 3, 4, 5, 124n3, 126n11
Su Shih, 99, 101
Su T'ien-chüeh, 92
Subterranean dwelling, 4
Succession, 12, 39-40, 113; collateral, 16; primogeniture, 12, 39-40, 84, 113
Sui dynasty, 5, 45
Sung dynasty, 63, 65, 75
Sung hsüeh-lei (sending blood and tears), 13
Sung Hui-tsung (Sung emperor), 20-21, 32, 99, 109
Sung Kao-tsung (Sung emperor, r. 1127-62), 34
Sung-mo chi-wen, 5
Sungari region, 7, 8, 17, 112
Superstratification, viii, 37, 140n52

Ta-chin chi-li (compendium of ceremonies of the great Chin), 85, 86
Ta-ting period (1161-89),

Index

57, 61, 62, 73, 75, 77, 82, 100
Ta-t'ung, 35
Ta-wei, 8
T'ai-hsüeh (national university), 100
T'ai-ho lü (*T'ai-ho* legal code), 85
T'ai-tsung [Abahai] (Ch'ing emperor), 116
T'ai-tsung (T'ang emperor), 81
T'ai-yüan, 21
T'ang dynasty, 5, 40, 45, 85, 87, 88, 93, 98, 114, 115
T'ang-kua An-li, 71
Tao-i (barbarians of the island), 105
T'ao Tsung-i, 98
Taoism, 48, 105-6, 114, 115, 162n84; Ch'üan-chen sect, 106-7; Ta-tao sect, 107; T'ai-i sect, 107
Tax(es), 9, 28, 33, 47, 49-50, 73, 106, 114; property money, 79, 83, 114. See also Economy
Te-Yün, 86
T'i-fa ling (head shaving act), 34. See also Jurchen
Tibetans, viii
Tieh po-chi-lieh, 27. See also Po-chi-lieh
Tien-ch'ien ma-pu-chün tu-chih-hui-shih (palace cavalry and infantry commander in chief), 63
Tien-ch'ien tu-tien-chien ssu (office of palace corps supervisor), 62
T'ien-hui, 55
T'ien-tsu (Liao emperor), 19, 20
T'ing-chang, 45-46. See also Officials, suppression of Chinese
T'o-ba, viii
T'o-sa po-chin chai, 10

Trade books, 109-10; with Liao, 14-15; with Koryŏ, 15; smuggling, 108; with Southern Sung, 108. See also Gold; Horses; Oxen
Tributary system, 15
Tso Chi-kung, 30, 32, 134n36, 138n36
Tsung-kan. See Wan-yen Wo-pen
Tsung-kuan (chief general officer), 46-47, 53
Tsung-ssu-p'in (lower fourth grade), 48
Tsung Tse, 34
Tsung wu-p'in (lower fifth grade), 48
Tu po-chi-lieh, 26. See Po-chi-lieh
Tu Shan-fu, 102
Tu Yüan-shuai fu (office of the grand marshal), 32, 33
T'u-tan (clan), 10
T'u-tan Ch'üan, 96
T'u-tan I, 100
Tun-en Ch'eng, 10
T'un-tien chün ("farmer-soldier" institution), 47
Tung Chieh-yüan, 102
Tungus, x, 4, 8, 18, 1 125nn6-8
Tzu-chih t'ung-chien (comprehensive mirror for aid in government), 99
Tz'u, 41
Tz'u-chang ("polished phraseology" of literature), 92
Tz'u-shih, 65

Wai-ch'ao (outer court), 65
Wan-hu (head of ten thousand men), 70, 90
Wan-sung lao-jen (the old men of ten thousand pine trees), 107
Wan-yen (clan), 10, 16, 17, 25-26, 47-48, 52, 63, 64,

99, 118
Wan-yen A-ku-ta (emperor, r. 1115-23), 7, 8, 17, 19-20, 26, 30, 45, 134n34, n36, 137n11, 138n30; founding of the Chin, 18; government, 27-28, 52; measures for centralization, 27, 28; population transferred, 28-29, 137n15; and sinicization, 32, 38
Wan-yen Ho-che, 26
Wan-yen Ho-li-po, 16-17
Wan-yen Hsi-yin, 12, 31, 36, 40, 41, 95, 141n4, n8
Wan-yen Hsün (emperor, r. 1213-23), 95. See also Hsüan-tsung
Wan-yen Liang [Hai-ling Wang] (emperor, r. 1149-61), 42-48; as usurper, 42, 142n34; invasion of the Southern Sung, 68-69, 70, 109, 110; policies, 43-48, 113
Wan-yen Nien-han, 20, 21-22, 26, 33, 34, 35, 36, 37, 39, 41, 138n35, 139n37, n41
Wan-yen Pa-hu-lu, 91
Wan-yen Po-ti, 101
Wan-yen P'o-la-shu, 16-17
Wan-yen Shou, 99-100, 107, 115, 162n82
Wan-yen Ta-lan, 34, 35, 39
Wan-yen Tan (emperor, r. 1123-49), 30, 37; reforms, 41-42, 139n41, 140n3, 153n22
Wan-yen Tsung-fu, 69
Wan-yen Wo-li-pu, 20, 21-22, 33, 36, 37, 138n36, 139n41
Wan-yen Wo-lu, 26, 30, 31
Wan-yen Wo-pen [Tsung-kan], 39, 40, 141n6
Wan-yen Wu-chi-mai (emperor, r. 1123-35), 11, 20, 27, 28, 30, 32, 35, 36, 37; policies, 29, 32, 33

Wan-yen Wu-chu, 13, 34, 35, 139n37, 141n8
Wan-yen Wu-ku-nai, 15, 16, 17
Wan-yen Wu-lu (emperor, r. 1161-89), 30-31, 142n34, 149n9; background, 69-70; rise of, 70-71; movement for revival, 71-83, 113-14. See also Shih-tsung
Wan-yen Wu-ya-shu, 17
Wan-yen Ying-ko, 16-17, 19, 26-27
Wan-yen Yün-chi (emperor, r. 1209-13), 95
Wan-yen Yün-kung, 99
Wang An-shih, 103
Wang Che, 106, 107
Wang Ch'u-i, 107, 162n82
Wang Jo-hsü, 103, 104, 106, 109
Wang Kuai, 88
Wang O, 93
Wang T'ing-yün, 99, 158n30
Wang Yün, 60
War, 11; Chinese, 23, 31; firearms, 23, 112; Jurchen, 9, 10, 17, 22; between Liao and Chin, 19; between Northern Sung and Chin, 20-21; Weapons, 91
Wei Dynasty, 5, 93
Wei-shao (emperor, r. 1209-13), 105
Wen-tu (clan), 10
Wo-chi, 4
Wo-tsu, 4
Women, 10, 13, 69, 70, 95, 96, 98
Wu-chi, 4, 5
Wu-ku-lun (clan), 10
Wu-kuo pu (Five Nations), 17
Wu-li Ch'ien (property money), 79

Yang Huan, 92
Yang P'u, 29-30
Yang Shih, 105
Yang Yün-i, 99, 101

Index

Yangtze River, 34, 69
Yeh-lü Chang-nu, 19
Yeh-lü Ch'u-ts'ai, 101, 107
Yeh-lü Lü, 101
Yeh-lü Ta-shih, 20
Yeh-lü Yü-tu, 21
Yellow River, 35, 90, 96
Yen-ching, 9, 19, 20, 21, 31, 35, 36, 44, 71, 107
Yen Ting-chi, 96
Yen-Yün region (ex-Liao territories), 20, 30, 55, 56, 133n28
Yin (protection), 61, 64, 66, 67
Yü-shih t'ai (censorate), 41. See also Censors
Yü-wen Hsü-chung, 31, 36, 40
Yü Yün-wen, 69
Yüan dynasty, ix, x, 46, 55, 58, 60, 66, 67, 93, 94, 97, 100, 102, 103, 107, 115, 116; drama, 101-3; provincial system, 90, 116
Yüan Hao-wen, 60-61, 66, 92, 99, 110
Yüeh Fei, 139n43

PUBLICATIONS ON ASIA OF THE INSTITUTE FOR COMPARATIVE AND FOREIGN AREA STUDIES

1. Compton, Boyd, trans. and ed. *Mao's China: Party Reform Documents, 1942-44.* 1952. Reissued 1966. Washington Paperback-4, 1966. 330 pp., map.
2. Chiang, Siang-tseh. *The Nien Rebellion.* 1954. 177 pp., bibliog., index, maps.
3. Chang, Chung-li. *The Chinese Gentry: Studies on Their Role in Nineteenth-Century Chinese Society.* Introduction by Franz Michael. 1955. Reissued 1967. Washington Paperback on Russia and Asia-4. 277 pp., bibliog., index, tables.
4. *Guide to the Memorials of Seven Leading Officials of Nineteenth-Century China.* Summaries and indexes of memorials to Hu Lin-i, Tseng Kuo-fan, Tso Tsung-tang, Kuo Sung-tao, Tseng Kuo-ch'üan, Li Hung-chang, Chang Chih-tung. 1955. 457 pp., mimeographed. Out of print.
5. Raeff, Marc. *Siberia and the Reforms of 1822.* 1956. 228 pp., maps, bibliog., index. Out of print.
6. Li Chi. *The Beginnings of Chinese Civilization: Three Lectures Illustrated with Finds at Anyang.* 1957. Reissued 1968. Washington Paperback on Russia and Asia-6. 141 pp., illus., bibliog., index.
7. Carrasco, Pedro. *Land and Polity in Tibet.* 1959. 318 pp., maps, bibliog., index.
8. Hsiao, Kung-chuan. *Rural China: Imperial Control in the Nineteenth Century.* 1960. Reissued 1967. Washington Paperback on Russia and Asia-3. 797 pp., tables, bibliog., index.
9. Hsiao, Tso-liang. *Power Relations within the Chinese Communist Movement, 1930-34.* Vol. I: *A Study of Documents.* 1961. 416 pp., bibliog., index, glossary. Vol. II: *The Chinese Documents.* 1967. 856 pp.
10. Chang, Chung-li. *The Income of the Chinese Gentry.* Introduction by Franz Michael. 1962. 387 pp., tables, bibliog., index.
11. Maki, John M. *Court and Constitution in Japan: Selected Supreme Court Decisions, 1948-60.* 1964. 491 pp., bibliog., index.
12. Poppe, Nicholas, Leon Hurvitz, and Hidehiro Okada. *Catalogue of the Manchu-Mongol Section of the Toyo Bunko.* 1964. 391 pp., index.
13. Spector, Stanley. *Li Hung-chang and the Huai Army: A Study in Nineteenth-Century Chinese Regionalism.*

Introduction by Franz Michael. 1964. 399 pp., maps, tables, bibliog., glossary, index.
14. Michael, Franz and Chung-li Chang. *The Taiping Rebellion: History and Documents*. Vol. I: *History*. 1966. 256 pp., maps, index. Vols. II and III: *Documents and Comments*. 1971. 756, 1,107 pp.
15. Shih, Vincent Y. C. *The Taiping Ideology: Its Sources, Interpretations, and Influences*. 1967. 576 pp., bibliog., index.
16. Poppe, Nicholas. *The Twelve Deeds of Buddha: A Mongolian Version of the Lalitavistara: Mongolian Text, Notes, and English Translation*. 1967. 241 pp., illus. Paper.
17. Hsia, Tsi-an. *The Gate of Darkness: Studies on the Leftist Literary Movement in China*. Preface by Franz Michael. Introduction by C. T. Hsia. 1968. 298 pp., index.
18. Hsiao, Tso-liang. *The Land Revolution in China, 1930-1934: A Study of Documents*. 1969. 374 pp., tables, glossary, bibliog., index.
19. Gasster, Michael. *Chinese Intellectuals and the Revolution of 1911: The Birth of Modern Chinese Radicalism*. 1969. 320 pp., glossary, bibliog., index.
20. Thornton, Richard C. *The Comintern and the Chinese Communists, 1928-31*. 1969. 266 pp., bibliog., index.
21. Lin, Julia C. *Modern Chinese Poetry: An Introduction*. 1972. 278 pp., bibliog., index.
22. Huang, Philip C. *Liang Ch'i-ch'ao and Modern Chinese Liberalism*. 1972. 200 pp., illus., glossary, bibliog., index.
23. Gerow, Edwin and Margery Lang, eds. *Studies in the Language and Culture of South Asia*. 1974. 174 pp.
24. Morrison, Barrie M. *Lalmai, A Cultural Center of Early Bengal*. 1974. 190 pp., maps, drawings, tables.
25. Hsiao, Kung-chuan. *A Modern China and a New World: K'ang Yu-Wei, Reformer and Utopian, 1858-1927*. 1975. 669 pp., transliteration table, bibliog., index.
26. Ryan, Marleigh Grayer. *The Development of Realism in the Fiction of Tsubouchi Shōyō*. 1975. 133 pp., index.
27. Suh, Dae-Sook and Chae-Jin Lee, eds. *Political Leadership in Korea*. 1975. 272 pp., tables, figures, index.
28. Wilhelm, Hellmut. *Heaven, Earth, and Man in the Book of Changes: Seven Eranos Lectures*. 1976.

29. Tao, Jing-shen. *The Jurchen in Twelfth-Century China: A Study of Sinicization*. 1976. 217 pp., map, illus., appendix, glossary, bibliog., index.
30. Ahn, Byung-joon. *Chinese Politics and the Cultural Revolution: Dynamics of Policy Processes, 1958-1966*. 1976.
31. Nowak, Margaret and Stephen Durrant. *The Tale of the Nišan Shamaness: A Manchu Folk Epic*. Forthcoming.
32. Norman, Jerry. *A Student's Manchu-English Lexicon*. Forthcoming.